Global Culture, Island Identity

Studies in Anthropology and History

Studies in Anthropology and History is a series that will develop new theoretical perspectives, and combine comparative and ethnographic studies with historical research.

Edited by Nicholas Thomas, The Australian National University, Canberra.

This book is part of a series. The publisher will accept continuation orders which may be cancelled at any time and which provide for automatic billing and shipping of each title in the series upon publication. Please write for details.

Karen Fog Olwig

Global Culture, Island Identity

Continuity and change in the
Afro-Caribbean community
of Nevis

hp
ap harwood academic publishers
Switzerland ◆ Australia ◆ Belgium ◆ France ◆ Germany ◆ Great Britain ◆
India ◆ Japan ◆ Malaysia ◆ Netherlands ◆ Russia ◆ Singapore ◆ USA

COPYRIGHT © 1993 BY

Harwood Academic Publishers GmbH, Poststrasse 22,
7000 Chur, Switzerland. All rights reserved.

HARWOOD ACADEMIC PUBLISHERS

Private Bag 8, Camberwell, Victoria 3124, Australia
58, rue Lhomond, 75005 Paris, France
Glinkastrasse 13-15, O-1086 Berlin, Germany
Post Office Box 90, Reading, Berkshire RG1 8JL, Great Britain
3-14-9, Okubo, Shinjuku-ku, Tokyo 169, Japan
Emmaplein 5, 1075 AW Amsterdam, Netherlands
5301 Tacony Street, Drawer 330, Philadelphia,
    Pennsylvania 19137, USA

LIBRARY OF CONGRESS CATALOGING-IN-PUBLICATION DATA

Olwig, Karen Fog, 1948–
    Global culture, island identity : continuity and change in the
    Afro-Caribbean community of Nevis / Karen Fog Olwig.
        p.   cm. -- (Studies in anthropology and history ; v. 8)
    Includes bibliographical references and index.
    ISBN 3-7186-5329-X
        1. Nevis--Civilization.   2. Nevis--Race relations.   I. Title.
    II. Series.
    F2084.049   1993
    972.973--dc20   93 -35262
                                                                        CIP

DESIGNED BY   Maureen Anne MacKenzie
               Em Squared Main Street Michelago NSW 2620 Australia

TYPESET BY   CGS Typesetters, Leighton Buzzard, Great Britain

FRONT COVER   The Methodist chapel in Charlestown, Nevis. From Thomas Coke, *A
               History of the West Indies*, vol. III. London, 1811.

Contents

Illustrations

Preface

This analysis offers a historical, anthropological perspective on the development of cultural identity in a global context. It does so through a case study of a West Indian community which since the 1600s has incorporated African and European cultural elements within a common framework of social life, in the process creating the basis for a culturally all-encompassing and geographically unbounded ''global'' or inclusive culture. This global culture has become extended to Western metropoles, as viable migrant communities in North America and Britain have become established during the course of this century, influencing the culture of the host societies. This discussion of global cultural processes therefore offers a historical, anthropological analysis of a phenomenon which has been associated with the ''post-modern'' times of the contemporary world.

The global quality of West Indian culture is seen to be related to the circumstances of slavery and colonialism which sought to suppress and make invisible the Afro-Caribbean community within the island society. For this reason the Afro-Caribbean people employed colonial institutions, to which they gained access, as frameworks within which to formalize and display a culture which they saw as their own. After emancipation these frameworks increasingly derived from migration destinations in the West Indies, North America and Britain, where waged employment was available. In the course of these historical processes a global culture emerged which was characterized by its ability to cultivate and promote a locally developed system of values and practices through the appropriation of external cultural forms.

Research for this book began in 1978, when, during a fieldtrip on St. John in the Virgin Islands, I interviewed a number of immigrant workers as part of a study on the impact of American mass tourism on island society. Many of the migrants were from Nevis, and upon completion of the research on tourism I began to study the system of migration which had brought so many Nevisians to the island. Nevisian migration to St. John turned out to be part of a larger pattern of transnational movement of people, goods and remittances which I suspected might have wider implications. The way in which this transnational movement sustained, and in turn was sustained by, a global community of Nevisians living in different parts of the world suggested that the traditional place-centred orientation of anthropology was inadequate. If even the smallest and most remote of islands was so global in scope, this was a subject which seemed to warrant more attention. During the 1980s fieldwork therefore was expanded to include not just the home island of Nevis, but also migration destinations in Leeds, England, and New Haven, USA.

More than eighteen months of research among Nevisians in the West Indies, North America and Europe suggested that not only were Nevisians closely integrated in a global community of social and economic ties of fundamental importance in daily life, but their whole cultural outlook was characterized by an outward orientation. Thus while those living on Nevis were preoccupied by cultural elements from the United States and Europe, Nevisians abroad cultivated the culture of their home island. This absentee culture, naturally, was related to the nature of the migration system itself, but it also was tied to the afore-mentioned period of colonial history where the island had been under external domination. Fieldwork therefore was complemented by extensive historical, anthropological research in published and unpublished sources, dating as far back as the seventeenth century.

If fieldwork was frustrated by the fact that Nevisian culture always seemed to be where I was not, a result of it being part of a wide-ranging, non-localized community, the historical research was troubled by the nearly complete absence of Afro-Caribbean voices in the records. The historical documents were authored by government officials, plantation owners and managers, travellers and missionary workers, who came from the colonial mother country of Great Britain. Their accounts reflected, naturally enough, colonial or British concerns. Though the Afro-Caribbean absence presented a historical, methodological problem, it could be seen to reveal an important theme in the evolvement of Nevisian culture. By critically examining the historical accounts it was possible to paint a picture of the way in which British institutions, brought to the island during more than three centuries of colonial rule, had been employed by the Afro-Caribbean population to establish a place for themselves and display a culture of their own.

The seeming evasiveness of Nevisian culture which long presented me with serious methodological and theoretical difficulties became a fundamental key to the understanding and interpretation of some of the cultural processes which have characterized Nevis through time. This case study in cultural development, involving processes of great complexity, sheds light on broader processes in the Caribbean as well as in other Third (or Fourth) World areas of the decolonizing world.

The prolonged and variegated research which forms the basis of this book was made possible by several grants. The University of Copenhagen supported fieldwork on St. John (1978), Nevis (1986–7), in Leeds (1987–9) and New Haven (1987) as well as much of the archival research in Great Britain. The Danish Research Council of the Humanities supported fieldwork on St. John (1979–80) and fieldwork on Nevis (1981–2). The Danish Council for Research on Developing Countries supported research on Nevis (1984, 1989), provided funds to acquire Methodist archival material as well as a grant which enabled me to write this book. This economic assistance is gratefully acknowledged.

I have also received help from a great number of people for which I am thankful. I have enjoyed generous hospitality and stimulating conversations in the homes of Gwendolyn and Mario Benjamin on St. John; Mary and Lionel Thompson and family on Nevis; Julia Wright and Max Farrar in Leeds; Mary Alice and David Lowenthal as well as Nina and Colin Prescod in London. The staff of numerous archives and libraries in Nevis, St. Kitts, Great Britain and Denmark helped guide me through their collections and find the relevant materials. Colleagues at the Institute of Anthropology have discussed a number of papers on Nevisian culture at institute seminars and encouraged the project. The book manuscript has benefited enormously by the careful critique lavished on it by Riva Berleant-Schiller, Barry Higman (who also helped by transcribing Antonia Williams' manuscript located at the University of the West Indies), Ulf Hannerz, Ulla Hasager, Daniel Miller, Sidney Mintz, Kenneth Olwig and Richard Price. My husband Kenneth and daughter Mette joined me on much of my global and historical odyssey. They helped steer me through some of its most difficult parts and made the pleasurable parts even more enjoyable. The entire project, however, would not have been possible without the active support, critique and encouragement from countless Nevisians throughout the world. I owe everybody a great debt of thanks.

PLATE 1   *The coat of arms of St. Christopher-Nevis.* Independence Magazine, *St. Christopher and Nevis, 19th September, 1983.*

Introduction

Prologue:
Nation-State and Global Community;
The Case of St. Kitts-Nevis

In 1984 a new nation-state was recognized by the world, when the prime minister of St. Christopher-Nevis was invited to give a speech to the General Assembly of the United Nations. The event was covered by the local government radio station and it generated a certain amount of pride among the population of this new nation who suddenly saw their tiny country of a little more than 100 square miles, inhabited by 50,000 people, in the center of world affairs. This event symbolized the international recognition of the autonomous nationhood of St. Kitts-Nevis, as the two islands are called locally. This political autonomy had been carried into effect in October 1983 with the signing of a treaty of independence from Great Britain, who had ruled the two islands since the 1620s with periods of French rule during the early history.[1]

While Kitticians and Nevisians enjoyed the attention that the international community accorded their small twin-island, the move for independence was hardly characterized by the nationalistic zeal often associated with the declaration of political autonomy. In fact, nationalism, understood as the belief that political entities coincide with ethnic ones and that the total population share a common culture which is closely linked to the division of labor and mode of production of the society (Gellner 1983:1, 37–38, 95), was only minimally present except at the most formal level. Independence did lead to the creation of an official set of national symbols, such as a flag, an anthem and a coat of arms. This had the purpose of "inventing some semblance of nationhood, and thus nation-state status" (1988:7), as Zelinsky has written of the use of such symbols more generally. This did not reflect a population united in a common pursuit of an autonomous political, social and cultural community. Rather the new nation-state was split by internal divisiveness which was caused, at least in part, by the nature of the two island societies which made up the nation-state. Whereas the larger island of St. Kitts was characterized by industrial sugar production tied to a strong labor movement, Nevis had long been an island of small farming based on household production. These social and economic

1

differences were seen to be of such fundamental importance that Nevisians only accepted independence with St. Kitts on the condition that they be granted internal self-rule. As a result, Nevis, the smaller island of 36 square miles with a population of less than 10,000, received its own assembly dealing with local legislation; its own premier; and its own representative of the British queen in the form of a governor.

The most prominent sociocultural ties which united the people within the twin-island state and which could be raised to national officialdom were those connected with the rule of the old colonial powers, the very political forces from which national independence had been declared. This culture figured prominently in the coat of arms which was decorated with such items as a poinciana flower, named after former French governor of St. Kitts, M. de Poincy; the French fleur-de-lis; the English rose; a sugar cane and coconut palm symbolizing the European plantation economy during colonial rule, as well as military objects referring to the many wars waged between colonial contenders in the waters off the islands (*Independence Magazine* 1983).[2]

National identity as defined above was not even present in great measure at the island level as a source of divisiveness. If the primary cultural foundation of the new nation of St. Kitts and Nevis was the rather anachronistic common European heritage of the colonial past, the people of the nation were united in a common absentee orientation, away from the island society to destinations of wage labor abroad. This cultural orientation away from the island was, interestingly enough, also symbolized, though no doubt unintentionally, on the coat of arms in the form of a lighter, a traditional means of transportation in (or away from) the islands (*Independence Magazine* 1983).

The local population had long recognized the undesirability of eking out an economically marginal existence on the two islands where the plantation system had experienced a long period of economic depression since the early nineteenth century. Few alternative economic opportunities had emerged except for small-scale subsistence level farming on Nevis and, in recent years, offshore-type industry primarily located on St. Kitts, offering employment at minimal wages. During the last 150 years the islanders therefore had emigrated to North and South America as well as Europe, leading to the establishment of migration communities in such disparate destinations as New Haven, Leeds, Toronto, and some of the more economically developed West Indian islands (Richardson 1983). For this reason the islanders did not regard their local territory or their colonial affiliation as their major frame of reference but had developed kin networks of a global dimension, and it was to these networks that they looked for access to resources wherever they were.

This did not mean that the islands had no significance except as places of birth which must be left as soon as possible. The islanders remained deeply attached to their places of birth, concretized in their homes, where they were reared and where relatives still lived, toward whom they had kinship obligations. Furthermore, migrants maintained a close affinity to the location of their childhood—the village of their childhood home and the surrounding areas where they grew up.

These areas of significance—the individual's kin network extending throughout the world and the home of the parental nucleus of this network—received important expression in extensive exchange relations. They involved, for the migrants, making monetary remittances, the sending of material goods and the provision of assistance for others to emigrate, and for those who stayed behind, providing assistance with child rearing and sending shipments of local produce from the native soil. Not only were the absentee islanders essential to the well-being of the local islanders, in that remittances from abroad were the main source of income on the islands, but they also played an important political role, contributing funds to local political candidates, campaigning in migration destinations, and in some cases even returning to their home island to vote.

The twin-island nation-state therefore did not include the majority of the people who identified themselves at Kitticians and Nevisians nor did it display any particular social, economic and political autonomy in the eyes of its populace. The Afro-Caribbean population of St. Kitts-Nevis certainly did not constitute an "imagined political community", another definition of a nation (Anderson 1983:15). Rather it was crosscut by a wide array of "imagined communities" of interpersonal relations extending from individuals or individual homes on St. Kitts and Nevis to similar entities in the migration communities with which flows of economic, social and cultural exchange were maintained. In this tradition of mastering and maintaining a variety of cultural and economic resources within relatively loosely defined networks, the islanders were more similar to peoples in kinship-based societies whose "economic and political survival" has been seen as dependent on "keeping options and connections open", a condition which is irreconcilable with "an unambiguous, categorical self-characterization such as is nowadays associated with a putative nation, aspiring to internal homogeneity and external autonomy" (Gellner 1983:13).

While nationalism may not be reconcilable with the social organization of stateless societies, present-day Kitticians and Nevisians have not shown any difficulty combining their multiple affiliations with statehood, mainly, it would seem, because the image of the nation which they have is rather different from that held in the Western countries where it developed. It would thus be a mistake to assume that the population of St. Kitts and Nevis was against the idea of political independence and nationhood *per se*. On the contrary, for the local as well as the absentee islanders statehood was quite a useful institution which provided a set of new options in their dealings with the outside world. For one thing, by declaring independence St. Kitts-Nevis was, as noted, put on the map in the international community of nations through its membership in the United Nations which conferred rights to participate in political debate. Also as an independent state St. Kitts-Nevis could bargain for foreign aid from the various international organizations. Furthermore, as citizens of an independent nation the local population would gain easier access to immigrant status in attractive destinations for wage labor abroad, particularly in the United States, where quotas for immigration from British dependencies are extremely low. In other words, the nation-state was important, not because it was believed to confer the sort of "internal homogeneity and external autonomy" associated with the development of modern nations in the Western world. It was important as a Western institution which offered a new framework of recognition and respect within which the islanders could communicate with the Western world, not as localized citizens in the new nation-state, but as members of the transnational communities. In other words, it was employed by the islanders as a means of projecting Afro-Caribbean "global" culture and identity.

This tale of a nation-state is just one example of many referring to a long tradition of seeking self-assertion and external recognition through the appropriation and manipulation of institutions of the dominant Western world. This book discusses the way in which the Afro-Caribbean community on Nevis since the 1600s has incorporated African and European cultural elements within a common field of social life, in the process creating the basis for a "global" or inclusive cultural context. While it developed within a particular island society, it has proved adaptable to conditions in different parts of the world and, along with similar Afro-Caribbean cultures, capable of further development in foreign societies, in the process exerting considerable impact upon the culture of the host countries.

GLOBAL CULTURE

The notion of global culture has emerged during recent years as anthropologists have realized the growing complexity of cultural expression, particularly in the Third World. Much of this complexity can be attributed to cultural flows extending primarily from the West to the Third World which have situated even the remotest villages within a global ecumene (Hannerz 1992). Formerly, Western social scientists had tended to interpret cultural contact and change in terms of homogenizing processes, whereby Third World countries exposed to Western economic and political dominance were seen to become Westernized culturally. The notion of global culture, however, does not imply a single, integrated cultural entity, similar to "the culture of the nation-state writ large". Rather it refers to the globalization of culture through transsocietal processes involving "exchange and flow of goods, people, information, knowledge and images" (Featherstone 1990:-1-2; see also Appadurai 1990, 1991; Hannerz 1992).

The absence of global cultural homogenization, despite intensive cultural interaction and exchange on a worldwide level, can be seen to be due to the processes of heterogenization which occur as global culture is incorporated into local contexts of life. The predominance of cultural forms associated with Western countries does not necessarily imply an acceptance of the cultural notions and values associated with these forms in the West or an understanding of their socioeconomic significance in the Western world. Once cultural "fragments" are removed from their original context, they are given a new meaning and function informed by the new context within which they are placed. This does not mean that the Western origin of the elements is insignificant or forgotten. On the contrary, they receive their special significance exactly because they derive from the West. Western cultural elements constitute, in many instances, the only concrete ties that Third World people can establish with what they conceive to be a vital center of power. They are, in other words, an important means whereby people in the Third World can engage in a dialogue with the dominant West, albeit an asymmetrical one. Global culture, in other words, involves "popular and local discourses, codes and practices which resist and play-back systemicity and order" (Featherstone 1990:2). Far from constituting an attempt at imitating Western culture, as the adoption of Western cultural forms may suggest, global culture rather involves a critical assessment of the dominant Western culture and society which produced the forms.

The driving force behind global cultural processes can be seen to be found in the tension between tendencies towards, on the one hand, cultural homogenization, deriving from the dominance of global flows from the West, and, on the other hand, cultural heterogenization, resulting from local appropriation of these flows (Appadurai 1990:95). In the study of global culture it is therefore important to focus not just on the various channels whereby external cultural elements are brought to the Third World but just as significantly on the ways in which these elements are incorporated into already existing culture. This means that the notion of globality should be expanded to refer to the comprehensive or inclusive nature of local cultural processes as well as the diverse geographical origin of many of their constituent elements. This use of the term is, of course, in agreement with the concept of globality in its wider sense.

The ability to incorporate and accommodate disparate, foreign cultural elements within local contexts of life has received little notice in anthropology largely, it would seem, because it is difficult to analyze through Western concepts of culture. According to Kapferer (1988) modern Western society is based on a principle of democracy and equality which is predicated on a notion of equal worth and thereby equal right. This also implies an idea of sameness, however, in that it is only by being alike or identical that it is possible to qualify for a status of equality. It is therefore not possible to incorporate those who display a cultural difference of any importance into such societies, because these people cannot be admitted as equals. In Australian society, dominated by descendants of English colonizers, this is seen by Kapferer to have resulted in the aboriginal population being delegated to an external "natural" sphere outside the social order. As a contrast to Western egalitarian society Kapferer points to hierarchical societies, where a place can be found for a variety of cultural conceptions, because the idea of hierarchy is based on the presence of inequality and thereby difference. The cultural diversity of hierarchical societies is not necessarily unproblematic, however, because there is often no agreement among the various population segments as to their position in the hierarchy, as illustrated by the struggle between Tamils and Sinhalese in Sri Lanka.

While the notions of equality and hierarchy may help us understand the possibilities of the emergence of cultural diversity in larger state societies, they are less useful for an understanding of cultural complexity among smaller population groups in the Third World. The incorporation and appropriation of foreign cultural elements which occurs here is not informed by membership in a larger, overriding social order of a state, but is typically the act of individuals who, operating within fluid sociocultural constellations and using their own skills and personal connections, engage in various forms of dialogue with the West. They operate from the vantage point of belonging to loosely structured groupings which allow for manipulation with a variety of resources, establishing a mosaic of crosscutting affiliations and practicing a multiplicity of identities, in the process creating a series of partly overlapping sociocultural fields of operation (Southall 1970). For these people the incorporation of a variety of cultural elements within a successful field of operation therefore is the very essence of sociocultural constituting.

THE GLOBAL NATURE OF AFRO-CARIBBEAN CULTURE

When examining the global nature of Afro-Caribbean culture it is necessary to look at the complex cultural processes which have taken place as enslaved, later free, people of African descent have sought to establish sociocultural fields and identities of their own within the strictures set down by an external colonial power. The African background of most of the people brought to the Caribbean was very much one characterized by "competition, movement, fluidity", "overlapping networks of association and exchange" and "multiple identities" (Ranger 1983:248). The Africans who arrived in the Caribbean constituted "heterogeneous crowds" rather than well-defined groups, and the cultural heritage they shared was primarily one of "deep-level cultural principles, assumptions and understandings" (Mintz and Price 1976:7, 9). One of the most vital aspects of this shared heritage would seem to have been the well-developed ability to create meaningful lives out of the disparate cultural practices and social relations which they encountered in the colonial societies.

The free ranging sociocultural maneuvering, known from Africa, was, however, very much circumscribed by the conditions of life presented by the European controlled colonial system. In the case of Nevis the early colonial system was molded by colonizers who came from the late medieval, early modern English society. This was based on an hierarchical patriarchal socioeconomic order, where differences in economic capability, social position and cultural outlook were expected and accommodated within an overarching, inclusive framework. Beginning with the seventeenth century and establishing itself in the course of the eighteenth century an entirely different social order of equality appeared. This was an exclusive one which accepted as equal only those who conformed to the culture of the emerging English middle class, which centered on notions of respectability.

These two English social principles of hierarchy and equality naturally presented the Afro-Caribbean population with fundamentally different frameworks of life, as far as their position within the colonial society was concerned. Whereas during the early period of slavery the Afro-Caribbeans were incorporated into the bottom of the society, below the British indentured servants, by virtue of their belonging to their owners' family-based farming enterprises, during the later period they became virtually excluded from the human ranks of society to be reckoned as part of the plantations' stocks. Thus while the colonizers tended to regard the early African slaves' cultural practices with a mixture of incredulity and curiosity, the later slave culture became increasingly condemned as immoral and animal-like.

Despite the fact that the slaves underwent a process of social and cultural marginalization in the colonial society, they created sociocultural spaces of their own in those crevices of the plantation society where they were outside their masters' sphere of control. These spaces emerged most importantly in connection with the system of social reproduction which the slave population developed. Even though the slaves were their owners' private property to be maintained by them, they were allowed, as a matter of economic expedience and convenience, to develop a reproductive system which enabled them to maintain themselves. In the process of doing so they created semiautonomous spheres of life in connection with, for example, provision agriculture, which came to provide a main source of subsistence, and family relations centered on the bearing and rearing of children. These practices and spheres provided an important basis for the emergence of the sociocultural fields which came to constitute the Afro-Caribbean community (Mintz 1974; Olwig 1985a).

The social institutions developed among the slaves to set down norms for "regular or orderly social interaction" had only validity within the slave population in that they received no recognition in the colonial society at large (Mintz and Price 1976:12). The situation of marginality or "social death" in which this society increasingly sought to place the slaves (Patterson 1982) could be countered, however, to some degree by the slaves' ability to exploit the cultural niches open to them in the more open social institutions of the pre-modern English society upon which West Indian society had been founded and which were still culturally viable. They were able to find social recognition for their culture, and thereby some rights for the Afro-Caribbean community, by displaying their culture through these somewhat anti-quated European institutions.

The establishment of an Afro-Caribbean cultural presence in the colonial society meant making use of Euro-Caribbean cultural forms to express an Afro-Caribbean culture. The globality of Afro-Caribbean culture therefore involved both the establishment of a common framework of life out of a variety of disparate cultural elements and practices and the display of this culture through an institutional framework which, though external to this culture, was nevertheless open to it. This interplay did not lose its significance after Emancipation. The freedom which they experienced as plantation laborers working in the same sugar fields and living in the same slave houses as during slavery was of such a nature that they continued to experience the social marginality that they had been exposed to formerly. Further-more, the English colonial society, increasingly organized on the basis of principles of equality and democracy, allowed equal rights only to those who adhered to English notions of respectability.

As shall be seen, the English culture of respectability was in many ways defined in opposition to both the popular culture of the common people, such as the culture developed by the Afro-Caribbean population, and the more stratified, inclusive British society which preceded it. It was therefore not possible, or desirable, for the vast majority of this population to find a place of recognition in the English colonial society which established itself after Emancipation and remained dominant until recent years. I shall argue that the importance of emigration must be seen, at least in part, in the light of the difficulty experienced by the islanders in reconciling the demands of the English culture of respectability, which became deeply entrenched in the formal socioeconomic system, with the realities of a viable Afro-Caribbean cultural system, which informed daily life.

The concept of global culture may reflect a new perception of complex cultural processes which fits the mood in post-modern Western society where global culture is seen as "opening up another space onto which can be inscribed speculative theorizations, thin histories and the detritus of the exotic and spectacular" (Featherstone 1990:2). From a Caribbean perspective, however, the complex social relationships and cultural processes which constitute global culture have a long past, a logic of their own and a spectacularity of surprising combinations that makes traditional ethnographic exotica look rather familiar. This rich and well-established global pattern may be seen to derive from "post-modern" historical antecedents in the Caribbean. Thus it may be argued that Afro-Caribbean culture is "pre-post-modern", having evolved not from primitive antecedents but rather out of the Caribbean plantation system, which in its organization and structure represented an early modern industrial form well before industrialization was a dominant factor in Europe (Mintz 1986:48–52). In the process they resisted, or "played back", the colonial "systemicity and order" contributing to the formation of the present-day transnational societies of the Caribbean which are not constituted within a localized area but in networks of socioeconomic relations between individuals living in the Caribbean as well as in other parts of the world. By analyzing the present-day transnational Nevisian community in the light of a global culture with deep roots, this book offers a historical perspective on a phenomenon which has been seen to be of more recent vintage.

A DETERRITORIALIZED COMMUNITY

The global quality of Afro-Caribbean culture springs not just from the many transsocietal flows which have met in the Caribbean, but also from the increasing deterritorialization (Appadurai 1991:192) which the Afro-Caribbean people have experienced as a result of outmigration in the wake of Emancipation. This book therefore also presents a new cultural perspective on another, perhaps more established, tradition of research on migration which has taken place during the last decades. Although studies of Caribbean migration have demonstrated a growing awareness of the importance of a "migration culture" or "migration tradition" which has led to the rise of non-localized, global communities (Thomas-Hope 1978, 1985; Marshall 1983; Richardson 1983; Sutton and Chaney 1987), most of the work done so far has tended to be characterized by socioeconomic and ecological analyses of sending and receiving societies based largely on statistical materials. This is also true for the research on migration from Nevis (Frucht 1966, 1968, 1972; Richardson 1983; Liburd 1984; Mills 1985, 1987), even where it has pointed to the importance of carrying out a cultural analysis of migration.[3] In this book migration is analyzed in light of the globality of Afro-Caribbean culture which has emerged out of transsocietal cultural processes. Within this context, deterritorialization therefore may not so much imply loss of local rootedness as a further cultivation of the cultural space which has emerged in the global encounter.

CULTURAL IDENTITY

The focus of this work is not on the development of a clearly demarcated, autonomous Afro-Caribbean culture, but on the assertion of cultural identity on the part of an Afro-Caribbean people living, first, in a colonial society dominated by a foreign power, later in an increasingly transnational community. This approach is related to a new awareness within anthropology and history of the importance of the cultural construction of identity among colonized people by such means as codification of customs (Keesing 1982, 1985), invention of tradition (Ranger 1983), or self-identification through consumption (Friedman 1990). They demonstrate how cultural identity is created by the projection of lived culture through reified culture, often that associated with the colonizers, such as anthropological texts, legal codes or the Bible (Keesing 1982, 1985), military drills and elaborate ceremonies (Ranger 1983), or material goods such as expensive Western clothing (Friedman 1990).

This emphasis on the interplay between local cultural practice and external cultural display in the establishment of cultural identity presents a new approach. The literature on cultural identity within anthropology has tended to be character-ized by two opposing points of view, where one has regarded a (primordial) cultural essence as primary to the development of cultural identity, whereas the other has emphasized the significance of external circumstances. In the Caribbean these two viewpoints are reflected in the cultural pluralist and the integrationalist approaches which stress respectively cultural separation and autonomy versus structural integration and subordination in a larger social context.

While the debate between pluralists and integrationalists has been dominant in theory on Caribbean culture (Austin 1983), the fruitfulness of combining both a pluralist and an integrationalist perspective within a single analysis has long been apparent in Sidney Mintz' more complex framework of cultural adaptation and resistance developed primarily in studies of Caribbean peasantries (1974). This framework views cultural development as involving both change (adaptation and integration) and continuity (resistance and autonomy). A similar dualism is expressed in a somewhat different way in Peter Wilson's (1973) analysis of the two coexisting cultural notions of respectability and reputation, which are seen to correspond to respectively colonial and locally developed cultural values that influence different spheres of social life in the Afro-Caribbean communities. Roger Abrahams' (1983) distinction between cultural form and cultural content presents yet another approach where the former is seen to be changeable and adaptive and the latter more resistant.

Such integrative frameworks are particularly useful in an area like the Caribbean where the societies were Creole in the sense that their culture cannot be seen to be the product of an indigenous culture which has evolved *in situ* without significant external interference or of one culture brought to the area from the outside, but must be seen to be created and molded by people of different cultural backgrounds existing within various historic contexts of dominance (Brathwaite 1978[1971]:xiii–xvi). Caribbean culture involves the development of collectively shared ideas and practices as well as the display of this culture within a wider social context, where it is not common to all.[4] The danger of working with such a dual framework, however, lies in the temptation to view Caribbean people as victims of a sort of cultural schizophrenia due to the coexistence of entirely different cultures which cannot merge.

This danger is related to the fact that the historical basis of Afro-Caribbean identity has not received much attention in Caribbean studies but rather has been treated almost as if it were an undercurrent disturbing the flow of research. This has recently been brought out in two publications, one dealing with Caribbean historical consciousness (Price 1985), the other with Caribbean cultural (and national) identity (Safa 1987). Price shows that, despite the fact that the past has long been recognized as an important aspect of contemporary Caribbean societies, the meaning of this past to Caribbean people has not been adequately interpreted in the scholarly literature. This is related to the fact that there has been little understanding of the importance of history in the creation of "collective" identity or of the more subtle ways in which cultural identity is given expression in different historical contexts. As a result it has been a commonly held view that Caribbean people have been either unimportant bystanders to, or helpless victims of colonial history, and that therefore they have no historical consciousness (1985:24–26).

The failure to recognize the historical basis of cultural identity in the Caribbean has contributed to the perception of Caribbean cultural identity as ambiguous, dependent and insecurely founded (Safa 1987:115–17). Safa suggests that this cannot be attributd to an "ill-formed culture" but can rather be seen to be "an indication of multiethnic, class-stratified societies whose elites have continued to deny recognition to their own 'folk' culture". For this reason, these cultures have been forced to find less visible avenues of cultural expression outside the formal institutions (1987:117–18). Both Price and Safa therefore call for more careful studies of the interplay between cultural identity and the expression of historical conscious-ness in the Caribbean.

A HISTORICAL ANTHROPOLOGY OF NEVISIAN CULTURAL IDENTITY

This work will analyze Afro-Caribbean culture in terms of the historical continuity and change in the formation and expression of cultural identity beginning with the earliest period of colonization and plantation slavery. It thereby will attempt to shed light on the issues discussed above which have tended to be neglected or regarded negatively as a problem within Caribbean research. Furthermore, by focusing on the way in which colonial institutions have been employed and transformed by the Afro-Caribbean people as they have sought to make their culture visible, I present a nuanced and dynamic analysis of the formation of identity through cultural interaction.

On the basis of a historical anthropological case study of Nevis I shall analyze the complex interaction between the development of Afro-Caribbean culture and the assertion of this culture within the wider West Indian society in order to gain a socially recognized cultural identity. Because of its particular history and its size it is possible to study continuities as well as changes in the formation and display of Afro-Caribbean cultural identity. During the early heyday of plantation society Nevis was a major center for sugar production; during the course of the eighteenth and nineteenth centuries, however, the island became a colonial backwater due to failing soils and a poor economy of scale. This provided a favorable climate for a cultural continuity going back to the Euro-Afro-Caribbean culture which had developed early on in the island's colonial history and this, in turn, has made Nevis an excellent field for students of popular culture and its historical development (Abrahams 1983). These same marginalized conditions, somewhat paradoxically, also favored a culture which encouraged islanders to migrate and yet maintain strong ties with their home island. This migration culture is therefore both international in scope and intensely local.

The size and homogeneity of Nevis coupled with its international extension make it an ideal place for the kind of comprehensive study which is necessary for an understanding of the global character of Afro-Caribbean culture, but which is less apparent on islands which appear to be more cosmopolitan in their display of a plurality of different cultures and "openness toward divergent cultural experiences" (Hannerz 1990:239). In this way Nevis presents an excellent opportunity to examine the way in which Afro-Caribbean culture has been formed out of global cultural processes.

This book seeks to document and analyze, on the one hand, the continuity that is apparent in the evolution of Afro-Caribbean culture through time, and, on the other hand, the varying Euro/Western institutions and cultural forms (or traditions) through which this culture has been displayed and projected, as the Afro-Caribbean population has sought to win recognition for its culture and thereby for itself. By showing how it has actively employed foreign institutions such as that of the Western nation-state as vehicles for the promotion and public assertion of Afro-Caribbean culture, I shall argue that these institutions which have been regarded as means of oppression were, at least in part, appropriated by those they were meant to control in order to be turned against their oppressors.

Three major structural frameworks will be delineated, each of which has presented the Afro-Caribbean population with different possibilities for making its culture visible. While they can be seen to correspond roughly to three historical periods, it is not the chronological order of the historical sequences, nor the many historical changes which occurred during these periods, that guide this discussion. This book, in other words, should not be regarded as a history of Nevis. The organizing structure behind the sections is rather the changing global frameworks within which local cultural practices have emerged and cultural identity has been displayed.

In Section One, "English Patriarchal Hierarchy, African Bondage", the interplay between English notions of patriarchy and African conceptions of belonging is discussed with respect to the early colonial society of yeoman farming based on English servants supplemented with African slaves (Chapter One), and the mature plantation society based entirely on African slaves (Chapter Two). It is argued that institutions connected with relations and values of sociability which early English colonists brought to the West Indies during the early seventeenth century came to constitute important loci where the growing African population was able to develop a sense of belonging and assert a social presence in the colonial society. This became of increasing significance as the slaves underwent a process of social marginalization with the emergence of large scale sugar plantations by the end of the seventeenth century. The situation of social death which is supposed to have characterized West Indian slaves therefore can be seen to have been negated by the way in which slaves on Nevis continued to cultivate institutions and traditions of sociability which belonged to an earlier era of patriarchal relations.

Section Two, "In Pursuit of Respectability", focuses on the English cultural framework of respectability which came to the West Indies in the form of religious and educational institutions thus offering the slaves new possibilities for seeking social recognition in the colonial society. Chapter Three discusses the concept of respectability, revolving around such virtues as proper manners, sexual restraint and hard work, which had emerged among the rising middle classes in Europe during the eighteenth century. It served as a means of demarcation *vis-à-vis* the lower classes where traditions of sociability still remained of importance. It is shown how on Nevis the adoption of norms of respectability became associated with upward mobility out of the marginalized Afro-Caribbean community and into the social ranks of colonial society. For those who remained part of the Afro-Caribbean community the cultural forms connected with respectability came to present an important institutional framework for the display of Afro-Caribbean cultural identity in the colonial society. The increasing importance of the culture of respectability after Emancipation is described in Chapter Four, which shows how respectability came to underwrite the new colonial order which emerged as the plantation regime declined. This benefited the small group of freed who were able to rise to middle class status in the colonial order of post-Emancipation Nevis. As a result, the Afro-Caribbean community underwent a further process of exclusion from colonial society.

The way in which the small middle class cultivated a "culture" of respectability through a rich array of traditions and institutions is analyzed in Chapter Five. Many of these cultural forms associated with respectability became appropriated by the lower classes who identified with Afro-Caribbean culture for the purpose of asserting their cultural identity. Afro-Caribbean cultural identity therefore involved not only the display of culture within external cultural frameworks, but the employment of the two widely different frameworks of sociability and respectability.

In Section Three, "Home Is Where You Leave It: Paradoxes of Identity", the long tradition of marginalization of Afro-Caribbean culture within the local colonial society, combined with the demise of the local social and economic context of life, are seen to lead to the deterritorialization of the Afro-Carribean community. Chapter Six demonstrates that the political decolonization of the island did not lead to greater social, economic and cultural emancipation, but rather to the final undoing of the local society with all its internal contradictions. In Chapter Seven, these contradictions are seen to be resolved by emigration to destinations abroad and the development of a transnational community of kin relations focusing on parental homes on Nevis. Western material culture, acquired through remittances from migrants, now provide a framework for the display of the Afro-Caribbean cultural practices which underline the global community. Chapter Eight discusses the cultural implications of this deterritorialization of Afro-Caribbean relations. It is argued that as the village-based Afro-Caribbean culture has ceased to be of practical relevance within the local society, it has obtained symbolic significance in the global community. The cultural forms associated with Afro-Caribbean cultural practices in the margins of the local society become obsolete external cultural forms. They can therefore be employed to display and cultivate a localized Caribbean identity which helps hold together the dispersed global community of Nevis.

This study draws on a variety of sources, ranging from government officials reporting on conditions in the colonial society; owners and overseers of sugar estates writing about plantation affairs; Methodist missionaries describing their work among the slaves and freed within the plantation society; Nevisians writing, on their own, about their culture and history, or reflecting, in discussions with me, about their lives, past and present. I have presented these various voices in whatever form of English they were expressed, without editorial comments where they do not conform to contemporary standard English. This expressive flexibility is a reflection of the formative role of these different people, as representatives of various cultural flows, in the complex cultural processes which led to the emergence of global culture and local identity among the Afro-Caribbean population of Nevis.

NOTES

[1] The French occupied parts of St. Kitts until 1713 when, with the Treaty of Utrecht, the entire island became British.

[2] The coat of arms, the flag and national anthem are presented in the *Independence Magazine* which appeared in 1983. While the former was a modification of the already existing coat of arms the flag and the anthem were chosen on the basis of a national competition which was held before independence.

[3] An important analysis of migration in Caribbean societies which sees the symbolic as well as socioeconomic significance of migration can be found in Patterson (1978). Frucht (1968), Philpott (1973) and Foner (1979) among others have discussed the importance of the networks which extend from Caribbean islands to migration destinations.

[4] Whereas very little research has been carried out on the cultural identity of the majority of the Afro-Caribbean population which has emerged and been defined within a colonial framework, a number of works have examined the identity of the ethnic minorities in the Caribbean whose locus can be found outside Caribbean colonial society. These include studies of the East Indians in Guyana (Drummond 1980, 1981; Jayawardena 1980), the Chinese in Jamaica and Guyana (Patterson 1975), and the Caribs in St. Vincent or Middle America (Drummond 1980; Gonzalez 1988; Gullick 1985).

PART I

ENGLISH PATRIARCHAL HIERARCHY, AFRICAN BONDAGE

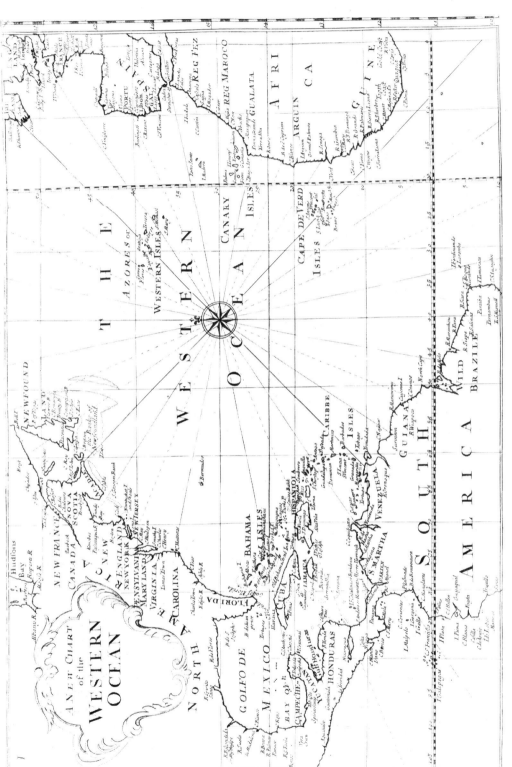

PLATE 2   *"A New Chart of the Western Ocean". Hans Sloane, A Voyage to the Islands of Madera, Barbados, Nieves, S. Christophers and Jamaica, London: BM for the author, 1707.*

CHAPTER ONE

Africans in English Patriachy

The colonial society which the English yeoman farmers created on Nevis after 1628 was rather short-lived. Within a few decades, the small farmsteads based on family labor and servants supplemented by African slaves, gave way to large-scale sugar estates owned by a small group of planters who cultivated the land entirely with African slave labor. The family-based, patriarchal society was replaced by a plantocratic society, and the African slaves were delegated to a marginal position outside the social ranks of this order. The plantation society was to dominate the island society well into the nineteenth century, and it had a profound social, economic and cultural impact on the local society which is still felt today.

In comparison with the overwhelming importance of the plantation society the early colonial society of small farmers has been seen as a brief phase in the incipient phase of colonization of primarily historic interest. In this section I shall argue that certain traditions and institutions associated with this early society survived the onslaught of the plantation society and came to provide socially acceptable frameworks for the evolvement and display of Afro-Caribbean culture. This was of utmost importance as the slaves underwent a process of increasing marginalization in the plantation society.

The first Africans who were transported as slaves to the small, conically shaped island of Nevis encountered a society of predominantly English farmers who cultivated a variety of crops such as tobacco, indigo, ginger, as well as subsistence crops. Until the middle of the seventeenth century the land was tilled primarily with the help of indentured laborers, and many of the farmers were themselves, in fact, former indentured servants who had received a piece of land after completion of their terms of servitude (Smith 1947:230; Bridenbaugh and Bridenbaugh 1972:175–203; Batie 1976). In the mid-1640s sugar cultivation began on Nevis introduced from Barbados via St. Kitts (Bridenbaugh and Bridenbaugh 1972:81), and, according to Charles Rochefort's *History of the Caribby-Islands*, by the late 1640s there were three to four Englishmen on Nevis "who subsist and live handsomely, by the trade they drive in Sugar, Ginger and Tobacco" (1666[1658]:20). The transition to sugar production was well under way on Nevis by 1655, when sugar was listed as the major export crop (Dunn 1972:122–23). The expansion of sugar cultivation entailed major social and economic changes as smaller farms were combined into large plantations which could provide the economic foundation for investment in the extensive processing equipment necessitated by sugar production. The small farmers continued to make a comfortable living on tobacco cultivation, however, until a restriction on trade was instituted which made it difficult for them to sell the crop at satisfactory prices and, during the 1660s, forced many of them to abandon farming on Nevis (CO1/18:29 April, 1664; CO1/33:23 September, 1655).

By the 1650s, when sugar production based on a slave labor force had begun to supersede tobacco cultivation as the main cash crop on Nevis, slaves constituted less than 20% of the population. The number of slaves increased dramatically during the following decades as the sugar plantations consolidated themselves on Nevis, and in 1678, when the census was conducted on the island, the 3849 "Negroes" outnumbered the White population of 3521.[1] By the early eighteenth century, when the conversion to sugar production was completed, the Black population exceeded 5000 and comprised close to 80% of the total population (CO186:11 May, 1722; Galenson 1981:120).[2]

As the large scale plantation system based on a slave labor force established itself, the remaining servants were upgraded and employed primarily as skilled artisans, overseers and bookkeepers. The slaves, on the other hand, came to be regarded and treated as brute stock over which the planters had absolute authority. The social marginalization which the slaves experienced was not, however, left unchallenged by them. They established a social presence in the colonial society, as will be shown, primarily by manipulating traditions and institutions of the English patriarchal order to which they gained access during the early period of colonization when they comprised an insignificant minority in the island society. In this development and consolidation of a presence in the island society the slaves found a vital resource in their African cultural background.

THE AFRICAN BACKGROUND

In their discussion of the role of African and European culture in Afro-Caribbean cultural development Mintz and Price have pointed out that the importance of the slaves' African background has tended to be discussed either in terms of postulated tribal origins of certain slave groups or in terms of a generalized African heritage. This approach is not valid, they argue, because the slaves did not arrive in the New World as members of particular tribal groups but as individuals torn from the sociocultural contexts within which they had lived in Africa. Furthermore, the slaves could not be said to have shared a single African heritage. They therefore suggest that the African influence in the New World not be sought in particular traits or traditions believed to have been retained more or less intact but rather in basic cultural principles and values which underlie cultural forms and behavior patterns (Mintz and Price 1976:4–5).

In the search for such fundamental principles the recent literature on Africa which takes a more regional and historically informed approach and discusses African culture in more general terms is helpful. The concept of the corporate tribe, once thought to refer to a basic socioeconomic unit in African social structure, has now been seen to refer to a historic unit which emerged as a result of changes which occurred in connection with the European colonization of the continent (Sharpe 1986; Tonkin 1990). It is not possible to view the slaves' African background in terms of tribal groups since most of the slaves transported to the British West Indies from the middle of the seventeenth to the end of the eighteenth century did not belong to any clearly demarcated socioeconomic entity which can be identified as a tribe. The socioeconomic framework which defined the most basic context of life for pre-colonial Africans was rather informed by the notion of kinship. As noted by Kopytoff and Miers in their discussion of African slavery, the concept of the person was closely related to belonging in a kin group which conferred social, economic and political rights as well as ritual protection (1977:17).

The power basis of kin groups fluctuated a great deal and depended on the ability of the group to attract a large following, people being regarded as vital re-sources from a political and social as well as an economic point of view. Kinship pro-vided "both the idiom and the metaphor for social and political relations" (ibid.:22). For this reason kinship did not merely constitute a principle of demarcating insiders from outsiders but it also embodied a means of incorporating strangers into a group. The kin ties which were extended to strangers were of a hierarchical nature and in-volved, at one extreme, the incorporation of slaves who against their own free will were placed under the authority of a master in a new kin group. At the other extreme, they entailed the incorporation of persons who voluntarily chose to place themselves under the patronage of particular persons in a kin-like position of dependence having given up membership in their own kin group for such reasons as "quarrels, threats, hunger, hope for a better life, or because they had committed some crime" (Kopytoff and Miers 1977:12, 24).

The situation of struggle and socioeconomic flux, where political control was not placed in a permanent headship which was usually inherited but rather sought by a number of competing patrons operating so as to further their power base as leaders of kin groups, is closely related to African notions of witchcraft. Rowlands (1985) suggests that much of Western and Central Africa is characterized by an ambiguous perception of power with deep historical roots. This is reflected in the belief that the possession of supernatural substances is a precondition for the assumption of leadership. If harnessed, this substance is beneficial and works for the welfare of the community; if uncontrolled, the substance is used for the amassing of wealth and personal power and hence dangerous and lethal for members of the community. Power, in other words, involves substances which must be controlled, and those leaders who demonstrate too high ambitions for centralized power in their person will be regarded as demonstrating a lack of control of this substance which leads them to become involved with sorcery. Accusations of sorcery therefore can be viewed as a means of preventing individual political leaders from concentrating too much power in their own person.

The connection between supernatural forces and power is also apparent in the importance attached to certain places as residences of particular spirits which can be cultivated and invoked by human beings, and many Africans have belonged to local religious cults drawing their membership from a number of kin groups. Through secret rituals involving various paraphernalia, such as masks, a participant established a close, personal relationship with a guardian spirit. This relationship was one of dependence and subordination to the guardian spirit. For this reason cult members became partly freed from the ties of subordination and dependence which they had with others, most notably senior members of their lineage, for which reason secret cults often became a challenge to the kinbased sources of power (Horton 1971:102–13). People in pre-colonial Africa therefore did not have one single-stranded identity as members of a particular kin group but moved in and out of "overlapping networks of association" (Ranger 1983:248).

The fundamental cultural principles and values which the Africans brought with them to the New World included both hierarchical and egalitarian notions. The kinship system was in some respects hierarchical in nature in that it depended upon the existence of relations between dependents and patrons who sought to build up a power base through a large following. These ties were expressed in kin terms and usually involved a process of incorporation and acceptance, and African institutions, ranging from households to whole societies, have been characterized as "strikingly absorptive of outsiders" (Kopytoff and Miers 1977:61). On the other hand, because power was not concentrated in central, permanent offices but rested in the ability of competing kin groups to attract followers, it tended to prevent the development of centralized hierarchical states and furthered more egalitarian social orders. This interplay between hierarchical and egalitarian tendencies is also reflected in the supernatural realm. The hierarchical tendencies were, on the one hand, underlined by the belief that supernatural power was held by those who succeeded in gaining a position of leadership. This power was believed to have been abused, however, if employed to establish a position of central control and leadership. The existence of spirits in different natural locales that could be consulted and invoked by the general population, often through membership in a cult, furthermore meant that there were alternative sources of power that presented a check on the uncontrolled amassment of wealth and power. These basic principles of incorporation through ties of patronage and dependence, of establishing different fields of sociocultural ties, and of harnessing supernatural forces to generate a power base must have constituted important guiding principles in the way in which Africans responded to their situation as slaves in the American colonies.

THE SOCIETY THE COLONISTS MADE

Nevis was one of the first West Indian islands to be colonized by the English, when a group of about 100 planters and servants from neighboring St. Kitts under the leadership of the Englishman Anthony Hilton settled there in 1628. They quickly put up a number of makeshift huts built of four to six wooden forks planted in the ground and covered with leaves of palms or plantain (Smith 1910[1629]:910; Bridenbaugh and Bridenbaugh 1972:37). Despite attacks by the Spaniards the following year, where all the houses on Nevis and St. Kitts were burned and the settlers had to flee to the mountain (SP16, vol. 151/20:5 November, 1629), the English maintained a colony on the island. When Charles Rochefort (1666:20) described Nevis a couple of decades later, in the 1650s, he characterized it as quite a civilized place where "Swearing, Thieving, Drunkenness, Fornication, and all dissolutions and disorders are severely punish'd". The English colonizers had left their old country in order to start a new and better life in the New World. Nevertheless they had brought with them sociocultural notions, closely connected with the society they had left behind, which came to have a fundamental impact on the colonial societies which emerged in the New World.

The social order of early modern England was a rather dichotomous one. It was characterized, on the one hand, by the old, medieval order, where everybody from the lowest laborer to the king were accorded their proper places in a great chain of reciprocal relations of authority and obedience, and, on the other, by an emerging, modern order of egalitarian, individualistic and competitive relations (Underdown 1985:9, 40). The old order was mainly to be found among the gentry and the poor in the village communities where the open field system still remained intact. Here life still revolved around the agricultural cycle of the year with its communal festival days centering on the church and involving rich as well as poor. The new order appeared among the incipient middle class which was emerging in those areas where the market economy and industry were becoming dominant. They believed in a society of hardworking and morally righteous families and regarded the cooperative activities and revelries of traditional village life as wasteful, if not ungodly. While the new order existed as an important model for change, which was partly realized during the Cromwellian interregnum, it did not become dominant until the eighteenth century, when fundamental socioeconomic change led to the transformation of the old, hierarchical order (ibid.:18, 40–42, 270–91; Hill 1984[1972]).

The early colonists reestablished in the New World one of the most important institutions of the old hierarchical order in the form of the patriarchal family. In the West Indies it was mainly based on the master-servant relationship which had attained great importance in early modern England. The majority of young people in English society who were capable of working but too young to marry and establish their own household were servants. They lived and worked in the household of their master and were regarded as members of his family. The inclusion of servants in the master's family was related to the fact that the family and the socioeconomic unit of the household were regarded as one and the same. In fact, early modern English did not distinguish between relatives and residents of a household meaning both by the term family. It functioned under the leadership of the patriarchal head who had virtually absolute power over his dependents, i.e. his wife, children, servants and apprentices (Laslett 1988:2; Kussmaul 1981:7).

Seventeenth century population censuses from the British colonies in the Americas reveal the importance of the family as a basic unit of organization which incorporated the majority of the population, including the African slaves, into a master-dependent relation. Following English custom the census takers regarded the family as "an independent economic unit" which consisted of "all those who lived under the control of the 'master of the family'" either in his dwelling or in his immediate surroundings. The censuses therefore listed all the people including all servants and slaves under the family master to whom they belonged (Wells 1975:298). The population census which was carried out on Nevis in 1678 follows this basic pattern, although there is some variation in the way in which the enumerators filled out the census lists. Whereas one enumerator listed all White adults by name, the rest listed only the heads of families by name and noted the number of White men, women and children, Negro men, women and children who belonged to their families. Some enumerators specified the presence of wives and children of the master in the family, however, such ties were not listed by all, making it impossible to ascertain whether the White members of the family were servants or related to the master by kinship or marriage. Thus we have no information about the relationship between the three White men, three White women, four White children, seven Negro men, fourteen Negro women, and ten Negro children who were listed under Captain Edward Earle, except that he was master of the family to whom they all belonged (CO1/42). On the basis of the census lists one can only conclude that all the members of a family were regarded as being primarily dependents of their master, whether or not this dependency was grounded in kinship and marriage, servitude or slavery. At this time, when sugar production was already well established, this meant that at least 8 families were listed as consisting of more than 60 persons whereas 45 contained more than 20 persons (Dunn 1972:129). While these families were quite influential, the island was still numerically dominated by smaller domestic units and c.1000 families were listed as headed by small farmers with less than 20 Negroes, two-thirds of them with no

Negroes at all, one-fifth holding 1 to 4 Negroes (Dunn 1972:129; Wells 1975:223).[3] The primary importance of the families as productive units is apparent in the 1678 census, in that it enumerated a number of units where no husband-wife-child ties were present such as "Francis Morton's family" which included 3 White men, 26 Negro men, 10 Negro women and 20 Negro children (CO1/42).

RELATIONS TO THE MASTER

The master-tie which formed the basis of the families was initially a modified form of the system of servitude which was so pervasive in England during the seventeenth century.[4] One of the important differences between the colonial and the English system was that the terms of servitude in the colonies were longer due to the expenses of transporting the servants across the Atlantic which were incurred by the farmers to whom the servants were bonded (Galenson 1981:8). The servants were required to give 5 or, from 1672, 4 years of service during which they were to be provided with clothing, food and housing. Upon completion of their terms they were to receive a small piece of land on the island but due to the continuous freeing of servants and the consolidation of smaller homesteads into larger sugar estates no land was available by the middle of the century and a bounty of 400 pounds of sugar was offered instead. The only alternative to low paid wage employment on the estates was emigration to other islands such as Jamaica (Smith 1947: 167, 230, Bridenbaugh and Bridenbaugh 1972:175, 275).[5] The long terms of bondage presented the colonial servants with conditions which were rather more harsh and inhuman than those they had known in England.[6] When servants began to work on large sugar estates cultivated by ganged field labor consisting primarily of slaves, servitude began to be referred to as White slavery (Beckles 1982:345).

The Africans who were brought to the West Indies during the first decades of colonization were placed at the bottom of the White family hierarchy just below the indentured servants. The attachment to a new social group via a position of dependence and deference toward a master of a family presented a familiar situation to the Africans, even though the physical, social and economic environment was entirely different. According to Rev. Robert Robertson, who became a rector at St. Paul's Anglican Church in 1707, newly arrived slaves regarded their master's ability to do things which to them were unknown and incomprehensible as proof of their special powers: "When the *newer* Negroes observe that we can read and write (or as they word it, *make paper speak*) and do many other things above their comprehension, they seem to take us for a sort of Superior Beings, made as it were on purpose to rule over them; they both admire, and fear, and hate us" (1730:32). New slaves perceived their masters' positions of leadership within an African conceptual framework where leaders were in possession of supernatural powers which were both to be respected and feared.

Initially, servants and slaves were accorded a basically similar treatment as dependents in the families. They labored together in the field performing the same kind of work (Smith 1947:256; Bridenbaugh and Bridenbaugh 1972:118); their clothing was made of the same sort of material, and they lived on basically the same diet consisting mostly of locally produced foodstuffs, although the two groups' food preferences were somewhat different (Ligon 1970[1673]:31, 37; Sainton 1982:55; Beckles 1989:95–97; Berleant-Schiller 1989:555). Also most servants and slaves occupied the same type of huts, simply constructed wooden structures with roofs of leaves, similar to the houses built by the first settlers on the island, and neither ordinary servants nor slaves were given beds to sleep in but had to make do with mats or hammocks (Bridenbaugh and Bridenbaugh 1972:37–38; Sloane 1707:xxx–xxxi, xlvii). The parallel situation of the servants and slaves as members of the family household is further apparent in the fact that slaves were exempt from labor on Sundays, despite the fact that they were heathen and therefore did not observe the Sabbath in a Christian fashion (CO1/38).

The most important distinction between servants and slaves was the limited duration of the servants' indenture in contrast to the slaves' bonding for life. Even this distinction was not juridically apparent when slavery began, thus in Barbados the legal difference between servants and slaves was not clarified until nine years after colonization, when the governor legislated in 1636 that all Blacks and Indians and their offspring were slaves for life unless other contractual arrangements had been made (Beckles 1989:31). The temporary status of the servants' indenture was not necessarily an advantage to the servants during their period of bondage, however, but rather led to a more careful treatment of the slaves who were the property of their masters for life (Ligon 1970:43). The servants' legal right to sue and bear testimony in court, which was denied the slaves, was relatively unimportant, because the courts were controlled by planters who would not be favorably disposed towards complaints on the part of servants (Higham 1921:176; Galenson 1981:171).

It was not until the latter part of the seventeenth century, with the conversion of the island's economy to sugar production, that the treatment of the two groups changed markedly. As a result the servants were gradually moved into a more privileged class of artisans and managers, and they disappeared entirely as a group from Nevis during the course of the seventeenth century. This transition was already apparent in the description from the 1680s by John Jeaffreson who owned a plantation on St. Kitts: "Slaves live as well now as the servants did formerly. The White servants are so respected that, if they will not be too refractory, they may live much better than thousands of the poor people in England, during their very servitude, or at least as well" (1878[1681]:257; see also Galenson 1981:95; Wells 1975:214; Pares 1950:22–23).

As the social and economic distance between masters and dependents increased with the change from small diversified farms to large sugar plantations, and the replacement of the servants with slaves which this change entailed, masters began to abuse the position of absolute authority they held towards their dependents. In 1682, for example, "An Act for preventing the Barbarism of Negroes" was passed in order to repeal a former act which had granted to the "master of each Negro executed" for felony or robbery "three thousand five hundred Pounds of Sugar out of the publick stock". The former act apparently was exploited by masters to exchange the dead bodies of undesirable slaves for sugar, and it had therefore proved too "grievous and burthensom to the Inhabitants of this island" (*Acts of Assembly* 1740:9). Masters' mistreatment of their dependents also became a public concern when it led to social disorder as exemplified by the preamble to a law from 1682. It noted that the "many thefts and robberyes committed in this Island by negroes have been for the greatest part occasioned through their masters not planting or allowing them any provision of soe Exceeding little that they are not able to subsist upon it". For this reason the law made it mandatory for "Every master of a Family, owner or Renter of Land of any Plantacon" to plant for every working slave, man or woman, "one thousand plants Ground in provision" fining offenders 1000 pounds, 500 of which were awarded to the informer (CO154/2). This introduction of slave rights in the legislation of the island was rather unique and, as shall be seen, it does not seem to have been enforced.

CLAIMING THE LORD'S DAY

In England the Anglican churches had represented an important, higher level integrative force in the local communities which commanded the respect of all members of the communities including the masters of families. In the West Indies the Church did not attain this central importance. Despite the fact that three churches had been built on Nevis by the middle of the seventeenth century (Rochefort 1666:20), the state of religion in the Leeward Islands was deplorable according to a report on the Leeward Islands by governor William Stapleton from 1671: "There may be 40 parishes in his government, to supply which he found one drunken orthodox priest, one drunken sectary priest, and one drunken parson who had no orders" (CO1/27). The situation of the clergy was sought improved in 1672 with an act for the maintenance of the ministry on Nevis which stipulated "yearly payments of 10 lb. sugar per poll for every person or persons [above 14 years of age], as well black as white [...] and fees of 100 lb. sugar for a marriage, and 300 lb. for preaching a funeral sermon", baptisms being free (CO154/1). This law had little effect by 1676 when the governor noted that it was impossible to report on births, christenings and burials since no records had been kept due to the scarcity or lack of ministers (CO1/38). Apparently this desperate state of religion in the islands provoked the colonial officials in England so much that a minister was sent out to each of the Leeward Islands in 1678 (CO1/42).

Even though churches had been established in the colonies and equipped with at least some clergy, the Church did not become the revered institution that it was in England, nor do the ministers appear to have held the position of authority and respect that they had in English society. When the Rev. Thomas Heskith, rector at St. John's Anglican Church towards the end of the seventeenth century, preached his farewell sermon on May 25, 1701, he thus began by regretting the "Immorality and loose Behaviour of too many of those who have preached the Gospel amongst you". He also lamented that even though there were a great many "Wellwishers to Religion" among the congregation, there were those "who make it their Business to discourage Religion and Virtue; to oppose and hinder the advancement of Christ's Gospel-kingdom; tho', at the same time, they are under all the Bonds and Obligations, all the awful and solemn Ties of Laws, whether Sacred or Civil, to protect and defend the Same". This ineffectuality of law was, according to Rev. Heskith, related to the fact that the island community was dominated by those most interested in "what's profitable", having "no aim in the whole Scheme of their Thoughts, but to gratifie their Ambition, their Interest and Malice with the Ruin of their Neighbours" (1702:1-2).

With the limited influence of the Church the authority of the masters was virtually unchecked in the island community, in particular as it became numerically dominated by slaves who had no protection in the legal system. As the smaller farms were consolidated into large plantations with the expansion of the sugar industry, the patriarchal heads turned into a plantocracy who were able to rule despotically on their estates having no local superiors, moral or legal, of any importance to whom they were responsible (Puckrein 1984:22-23). The social order which became established in the colonial societies of the West Indies in general was a truncated one consisting of a large number of small hierarchies, the heads of which were free to pursue their own interests with few, if any, formal restrictions from the colonial society of which they were part. While the Church had little impact as a unifying institution of authority and respect in the local community it helped institutionalize the Sabbath as a day where no work was performed for the masters. This enabled the slaves to claim the day for their own purposes.

During the early period when the slaves constituted a fraction of the population they were left to themselves when masters and servants observed the Sabbath. This was initially mainly because the English colonists did not know how to include people who spoke a foreign tongue and acted in a strange fashion in their sociocultural activities. Writing about early colonial times Robert Robertson suggested the following explanations for the slaves not being brought to church: "the Number of the Whites, or Christians, [was] considerably greater than that of the Blacks, or Heathens; and the Heathens then, and for some Years after, were little acquainted with our Language and generally speaking either very stupid or very perverse. Most of the whites thought they did pretty well in keeping up the Face of Religion among themselves on the Lord's Day"; this led to "the Slaves or Blacks being [...] in a manner overlook'd and abandon'd" (1730:45). This granting to the slaves of a weekly day where they were allowed to do what they pleased presented a possibility for the slaves to create a community of their own outside the control of their masters. Robertson thus added that some of the slaves "as were naturally industrious, or ambitious of making a finer Figure than their Fellows, or had several wives to please and gratify, employ'd the Day in labouring for themselves, others made it a Day of Rest, and the far greater part a Day of Sport, till the thing was found, when it came to be look't into by the Publick, to have grown to such a Head as not to be soon or easily crush'd; the Slaves claimed the Lord's Day as peculiarly their own, and without doubt many of the Masters were not fond of disputing the Point with them, as believing that this unbounded Liberty of doing what they liked on the Lord's Day made their Slavery sit the easier all the rest of the Week" (1730:45).

There is only rather scanty information on the sort of "labouring" which the ambitious and industrious slaves did for themselves during the early period of slavery. Ligon did not report on much economic activity on the part of the slaves on Barbados, except to say that they collected bark on Sundays and made ropes out of it, which they "truck away for other Commodities, as Shirts and Drawers" (1970:48). Some of the acts which were passed during the latter part of the seventeenth century on Nevis suggest that the slaves were involved in a variety of activities. An act from 1675 which prohibited the use of poison to kill hogs, goats and fowls straying into others' fields—a practice which had been common among Whites and slaves— indicates that slaves cultivated fields of their own and possibly also kept animals (CO154/2). The nature of this cultivation is described by Hans Sloane, who visited the West Indies, including Nevis, during the 1680s. He wrote that slaves were given free time on Saturdays in the afternoon, Sundays, Christmas and Easter holidays as well as other "great Feasts" "for the Culture of their own Plantations to feed themselves from Potatoes, Yams, and Plantans, etc., which they Plant in Ground allowed them by their Masters, besides a small Plantain Walk they have by themselves" (1707:lii). The slaves on Nevis apparently were not able to maintain themselves on such provisions, since it was felt necessary to pass a law in 1682 requiring masters to plant a certain amount of ground provisions per slave to avoid the many crimes committed by starving slaves (CO154/2).

The tradition of using the Sunday as a "Day of Sport", which Robertson also mentioned, emerged early, judging from Richard Ligon's description of Barbados from the 1640s.[7] He noted that the slaves there met every Sunday afternoon to play and dance together, men and women in different groups, and he described their rhythm, singing and dancing style as quite distinct, and pleasant. The main instruments were "kettle drums [...] of several sizes", the smallest drum being played by the best drummer and others being played "as Chorasses". The drums had only one tone, and therefore the music was not based on tunes but rather on the fact that "they varie their time, as 'tis a pleasure to the most curious ears" (1970:48, 50). The generally positive attitude towards the slaves' music, which Ligon's description reflects, changed drastically during the latter part of the seventeenth century as witnessed by a number of acts which attempted to control the slaves. On Nevis an act from 1675 "ordered and enacted" that "no master or mistress of a family suffer his or her negroes to ramble to and fro; to carry any unlawful weapons clubbs or staves, and that he or she permit no loud Singing and cawerous outcryes, extraordinary noyse of Drums; any uncivillityes or disorders to be among his or her slaves, about house or plantation" (CO154/2). This apparently did not discourage the slaves, and it was found necessary to pass more legislation to deal with the matter such as a series of acts from 1737, attempting to suppress "the common Practice for negroes to meet in great Companies on the Sabbath Day, feasting, drinking, and gaming". These gatherings also included slaves from the neighboring island of St. Kitts who arrived on Nevis in "Barklogs, Boats and Canoes [...] on the Sabbath Day, to feast and carouze". The acts also included a prohibition against any sort of drumming among the slaves, whether or not it took place on Sundays (*Acts of Assembly* 1664–1739:131, 133).

Hans Sloane provides an explanation for this change in attitude toward the slaves' music and dance. He notes that the slaves "formerly on their Festivals were allowed the use of Trumpets after their Fashion, and Drums made of a piece of a hollow Tree, covered on one end with any green Skin, and stretched with Thouls or Pins. But making use of these in their Wars at home in *Africa*, it was thought too much inciting them to Rebellion, and so they were prohibited by the Customs of the Island." Instead of drums the slaves used lute-like instruments made of "small Gourds fitted with Necks, strung with Horsehairs, or the peeled stalks of climbing Plants or Withs." Some of these instruments were also made of wood and were decorated with carved figures. The dancers, who displayed "great activity and strength of Body", had "Rattles ty'd to their Legs and wrists, and in their Hands" and were "keeping time with one who makes a Sound answering it on the mouth of an empty Gourd or far with his Hand". The Dancers often were decorated either with cow tails which were tied to "their Rumps" or with "odd things" which gave them a "very extraordinary appearance" (1707:xlviii–xlix, lii).

The incitement to rebellion which the White population identified with the slaves' music and dance may have been realistic but need not have been connected with the usages of drums in wars. More fundamentally, the performance of music and dance in local groups which drew their membership from different kin groups was in Africa associated with secret cults, which constituted an important means whereby the concentration and centralization of power in heads of kin groups was challenged. Music and dance may well have played a similar role as vital elements in the gatherings of slaves from different plantations which sought to check their White masters, who probably have appeared to the slaves to have made excessive use of their special powers and therefore to have been lethal to the slave community. That the music and dance performed by slaves had a higher purpose than that of providing entertainment is suggested by Sloane who described these dances as "Ceremonies"; however, he did not regard them as religious, because they were not "Acts of Adoration of a god" but "for the most part mixt with a great deal of Bawdry and Lewdness" (1707:lvi).[8]

Not all the free time activities in which the slaves engaged pointed in an African direction, however. Some of them involved both servants and slaves who were drinking and gaming together, particularly on Sundays and holidays and in connection with the "rum punch house". These social activites may well have taken place within an English cultural framework which had been established by the servants during the early period of colonization before the slave population was of any significance. In England servants had been used to participating in a great number of social events which took place in the community and were outside the farmers' control. Many of them were tied to the agricultural cycle and the church-year: May games, Whitsun Ales, morris dancing and maypoles which were often held on church-grounds, the burning of bonfires at midsummer which coalesced with the celebration of the nativity of St. John the Baptist, or various midwinter celebrations such as the yule log, the wakeful ketches, mumming and ceremonial dancing combined with the observance of Christmas (Thomas 1971:47, 65–66, 71; Malcolmson 1973:26; Underdown 1985:14).

Such celebrations created a framework of social intercourse which cut across the individual households, emphasizing the importance of neighborliness and cooperation within the village. At the same time they accepted the integration of the village patriarchs into the wider vertical structure of authority and deference—relations of deference toward the local landowning gentry, and of authority toward the servants and poor in the parish. The celebrations also served as important symbolic settings where the superiors could display their privileged position *vis-à-vis* the inferiors and where the inferiors could demarcate the rights they had in the common resources controlled by the privileged. They provided, furthermore, settings where some degree of hostility could be expressed against the structures of authority including those associated with masters (Malcolmson 1973:76, 79). This is apparent, for example, in the mummings which occurred at Christmas as well as on Plough Monday and at Whitsun Tide, where it was common for costumed people to sing and play—often satires—in homes within the community, particularly those of the better-off. The mumming also involved solicitations, and thus presented the possibility for the poor of earning some money (ibid.:57). In the towns a similar custom allowed apprentices to collect "boxes" from their masters' customers, thus giving the name "Boxing Day" to the second day of Christmas. Likewise, some traditions involved the assertion on the part of the villagers of their right to use estate land for certain purposes, others were arranged by the gentry or farmers after the completion of major agricultural tasks, such as the harvest which was celebrated with a harvest dinner, as a measure of appreciation of the work of their agricultural laborers (Malcolmson 1973:60; Bushaway 1982:38–42, 52, 124).

The alehouses which began to appear during the sixteenth century constituted a popular meeting place for servants who often went there daily to be with other servants outside their masters' control (Clark 1978:49–52, 61; Burke 1978:109; Kussmaul 1981:43). They became more important as the Puritans denounced the many festivals which took place in the church and churchyard, not the least church-ales, which often were associated with these activities. A great deal of the traditional games and rituals therefore were moved to the alehouse and its yard, such as the Christmas mumming and the May Day celebrations. Mystery plays which formerly were performed in the church now could be seen in depictions by folk artists on the walls of the alehouses. Alehouses also became places to arrange cockfights, play cards or backgammon, and to throw dice (Clark 1978:62, Burke 1978:109). Even though the alehouses provided a place where many of the traditions of medieval society could be continued, they were a less inclusive setting than had been the village church.[9] Often the leading members of the local society were absent from the alehouse, and it therefore did not come to symbolize any sort of village unity and community spirit but rather the social marginalization of the poor. The alehouses were clearly less respectable than had been the churches, not just because they were entirely secular, but because they became associated with more suspect activities, such as gambling, prostitution or the formation of casual sexual liaisons as well as criticism against the political power structure (Clark 1978:59–72).

Laws against the profanation of the Lord's Day on Nevis show that some of the White population had been carrying on many of the social activities which they knew from England on the Sabbath. An act from 1659 thus noted, among the misbehavior taking place on Sundays, "loud talkeing, singing of songs or any gaming" suggesting the maintenance of English gaming traditions among the White population.[10] This merrymaking involved both masters and servants, and a fine of £200 was instituted for offending masters while servants were to receive corporal punishment (CO154/1). The practice of "gaming" among the White population was also noted in a code from 1675, which included it among the "enormities committed" on the island "by profanation of yᵉ Lords Day" (CO154/2). While this sort of merriment on Sundays was condemned as disorderly and ungodly, Nevis was hardly a Puritanical society where any sort of festivity was banned. The uncontrolled communitywide revelries were, however, looked upon with growing concern by the sugar planters who were dependent on a great number of bonded laborers, the vast majority of them African slaves. In 1675 an act was passed which banned "the unchristianlike association of white people with negroes" and instituted corporal punishment for "all such white people as shall be found soe spending their times on the Lords or other Dayes in drinking playing or conversing with negroes" (CO154/2). A similar law was passed in 1697, which instituted public whipping for White persons who were "found with any negroes at play or assisting them with light, liquor or otherwise" (CO155/2).

On Nevis most of the social activities which involved the Black and White lower segment of the population took place either on plantation grounds or in the taverns where people met on weekdays and, against the law, on Sundays and holidays (CO155/2).[11] Some of the drinking and sporting also involved the upper level of the hierarchy in the sense that masters usually donated food and drink for celebrations which occurred in connection with festivals. In the process they reaffirmed their superior position in the local community and thereby the set of rights and obligations which were inherent in the relationship between masters and dependents. On Nevis it had apparently become a tradition for masters to give special rations of fish or meat at Christmas and other festivals, as can be seen in the planter William Stapleton's instructions from the latter part of the seventeenth century to his deputies "To allow the negroes fish, or flesh at Christmas, or other festivals as I have used to doe" (SM2/8). Furthermore, from an early date it became customary to grant the slaves two to three days off from work at Christmas and Easter, a tradition which came to be much regretted because of fears that the great crowds of people from different plantations would lead to trouble. Since customary festivities were perceived to be sacrosanct, and hence unwise to stop, the White inhabitants of the islands allowed them to continue but began to keep guards and patrol highways at night during festival times (Robertson 1730:45).

Several of the laws against drinking and playing also referred to the social mingling which took place in Charlestown and other places of trade in association with the holding of the market as a part of the English tradition of combining business and such forms of pleasure as the imbibing of alcoholic beverages. In England, markets and, in particular, fairs had been important as public settings for young men and women to meet outside the confines of the family and as places of recreation where entertainment and dancing coud be enjoyed (Burke 1978:111; Malcolmson 1973:20). Markets were well established on Nevis with their own appointed clerks, as shown by an act passed in 1672 to prohibit "the use of any scales, weights, etc., not first allowed by the Clerk of the market" (CO154/1).[12] In 1676, five places of trade were listed for Nevis, of which only the ones in Charlestown and Morton Bay, where there were a few houses, were deemed considerable (CO1/38). The Whites on Nevis were apparently dependent upon the market for many of their provisions, and in 1691 an act prohibited the buying of provisions in quantities cheaply in order to sell it at excessive prices. Another act from 1700 stipulated that meat must be sold at the public market in Charlestown also in pieces or joints of meat that the poor could afford (*Acts of Assembly* 1740:12, 15). Besides the trade which took place at this official market, more unofficial bargaining seems to have occurred, at least on Sundays, judging from the act against profanation of the Sabbath passed in 1675 (CO154/2). Slaves participated in trade early on, although initially it may not have been entirely above board. Records thus indicate that they were involved in the sale of stolen goods such as sugar or molasses used for the distilling of rum (*Acts of Assembly* 1740:22-23) for which reason the colonial government demanded that slaves should be in possession of a licence to sell any produce (CO1/26). This was not enough to curb the illegal trade, and in 1686 an act was passed, stipulating that the punishment for slaves stealing goods in the value of 100-300 pounds of sugar was to be the loss of one ear for the first offence, the loss of the other ear or 60 lashes for the second, and death for the third offence (CO1/58). Not all of the slaves' marketing was based on illegally acquired goods as the colonial records might lead one to believe.[13] By the eighteenth century, the slaves' trading with their own produce became entirely dominant on the Nevisian markets (Robertson 1730:12).

The growing population of slaves who, unlike the servants, could not look forward to any freedom of their own were proving more and more difficult to control, as they were exposed to the increasingly harsh regime of the sugar plantations. The latter part of the 1600s saw the passing of a number of acts for the better governing of the slaves. In 1686, one act was passed stipulating the punishment for slaves "abusing or threatening any person" to be thirty lashes at the public whipping post; another act ordered that slaves who refused to stop tumultuous behavior be punished with thirty lashes, and that masters or mistresses who did not prevent slaves from behaving this way were to be fined (CO1/58). In 1693 laws concerning the taking of runaway slaves were added (CO155/1). Similar acts and regulations were repeated or elaborated on during the eighteenth century in continuous efforts to institute some controls on the slaves who were perceived as constituting a growing threat to the social order through their maroonage and violent individual protests against oppressors. In 1725 the Whites' worst fears seemed to be confirmed when a supposed plot among the slaves to rise against the White population was discovered (CO186).[14]

FROM PATERNALISTIC HIERARCHY TO INDUSTRIAL SLAVERY

As large sugar plantations replaced the smaller farm units which had characterized early colonial society on Nevis, and as large slave groups came to constitute the predominant labor force, masters became less paternalistic in their outlook and began to treat their dependents more as necessary stock on the plantation than as members of their families. There were no official institutions which regulated the relations between masters and slaves, nor were there any formal structures which incorporated both masters and slaves in a common moral community. The many acts which were passed beginning with the latter part of the seventeenth century increasingly conferred on the slaves a status characterized by "subordination and lack of rights" (Goveia 1965:47–48), and the system of slavery which emerged has rightly been described as one which placed the unfree in a position of institutionalized marginality or social death (Patterson 1982). This social marginalization of the slaves was countered, however, by the informal fields of social and economic ties which the slaves had developed both amongst themselves and with White servants and masters, perhaps guided by the African principle that a social presence and identity is sought through the establishment of a multitude of relations. Some of the ties were confined to the slaves, and rather demarcated slaves as a separate group *vis-à-vis* the White population, while others were extended to White servants and masters, and rather more established for the slaves a place within the colonial society. Both sets of relationships became of the utmost importance to the slaves, as they tried to negate the position of social death which was accorded them in the mature plantation society.

NOTES

[1] This rapid increase in the slave population on Nevis was made possible, among other things, because the Royal African Company, which had monopoly on the transatlantic import of slaves, placed its headquarters in the Leeward Islands on Nevis in 1672 (Higham 1921:150; Pares 1950:22). Of the White population 800, or 23%, were listed as Irish; 51, or 1.5%, as Scotch (CO1/42). Unlike the neighboring island of Montserrat, where the Irish constituted the predominant part of the population and maintained their Catholic faith, the Irish on Nevis seem to have been assimilated in the English population, judging from a 1671 report which characterized the inhabitants of Nevis as loyal and unanimous in their Protestant religion and membership of the English Church (CO1/27).

[2] The decline in the White population was partly caused by the emigration of a large number of small farmers and servants from Nevis. In 1656 "about 1,400 men, women, and children" were reported to have embarked with "their goods and servants" for Jamaica which had been captured from the Spanish by the British in 1655 (SP25/77; CO1/3; CO185). When a

malignant fever killed 1500 of the White population around 1690 (CO152/38:15 February, 1691), a final death blow was literally dealt to the small farmers.

[3] A great number of these units consisted of one individual or two persons who appeared unrelated (CO1/42). This probably reflects the increasing socioeconomic difficulty in establishing a family, as the larger planter families began to monopolize the socioeconomic resources of the island. Dunn and Wells use the term "slaves" even though it does not appear on the Nevis census, where only the term "Negro" is used.

[4] The basic relation upon which the family of the colonial society was built was primarily that of servitude between master and servant (or slave) and only secondarily kinship and marriage. This may partly have been due to the dearth of women, as reflected in the 1678 census which enumerated only 828 White women as compared with 1534 White men (CO1/42). It also reveals the fact that the families here were mainly economic enterprises, rather than social entities, and that the labor needs were of a sort which increasingly required a large work force instead of a smaller unit of cooperating relatives.

[5] A total of 1600–1800 people, small farmers and former indentured servants, seem to have emigrated from Nevis, St. Kitts and Montserrat in the mid-1650s, however less than 80 were still alive in 1660 (Bridenbaugh and Bridenbaugh 1972:203). During the 1680s a number of people also left for Antigua (CO155/1). When the English captured Jamaica, its Indian population had been decimated by the Spanish and the island was inhabited by approximately 2000 Spanish and Africans, half of them slaves (Higman 1988:8).

[6] Servants could be sold for the remainder of their terms to another master, implying the perception and treatment of them as commodities. The prolonged period of bondage also made it difficult for the servants to marry. As was the case in England, servants were not allowed to marry without the consent of their master, and both fornication and the birth of bastard children were punished by public whipping of both the man and the woman. The woman, furthermore, was often punished for the loss of labor caused by her pregnancy and the cost of bringing up the child which this entailed by having to give an extra year of service (Smith 1947:270-74). Such regulations placed the servants more on the level of the slaves than that of members of their master's family (Galenson 1981:8-9). It is important to remember, however, that within the patriarchal family, the type of relations which develop depend not so much on the servants' formal, legal position in the society as on the treatment which they are accorded by the particular master, under whose absolute control they live and work. Thus the position of the servants *vis-à-vis* their masters can have varied a great deal according to the individual disposition of the master and the type of farming operation and his labor needs.

[7] For an analysis of the early development of music as a means of cultural expression among slaves on Barbados see Handler and Frisbie (1972).

[8] This perception of the slaves' dance as lewd may reflect European "racist notions of 'African-ness'" as Maurer has suggested in a recent article on Caribbean dance (1991:11). It is possible, however, that the slaves intended their dances to be sexually provocative as a means of social protest. This would be in continuance of a traditional African form of social sanction employed by women which involved obscenities and sexual abuse (Ardener 1973).

[9] The traditional role of the church as a symbol of village identity and cooperation was increasingly challenged by the upwardly mobile who sought recognition of their newfound wealth in the form of higher social status. Rather than seeing the church as a unifying institution they desired to employ it as a forum within which to seek this status, and

advocated, for example, the renting of private pews in front of the church for the well-to-do (Underdown 1985:29, 31).

10 There do not appear to be any existent detailed descriptions of the nature of the social activities which the White and Black population participated in, separately or together, during the seventeenth century. This may be because they were such an accepted aspect of social life that they did not, unlike the Africans' dancing, deserve special notice. There is much to suggest, however, that the "games" and "plays" that Blacks and Whites shared, according to the Nevisian acts which attempted to banish them, included English sports brought to the West Indies by the first settlers. Some of the early European explorers and settlers of the New World actively encouraged their people to continue recreational practices that they knew from home. When Sir Humphrey Gilbert voyaged to Newfoundland in 1583 he thus brought with him "Morris dancers, Hobby horses, and Maylike conceits" for "alurement of the Savages" and "solace of our people" (as cited in Story 1969:168). In other contexts the festivities associated with the old order could become a means of protest against the modern order. In New England during the 1620s Thomas Morton, who became a royalist during the civil war, thus "encouraged servants to revolt against their masters, danced round a maypole and 'maintained (as it were) a school of atheism'" (Hill 1984:340). It was in the colonial society of servants and small farmers that festivity and pleasure would have been seen as a way in which to mark the mutual interrelationship of rights and duties which tied the rich and poor together in a rural society, and English rural traditions seem to have become a natural part of the recreational life in the early colonies. This is the only reasonable explanation for the fact that Christmas traditions, in a form recognizable as varieties of traditions known from seventeenth century English society had become established as an accepted part of island life during the nineteenth century. It was during the seventeenth century that they were most viable in their homeland and that the island society most resembled that of the homeland. That such customs could have become established at a later date, when they were fast becoming antiquated anomalies in England and when there were few English servants and small farmers on the island, is highly unlikely. Once the Christmas mummings had become a tradition in the early West Indian colonies, engaged in by the lower segments of the society which included an increasing number of slaves, it was not possible to undo them, even when the slaves used them to display their own music and dancing style and planters regarded them as increasingly unpleasant and potentially dangerous. Even though there are references to the use of maypoles in New England during the seventeenth century, it is significant that such English rural customs eventually disappeared there entirely. This has been seen to be related to the merging of different cultures which took place in the North American colonies (see the following chapter; Bushman 1984:371-73).

11 The importance of the taverns is apparent in the public accounts of Nevis from 1672-81, levies on tavern licenses constituting a major source of income (SM2/3).

12 The importance of this early colonial establishment of a market finds a parallel in Mintz and Hall's seminal work on the internal market system in Jamaica, which states that on that island the first "legally established market place [...] was created in Spanish Town [...] in the year 1662, seven years after the English occupation, at the request of the English settlers". This market was "set up quite matter-of-factly according to English law" (1960:13). It is interesting that Jamaica was settled, among others, by a large number of farmers and servants from Nevis. Even though an appalling number died within a few years,

the fact that the colonies originally were settled by people who came from other West Indian islands meant that the same sort of institutions, such as the market, were likely to have been established in the different colonies. This does not mean that the later market system which became entirely dominated by the Afro-Caribbean population should be regarded as of English origin. As shall be seen, the colonial authorities merely established an institutional framework within which the Afro-Caribbean population were enabled to further develop and assert an economic, and cultural, system of their own. Furthermore, the market structure which the colonial government set up in the English colonies was not particularly English, but rather an integral part of the European peasant societies of the times.

[13] This is apparent in Ligon's description of the Barbadian slaves' trade with ropes they had made out of bark (1970:48).

[14] It is not certain that an intended plot had, in fact, been uncovered, since very little evidence was forthcoming to shed light on it. The primary evidence seems to have been that of a slave who informed his mistress of having overheard Negroes talk about rising against the Whites and having appointed a captain and a lieutenant for the purpose (CO186/1). This "plot" may have been similar to the one which was rumored in St. Kitts in 1770 where, according to Gaspar's careful inquiry, it was " 'nothing more than a Meeting every Saturday night of the Principle Negroes belonging to Several Estates in One Quarter of the Island called Palmetto Point, at which they affected to imitate their Masters and had appointed a General, Lieutenant General, a Council and Assembly and the other Officers of Government, and after holding Council and Assembly they concluded the night with a Dance' " (1985:212). Such meetings, in turn, are reminiscent of "Negro election day" festivals which slaves staged in New England during the latter part of the eighteenth century, where Black officers were granted symbolic power over the White community, real power over the Black community (ibid.:213).

Chapter Two

Afro-Caribbean Culture, Euro-Caribbean Institutions

THE PLANTATION SYSTEM: DEPRIVED SLAVES AND EXTRAVAGANT PLANTERS

Descriptions of Nevis from the eighteenth century paint a picture of an island entirely dominated by sugar plantations. James Rymer, a surgeon who spent several months on Nevis during the 1770s, described the island as a patchwork of sugar plantations, bordered by trees and bushes, which he found quite enchanting: "taking in planters dwelling houses, their different works, etc. together with the negro huts situated in clusters at some little distance from the masters abode, the prospect of the Island is altogether pleasing and agreeable, being variegated with trees and shrubs and fields of sugar canes, whose several never ceasing vegetations confirm the constant spring" (1775:3). Behind this pleasing view of the eternally green, fertile island, however, was a harsh plantation system. William Smith, minister at St. John's Anglican church from 1716, found that most of the slaves' lives revolved around the work routine on the plantations. "During Crop-time [the harvest season, which usually began in February and finished in July], they work night and day almost incessantly."[1] Outside the harvest season, slaves were employed "howing Canes or digging round Holes to plant them in, (perhaps forty Persons in a row)". For this toil, the slaves were rewarded with "Salt herrings, and [. . .] Potatoes, which are sweet, and of the *Spanish* kind". Smith added, however, that he had observed some slaves eat "Dogs flesh" and also knew "some of them to be fond of eating Grashoppers, or Locusts; others will wrap up Cane Rats, in Bonano-Leaves, and roast them in Wood Embers", indicating that the amounts and variety of foods provided by the planters was insufficient. The slaves lived under close supervision of the planter: "They live in Huts, on the Western Side of our Dwelling-houses, so that every Plantation resembled a Small Town; and the reason why they are seated on the Western side, is, because we breath the pure Eastern air, without being offended with the least nauseous smell; Our Kitchens and Boyling-houses are on the same side, and for the same reason" (Smith 19745:217, 225–33, *et passim*).

By the early part of the eighteenth century, the slaves had become indispensable to the successful running of the large, industrial sugar plantations; in the process they became deprived of any identity or status in the colonial society, except that of constituting a source of labor force at their masters' disposal. This

39

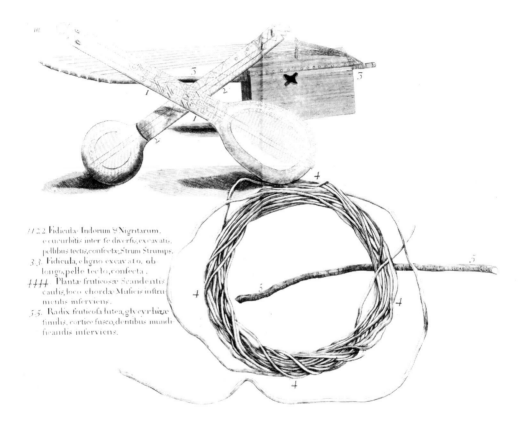

1.2.2 Fidicula Indorum & Nigritarum,
    e cucurbitis inter se diverfis, excavatis,
    pellibus tectis,confectæ,Strum Strumps.
3.3. Fidicula, e ligno excavato, ob
    longo,pelle tecto,confecta.
4.4.4.4 Plantæ fruticosæ Scandentis
    caulis, loco chordæ Musicis instru-
    mentis inferviens.
5.5. Radix fruticosa lutea, glycyrhizæ
    fimilis, cortice fusco,dentibus mundi
    ficandis inferviens.

PLATE 3   *Music instruments. Hans Sloane's* A Voyage to the Islands of Madera,
               Barbados, Nieves, S. Christophers and Jamaica, London: BM for the Author,
               1707.

treatment as nothing but brute labor was worsened by the fact that many of the owners of large sugar plantations chose to live in England and run their plantations through overseers and managers whose immediate concern was to profit themselves and to show a profit to the owner, regardless of the treatment of slaves which this might entail and the effects it might have on the profitability of the plantation in the long run. The status of the slaves is evidenced by letters sent by overseers to absentee planters which regretted the ill condition of the slaves, caused by insufficient food and clothing, because it led to low productivity on the estate. The following complaint from 1790 by George Webbe Daniell, an estate manager, may serve as an example: "The Negroes are now naked, and I am obliged to lessen their weekly allowance as our Insular supplies are scarce and very dear; not even a Barrel of Herrings has been sent out; this will prevent in a great measure, that regular roteen of Business which is indispensable upon West Indies property" (BM:21 July, 1790).

The treatment of the slaves as brute labor naturally precluded their being christened in that this would have admitted them to the Christian community on the island and thus given them an identity which, as Rev. Smith noted, they would be able to exploit in other contexts: "When a slave is once Christened, he conceits that he ought to be upon a level with his Master, in all other respects; in consequence whereof, he presumes That if his Master corrects him, for ever so great a Fault, he is at full liberty to send him out of the World, by a Dose of Poison." He described how a baptized Black woman had poisoned four White persons and concluded, "if even the whole Country was so mad, as to set about such an odd Conversion, the effect would then be a general Rebellion, and Massacre, of us Whites. This is Truth." Smith also noted that, "a Negro cannot be Evidence, in any respect, against a White Man: if he strikes a White Man, the Law condemns him to loose the Hand he strikes with; and if he should happen to draw Blood, he must die for it. If a White Man kills a Black one, he is not tried for Life; however, the Law obliges him to pay Thirty Pounds, *Nevis money*, to his Master, for the loss of his Slave. You will say, that these Proceedings are very despotick: But if you consider, that we have near ten Blacks to one White Person, you must own them to be absolutely necessary" (Smith 1745:230). None of the Anglican churches on the island displayed any interest in the conversion of slaves to Christianity at this time (*The Fulham Papers* 1965:118, 343).[2]

By refusing to include the slaves in the Christian community, the Church, which had been an important unitary force in English society, therefore actively helped maintain the slaves in a situation of social death. This death could be more than social, however, with a legal system which denied the slaves the right to bear witness in court allowing owners to underfeed and overwork their slaves to death. Even brutal outright murder of slaves went unpunished according to Smith, who wrote that a parishioner had killed one of his slaves "in a barbarous manner", for which act the slave owner received no punishment (except for the economic loss which he suffered by destroying his own property). If there was no legal system to protect the slaves many of the planters still appeared to wish to project an outside image of themselves as patriarchal masters basically concerned with the welfare of their dependents. Thus Smith added that the parishioner, who murdered his slave, "underwent a grievous Punishment; for (excepting his own Relations) not a single Gentleman would ever vouchsafe to converse with, or pay him a Visit, after he had committed the horrid Fact" (1745:233–34). The ability to maintain a well-run plantation without harsh treatment of the slaves clearly granted to the planters a certain amount of prestige. Sir William Stapleton, for example, wrote with pride to his manager after he had moved to England: "my plantation was always famous for provisions and ye looks of my slaves" (SM, Additional MSS:28 September, 1726).

It was not uncommon for the planters, or managers in their place, to continue earlier paternalistic social practices by admitting select slaves into their "family" circle, and some slaves seem to have been able to make the best out of this possibility for advancement. An example of this is Frank, belonging to the Stapleton family, who was recognized as an "extraordinary good Negro" and made an overseer in 1724. The manager, Joseph Herbert, suggested that this promotion should receive special recognition and wrote to the owner that it would "be of service" if a "hatt or some such thing" be sent to Frank for "his encouragement". The following year, Frank was somehow implicated in the slaves' supposed plot to rise against the White population. Two slaves were hanged "without any confession material", but Joseph Herbert and the attorney of the estate witnessed at court in Frank's defense and succeeded in sparing his life by shipping him to England. He stayed there until 1728 when he was sent to Antigua, and the following year he returned to Nevis after being pardoned by the governor of the Leeward Islands. During Frank's absence in England he was missed a great deal by Joseph Herbert who was careful to take "due care of Frank's house and stock". He disposed of some sheep for Frank, giving him the £9.14 which he received for them; he gave seven sheep to Frank's wives and children at his request, and delivered 19 sheep to Frank upon his return to Nevis. Frank sent several letters to Joseph Herbert during his absence, often complaining about poor treatment, and when Frank wrote that he was "in want of the necessaries of life" during his stay on Antigua, Joseph Herbert sent him some money. Before Frank returned to Nevis, the owners considered having him christened, because several people on Nevis "wanted his head". Frank proved to be a "very ungreatfull rogue", however. After less than 10 weeks on Nevis, during which time he disposed of his sheep, he fled to St. Kitts, and later Jamaica. Joseph Herbert concluded that "such extraordinary privileges" as Frank had received "induce some negroes to think they are above their fellow slaves & consequently puts 'em upon suitable attempts" (SM4/3:21 November, 1725; SM4/5:4 May, 1724, 29 September, 1725, 12 June, 24 June, 1726, 25 May, 1728, 1 August, 1729, 20 June, 1730; SM4/11: 1 June, 1726).

As part of their image of themselves as patriarchal masters, the planters sought to uphold the sort of life style which was associated with the old English gentry. They usually lived in spacious residences, which were centers for a luxurious way of life that included a great deal of entertaining. The lavishness of the planter class must have reached a high point, when, in 1787, week-long festivities were held in connection with the visit of Prince William Henry, later King William the Fifth. They included a sit-down dinner for 100 gentlemen and a ball, which was attended by 70 ladies, as well as horseraces and cockfighting (Pares 1950:74). The admiral to be, Lord Nelson participated in the events. He wrote the following about John Herbert, the uncle of his future wife, who was one of the wealthiest planters: "Although his income is immense, yet his expenses must be great, as his house is open to all strangers, and he entertains them most hospitably. I can't give you an idea of his wealth, for I don't believe he knows it himself. Many estates in that Island are mortgaged to him. The stock of Negroes upon his estate and cattle are valued at 60,000£ sterling: and he sends to England (average for seven years) 500 casks of sugar" (Nicolas 1845:162).

The men, in particular, engaged in the sort of social life which was associated with the landed gentry. Cockfights were popular pastimes for planters, and they displayed great interest in their cocks, some of which were sent out from England (Pares 1950:73). According to Rev. Smith, "excellent Game Cocks" were bred on Nevis, just as most plantations could "show a fierce Bul-Dog" indicating that dogfights also were popular (Smith 1745:217). John Baker, who lived on St. Kitts during the 1750s as a barrister and solicitor general for the Leeward Islands, described interisland cockmatches held on Antigua in 1755, attended by "very many gentlemen" from St. Kitts and Antigua, who did a fair amount of betting at the cockpit. In connection with this tournament, a number of other social events took place, such as hazards at the cockpit or in private homes, card games of whist, dinner parties, balls and concerts (Yorke 1931[1751–57]:80–82). The most common pastime, however, was drinking (Pares 1950:73). Much of it took place in private clubs such as the "Rebellious Club", where young Michael Smith drank himself to death in 1752 (Yorke 1931[1751–57]:67, 71). Men also enjoyed a great deal of sexual license with their slaves, who, as their property, were in a difficult position to refuse them.

Such license was not extended to the ladies, who lived much more confined lives. They spent most of their time indoors, keeping their activities to a minimum being attended by slaves who took care of all the domestic work (Bush 1981; see also Olwig 1985b). Their social life revolved around visiting other, similarly situated women, chatting and drinking tea. Thus when Nevisian planter John Pinney held a cockfight at his estate, he arranged for tea to be served for the ladies (Pares 1950:73). Apparently it was important for the women of the planter class to maintain their pale complexion, a symbol of their position as well-attended women who did not have to perform any kind of work outside the house (or inside for that matter). This concern led them to submit to a painful treatment, whereby they rubbed their skin with a poisonous nut, which caused it to swell and come off in large flakes within a couple of weeks, so that the women's "new Skin looks as fair as the Skin of a young child" (Smith 1745:30–31).

The extravagant life style of the planter class can, in many ways, be regarded as an exaggerated version of that which was associated with the landed upper classes in Europe. It involved the conspicuous display of a privileged life in luxury that made tangible the powerful position of the planters. This life style was emulated by the managers who took over the running of many of the island's estates when the planters, on occasion, chose to relocate in England in order to join the aristocracy there. This was accepted, to a certain extent, by the plantation owners, who realized the importance of the overseers maintaining a proper public appearance within the wider plantation society and presenting a certain position of wealth (and power) *vis-à-vis* the slaves. Thus an overseer of a large sugar plantation living with his family on an estate was entitled to a fairly impressive amount of service on the part of the slaves. In the case of George Webbe Daniell, who managed a large sugar plantation during the 1780s, "three women servants, one Cook, two House boys and one man in the Stables" were considered the proper allowance (SC, Bundle 17:September, 1783). Many of the overseers, who were single, cohabited with one of the domestic servants. This was the case with John Queely, overseer at the Nevisian estate Russell's Rest. During his previous employment on a plantation on St. Kitts he had lived with a slave woman, with whom he had six children within the span of nine years (BC:5 August, 1774).

With the planters absent it was tempting for the overseers to lead a more leisurely and luxurious life than they were entitled to. John Queely thus prided himself with having been much more efficient and honest than was generally the case, explaining: "I have not (like many managers I could name) spent my time in feasting and visiting abroad, or in ease, luxury and indolence at home: I have not like them employed the proprietors negroes in fattening beeves, nor applyed their cats corn & molasses, in feeding herds of swine, or flocks of sheep and poultry." Such behavior was, he stated, often occasioned by an ambitious wife who would like to be known as a generous hostess: "Women in general are in this part of the world emulous of being thought hospitable good house keepers, and they stop at no expence, which as they conceive it may entitle them to that characteristic, let the means of supporting it come from what quarter it will" (BC:5 August, 1774).[3]

The importance attached to luxury and hospitality on the part of the White upper class of course drained the sugar estates of economic resources and must have contributed further to the exploitation of the slave labor force. This seems to have been the case when David Stalker lost 28 slaves, owned by absentee planter Sir William Stapleton, because of his "barbarity and hard usage". This maltreatment of the slaves may have been related to his heavy drinking, which eventually led to his death (SM:20 May, 1738; Johnston 1965:186). Planters sought to curb this misuse of their property by providing managers with detailed instructions about the extent of their privileges and by appointing local attorneys to check on the plantation, or even sending out spies from England to report on the plantations' conditions. Usually planters do not seem to have had satisfactory control over their plantations during their absence in England, and Pares describes the absentee planter as faced with the choice between "eternal friction on the one hand and a gentle decline into bankruptcy on the other" (Pares 1950:141–59; Gay 1964[1928–29]:152).[4]

THE CREVICES LEFT FOR THE SLAVES

Throughout the West Indies, slaves were not only socially marginalized laborers toiling in the sugar fields and eking out a miserable life on the meager handouts of their masters. From early colonial times, the slaves succeeded in establishing relations of their own which were crucial to the shaping of the conventions of life which could form the basis of a distinct Afro-Caribbean culture. These relations can be seen to have developed in what Mintz, in a discussion of Afro-Caribbean peasantries, has termed historical and ecological "crevices in the societies". Historical crevices comprised those "*time periods* when European control faltered or was relaxed", whereas ecological crevices were found in those "*geographic* spaces where the plantation could not work" (1985:131). The early seventeenth century presented a period of relatively lax European control of the slaves, they being more or less left on their own when they were not used in the fields. This was seen to lead to the establishment of certain traditional rights among the slaves, which proved difficult to banish, when the planters sought to tighten control over the slaves by the end of the century. As shall be seen, these traditions retained their importance as institutional frameworks within which the slaves were able to maintain their cultural and social presence in a society after they had been entirely marginalized.

One of the most important geographical "crevices" came to be found in areas which could not be used in plantation cultivation, and which therefore were left for the slaves to use for the own agricultural activities in their provision grounds, as they were called. They presented physical spaces where they, in relative isolation from their masters, were able to develop a socioeconomic system of their own which proved to become a fundamental basis of the Afro-Caribbean community. The planters allowed their slaves to exploit these crevices, because they did not interfere with production on the plantations (they may even have sustained it), partly because the masters realized that they were unable to control all spheres of the slaves' lives. On Nevis, most of the plantations included mountainous as well as flat land, and many were bordered by tree-covered ravines, or guts, which cut through the low areas carrying water from the rainy higher levels to the sea. While the lowlands were covered with sugar fields, the mountains and guts were unsuited for large-scale agriculture and therefore were left for the slaves to use for their own subsistence cultivation (PP, Miscellaneous:53; Rymer 1775:3; Ramsay 1784:77). This was initially allowed by the planters, because they believed these grounds constituted a convenient and inexpensive means of feeding the slave population (Mintz 1974).

While the "ultimate effect" of these agricultural practices on the slaves' state of nutrition can be questioned (Higman 1984:212), this was perhaps not so much due to any inefficiency on the part of the slaves' provision cultivation. It was rather because many planters were tempted to force the slaves to depend on provisions from their grounds alone for sustenance or to reduce the allotment of foods, thinking that the slaves would be able to manage on their own. Slaves were not able to rely exclusively on the provisions that they could grow on their own grounds, however, due to periods of drought or excessive rain, which made any sort of planting impossible during certain periods of the year (BC:6 December, 1774; SC: Bundle 15:Plantation Accounts 1770–74; Gay 1964:160; Ramsay 1784:79; Pares 1950: 126–27).[5] Even if the nourishment obtained from the grounds was insecure, they nevertheless became crucial to the slaves because they made it possible for them to establish their own tradition of small farming relatively unhindered by the planters (Mintz 1974; Higman 1984:212; Olwig 1985a).

On Nevis slaves usually had small gardens around their houses as well as larger provision grounds further away from the estate grounds. It was common practice to give the slaves free time on Saturday afternoons, at least out of crop-time, to perform their agricultural tasks (Robertson 1730:12). Slaves were quick to regard the time allowed them for cultivating the grounds as a right. This led John Pinney to instruct his manager to vary the day of the week that he gave the slaves time off to work in their grounds and sometimes even to suspend the granting of free time for several weeks, in order that "they should not come to think they had a customary claim to Saturday afternoon" (Pares 1950:131).

Even though some planters sought to institute certain measures of control, the slaves' provision gardening nevertheless attained considerable cultural significance for the slaves. This is revealed indirectly during the latter part of slavery, when English Methodist missionaries in their efforts to convert slaves encountered Afro-Caribbean cultural expressions related to the farming of provision crops (some of which were of African origin). Farming thus presented the most powerful image for the slave, Bean, when on his death bed he wished to impress on his son the importance of leading a good Christian life: "God bless you my child. Take care to be a good boy. I have set you a good example, follow your father to heaben, keep from ebery ting dat is sinfa and God will bless on you, if you save him good heart make ebery thing prospa you take in your hand, when you plant cassada he make um come up good when you plant tanja when you plant potatoes he send rain from heben and he grow good" (C25: 21 May, 1802). Another missionary report shows that the slaves closely followed the changes of the moon and had definite ideas about the kinds of weather which followed, indicating that the cycles of the moon may have been an important guide for the planting of crops (C355:28 August, 1828).

Apart from these scattered descriptions of the slaves' farming from the early 1800s, the historical records from Nevis are rather silent about the slaves' provision cultivation, including the organizational structure of their farming and the agricultural techniques which they employed.[6] This lack of information was no doubt largely due to the fact that much of the farming occurred outside the plantation system proper and thus was of little concern to the White population, who may even have been relatively ignorant about the details of these matters. It was not before the condition of the slaves, and the very institution of slavery, became subject to severe criticism in Great Britain that descriptions of the slaves' provision grounds, which offered insights into the more human side of slavery, began to appear. One such description is found in Nevisian planter James Tobin's *Cursory Remarks*, in which he sought to refute the attack on West Indian slavery levelled by Rev. James Ramsay on St. Kitts. According to Tobin slave couples planted the ground around their houses in "lime, lemon, plantain, banana, and calabash trees", and they planted "what may be allotted them in other parts of the plantation, in cassada, yams, potatoes, &c for use; and in cotton, pot-herbs, fruit, &c for sale". The money procured from the sale enabled them to "purchase a hog, which is soon increased to two, or more, with the addition of goats, and poultry, if they are successful, and industrious" (1785:94–95). The testimony on slavery found in the House of Commons Accounts and Papers from the 1780s and 1790s also includes references to the slaves' provision cultivation, in great measure in order to determine the nutritional state of the slaves (Dirks 1987:56–96).

Even these accounts from the latter part of the eighteenth century reflect little understanding or knowledge of the details of the actual agricultural practices of the slaves. This may be related to the seemingly irregular way in which the slaves cultivated their land. In his study of Jamaican plantation maps from the eighteenth and nineteenth centuries, Higman thus found that few maps clearly demarcated the areas of provision cultivation on the part of the slaves, apparently because they were unable to determine their exact extent. As one attorney for several absentee plantation owners during the early part of the nineteenth century explained, "It is not customary in Jamaica to make any survey of the land cultivated by the negroes, and they generally cultivate it in a straggling way, here and there where they find the best soil; if they had land enough to go upon, they cultivate that which is most easily cultivated and most productive, so that it is impossible to form a judgment of the extent of it in the aggregate" (Higman 1988:261). This perception of their provision cultivation as "straggling" is caused by the slaves' common practice of cultivating the land in swidden agriculture, whereby they cleared the ground by cutting and burning the underbrush and smaller trees, so that they planted under the larger trees. In this way the slaves' grounds were not large, open areas, as were the sugar fields, but rather appeared as ground cover under trees. Furthermore, the slaves' provision grounds were not permanently located in one spot, because this type of agriculture usually was associated with a certain amount of mobility, whereby new spots were cleared in order to regenerate the soil of the old plots (Mintz and Hall 1960:7; Olwig 1985a:46–50).

Throughout the eighteenth century, the most detailed information about the slaves' economic activities and their social and cultural importance derives primarily from descriptions of the market where the slaves sold their produce. While the market seems to have been patronized primarily by the White population during the seventeenth century, during the eighteenth century, when the White population of small farmers and laborers had virtually disappeared from Nevis, the market became entirely dominated by the slaves. In his description of the market, which was held Sunday morning in Charlestown, Smith thus characterized it as a place "whither Negroes bring Fowls, *Indian corn*, Yams, Garden-stuff of all sorts, etc." (1745:231–32). It was no longer acceptable for the White population to trade at the markets, perhaps because they were held primarily by slaves and on Sundays, and Robertson noted that only Jews[7] and "the looser sort of *Christians*" traded with the slaves (1730:12).

The importance of trading to the slaves is apparent in two acts which were passed by the local assembly during the 1730s in order to prevent the slaves from selling stolen goods. The first act from 1737 reaffirmed the requirement that slaves must have licence to sell "any Goods, Wares, Merchandizes, Rum, or any other strong Liquor, either for themselves, or for their Owners, or for any other Persons, in any House, or in the publick Street, or in the Country". The act did not prohibit the slaves from "selling, or exposing to Sale any fresh Fish, fresh meat, Poultry, or any Produce or Manufacture of this Island, except Rum, and other strong Liquors" (*Acts of Assembly* 1740:133). In the amended act from 1739, the goods excluded from the requirement of licence were "Greens, Herbs, Grass, Wood, Roots, Food made of Roots, Crabs, fresh Butter, fresh Fish, and the Slave's own particular Manufacture" (ibid.:139). A description of a scare of French invasion which was rumored in 1778 provides further information on the sort of meats and manufactured goods which were traded by the slaves. The slaves had killed "hogs, sheep, etc., and brought them to market on Sunday [...] in the hopes of getting a little cash and to prevent their falling into the hands of the French. Upon hearing the alarm, they threw away their meat and destroyed other provisions—broke all the earthenware at market in the streets" (Pares 1950:94). The Methodists, who initiated their missionizing activities on Nevis in the 1780s, noted with dismay that two markets were held on Nevis on Sunday mornings, even though they constituted a serious break of the Sabbath. They were both reported to attract several hundred people who were "busily employed in buying and selling" (C301:26 March, 1827; C330: 7 January, 1828).

Despite their general appearance as busy places of trade, the economic importance of the markets has been questioned in an ecological study, which suggests that most individual exchanges were petty and that "too many writers [...] have confused activity with prosperity" (Dirks 1987:74). There is no doubt that many slaves attended market, even though they had little produce to sell and no need, or means with which, to purchase anything. The fact that many chose to make the long journey to market, even though they had little economic incentive to do so, demonstrates the great importance that the market had as a place, where slaves could congregate in order to chat and drink together. This is also apparent in the Methodist reports, where the missionaries express regret at the fact that many of their congregation attended market on the Sabbath, which remained market day on Nevis until the abolishment of slavery. One missionary noted how the slave "very frequently comes out of the market to preaching or to his class meeting, & immediately from there ordinances to mingle in the crowd and dissipation of the market again, his thought probably having been there the whole time" (C449:3 May, 1832). The social importance of the market is also apparent in another missionary report, where it is stated that the slaves washed and put on clean clothes before attending the market (C255:30 October, 1824), indicating that they regarded it as a place to show off their best. This central position of the market within the slave community was not lost upon the planters. Thus it was common practice for the planters to punish "a very refractory Slave" at the market, because they thought that the slaves would "be disgraced by a Public punishment in the Market place", and hoped "that a fear of this disgraceful Exposition would operate an amendment of Conduct" (HE:f.3).

The market clearly was not only, or perhaps primarily, a place where slaves could exchange their garden produce in order to obtain goods that were necessary for their survival. The markets also presented the slaves with a public forum within which they could display and trade their farm produce and thereby assert the significance of their provision agriculture. At the same time the market, as a public gathering place, provided a space where the slaves could congregate in large groups, exchanging gossip and forming a "public opinion" on important matters outside the control of their masters. The market, in other words, allowed the slaves to remove themselves from the margins of the society as socially dead brute labor and show publicly that they were semi-independent small farmers and traders within the colonial society. Since the slaves made this public statement within an institution which was recognized by the colonial society, it could not be ignored or made illegal by this society.

SOCIAL RELATIONS

Even though socioeconomic relations of vital importance developed among the slaves in connection with their provision cultivation, these relations remained informal and were not safeguarded by legal protection. As Nevisian planter Richard Nisbet explained, the slave had no legal right to the "few profits which [. . .] [he] can derive from his industry"; no right "to a certain fixed and due proportion of time to be appropriated to [. . .] [his] own use and advantage"; no right to be "fairly tried before he is sentenced to severe punishments". The food that the slaves were given and the free time they received to grow own produce or attend a funeral of a relative or friend had to be begged for (1789:36). The slaves remained in a formal position of complete dependence upon their masters, who in the act of conferring occasional privileges on their slaves only reaffirmed their authority *vis-à-vis* their slaves. The importance of masters possessing absolute authority and respect on estates is apparent in the problems which many newcomers to a plantation encountered. Thus it was common for the slaves to "try their new Master", often called a "Salt Water Buckro" by staging various kinds of disobedience in order to see whether they could challenge his control over them and thus break down his position of authority on the estate (HE:f.47; PP, Letter Books, No. 3:3 April, 1766).

This patriarchal system precluded official recognition of any sort of social structure among the slaves, since it might entail acceptance of alternative structures of authority which might pose a threat to the planters' power (Goveia 1965:94–95). The slave laws disregarded the possibility of enduring ties of importance among the slaves, including those ties which arise from family life. The Leeward Islands slave law of 1798 regarded it as "unnecessary and even improper" that the slaves were married by religious ceremony, and thought it sufficient that planters every New Year's Day convene the slaves to " 'enquire which of them have a husband or wife.' " (Higman 1984:351). Nothing was done in the Leeward Islands to protect families belonging to the same estate from being separated, when a slave population was sold to pay for debt (Goveia 1965:143–44). An example of the results of this practice is found in a Methodist report, which describes a woman, who had lost her husband ten years previously, when he was sold off to St. Vincent. She still heard from him and had continued to regard him as her husband throughout all these years (B55:29 May, 1820). This lack of interest in slave families was also due to the fact that during the early part of the eighteenth century the planters were not particularly interested in encouraging the birth of children on the part of the slave women, even though they would belong to them. This was, according to Rev. Robertson, because the lost labor from the mother combined with the high death rate of the children and the cost of rearing them until they could work quite simply did not make the breeding of children profitable (Robertson 1732:44).

Even though children were regarded as largely burdensome to the planters during the early part of the eighteenth century, when ample supplies of relatively inexpensive African slaves were available, the planters were not able to prevent slave women from becoming pregnant and bearing children (some, in fact, actively contributed to this themselves through their sexual exploitation of their slave women). Furthermore, during the last decades of slavery when the transatlantic slave trade had been abolished the slave population had to be replenished through the birth of slave children. According to Nisbet, slaves born in Africa were the most prone to live in husband-wife relationships, because they had not been "subdued and perverted by having growing up under slavery" (1789:21). The importance attached to this tie was, probably more significantly, related to the fact that it constituted, for the African slaves, the primary way in which to compensate for the loss of "kindred and of friends" which they had experienced (ibid.:9). Some husband-wife relations included polygynous unions, particularly those involving men who had improved their position on the plantations, either through hard labor in their provision ground, or by being an artisan or overseer of other slaves (Robertson 1730:45; SM4/5: 1 August, 1929). Within the slave community polygyny therefore might very well have been a mark of superior status; however, to the White population it was pointed to as a mark of their heathenness and slave status.

As slaves bore children, large kin groups emerged on the estates consisting of the descendants of those slaves who were imported from Africa. Since the children always belonged to, and resided on, the estate of their mother's owner, these kin groups tended to have a strong matrilateral bias, with some of the fathers living on other estates with their respective kin groups. In 1817, nine years after the African slave trade had ceased, less than 15% of the slaves on Nevis had been born in Africa. Since more than 80% of the slaves belonged to estates with more than 50 slaves at that time (Higman 1984:105, 116), most of them must have been living within large networks of interrelated kin. This is illustrated for Nevis in documents pertaining to a court case, where "a West Indian estate" is described as "an union of families", and one Nevisian slave family of 32 is referred to, which consisted of the children, grandchildren and great grandchildren of one African slave (*Case in Nevis* 1818:12, 39).[8] The significance of the plantation based family network is attested to by the fact that it was customary for the slaves to bury the dead "at the door of his own house" (B55:14 August, 1820) and thus near the family which still lived there.

As was the case with the slaves' economic activities, the records are not very forthcoming with information on the importance of the family in the daily life of the slaves.[9] Several references show that the family offered important protection in times of crisis. In the case of severe illness, or death, the family thus congregated to show their support, and, as in the case of Bean, to receive the blessing of the departing member of the family (C363:4 December, 1828; C25:21 May, 1802). The family was also of importance in its attempt to offer whatever help or protection it could muster, when problems arose on the estate with the planter or manager. Thus one driver (a slave in charge of the field slaves) became so incensed at seeing his mother flogged, that he plotted with another slave to murder the owner (B64:26 November, 1829). The situation was more complicated on another estate, where the driver was ordered by the planter to whip two slaves, for having received stolen goods, who happened to be his son and stepson respectively. The other slaves immediately protested loudly, in particular two women, one of them the half sister, the other the cousin of the two men (*Case in Nevis* 1818:12, 8).

Mintz has suggested that economic cooperation between spouses was important in provision cultivation and marketing with the husband concentrating on cultivating the ground, the wife on marketing the produce. This was important in a society where men and women performed the same sort of work in the field, providing no basis for a sexual division of labor. The significance of this cooperation for the formation of a marital relationship between spouses is suggested by evidence to the practice of breaking a relationship between couples by the cutting down in two of the *cotta*, the head gear in which produce was placed when it was carried to the market (Mintz 1974:217). The close connection between the marital tie and the establishment of a functioning domestic unit involving small farming, among other things, was certainly emphasized by James Tobin in his defense of slavery. According to Tobin, a young man began to assert his independence toward his own family at the age of 18-20, when he thought of "building a house for himself, and, at the same time, of connecting himself with some particular woman as a wife". Although he might not "abide strictly by the first choice" in marital partner he apparently began "to consider himself as settled," and the couple continued to "improve their settlement, and plant the ground around it as well as what may be allotted them in other parts of the plantation" (1785:93-94). In Tobin's view, the main threat towards this domestic idyll was the bad habit of taking an additional wife, which some of the most prosperous men indulged in. Even though the realities of slavery were much harsher than the picture drawn by Tobin, there is no doubt that the domestic economy which developed around provision cultivation constituted an important area within which family relations received concrete importance. This is also supported in my own study of slavery on the former Danish West Indian island of St. John, where court records showed maternal relatives and spouses to be important sources of help and cooperation in the slaves' subsistence economy (Olwig 1985a).[10]

Despite their refusal to grant any formal recognition to the slaves' families—however they were defined and demarcated—planters did recognize the importance of families in child rearing. Thus one of the many instructions left to the overseer by planter John Pinney stated that if any "creole field negro Boys or Girls" should be offered for sale, he should purchase them if they were "healthy and of a very good family" (PP, Miscellaneous:54). The only social unit among the slaves, which the planters recognized, was that of the household itself, in that they, according to Tobin, usually gave money or materials to the building of a new house and donated rum and food, as well as a free Saturday afternoon, when the slaves helped the new houseowner with "covering" the house (1785:66).[11] The slaves had no right to this help from their masters, since, as Nisbet noted, it was a favor which the slaves had to beg from their masters (Nisbet 1789:36–37). The planters' involvement in the construction of a new residential unit, which often also implicated the establishment of a new marital tie, therefore should not necessarily be seen as an official sanction of a new family among the slaves on the part of the planter. The spouses could not prevent the master from separating a family through sales, nor could they bar their master from punishing members of the family, if he so chose. The master had individual rights in all slaves and did not defer to any social relations among the slave population.

A RESISTANT CULTURE

In the face of the masters' attempts to retain absolute formal control over their slaves, many slaves resorted to various forms of overt and covert resistance. One of the most important forms of open resistance was maroonage to the forested mountain areas and ravines which presented convenient hiding places, and managers of plantations apparently calculated on a certain number of their slaves to be absent from the estate. When Joseph Herbert made an inventory of the estate's labor force, he listed a total of 95 workers, of whom generally 4 were run away (SM6/3:May 17, 1731). While most of the runaways acted on an individual basis, slaves sometimes staged more collective forms of maroonage, as for example, when most of Lady Frances Stapleton's "Negro men went away" for about 14 days. Significantly, they received no punishment, when they finally reappeared after a messenger was sent out asking them to return (SM7/1:14 May, 1725).[12] Slaves also attempted at times to present their demands towards the plantation authorities in larger pressure groups. Frances Stapleton's slaves, a few years previously, came "in a body" to the attorney of her estate swearing that if certain named persons "came to live on yᵉ plantation, they would all run away". They were dismissed with no promises except the assurance that whoever became manager of their estate, they would not be "ill used", the attorney noting that if one were to give in to such acts on the part the slaves "there wou'd be little good expected from them". Furthermore, he admonished the slaves that they "should obey whoever wee put on Manager or else be severly punish't" (SM7:23 March, 1722/3). Such direct acts of protest on the part of the slaves could not be tolerated in a plantation regime which depended upon the masters holding a position of power and authority toward their slaves. For this reason, clandestine or indirect forms of resistance were more prevalent and, perhaps, also more effective.

Religious beliefs and practices which invoked supernatural powers became an important means whereby the slaves challenged their masters' position of power. One such belief revolved around the conviction among the slaves that they would return to their "Native Country" after death, for which reason, it was a fairly common occurrence among new slaves to commit suicide (Smith 1745:228–29; see also Sloane 1707:xlviii). On 21 July 1731, Joseph Herbert thus reported that 3 of the 5 newly purchased slaves had gone "into the woods on a Sunday and hang'd themselves" (SM4/5). These slaves had literally taken their own lives to remove them from the sphere of control of their masters and in order to restore them in their homeland.

Mortuary practices among slaves in the West Indies constituted an important locus where a feeling of community was generated within the slave group and against the White population. An important institution was found in overnight wakes where great numbers of slaves gathered to spend a last night with the dead. Such wakes were festive occasions, where those gathered drank, danced, sang and told stories about important ancestors and spirits and the White man who no longer had any power to bother the deceased. The funeral itself also took place at night, and was attended only by the slaves, the Whites realizing that they were unwanted at these occasions (Abrahams and Szwed 1983:168, 176). These funerals were, like the wakes, known to be joyful events, and according to Rev. Smith they were attended by many slaves who sang and drank and called out to the dead (1745:231).[13] The link to deceased kinsmen was maintained by the slaves congregating in their free time "at the Grave of their deceased Kindred" in order to "Feast, Dance, and Carouse" (Robertson 1730:12–13). These customs, where slaves gathered on their own in order to engage in dancing and singing practices celebrating deceased relatives, and berating the White population, are indicative of the further development of cults among the slaves similar to the secret societies. Whereas in Africa the heads of kin groups and ancestors represented powerful figures in the formal social organization, in the West Indian slave societies, where all formal power rested with the White masters, ancestors who had passed away came to represent alternative sources of power, like the guardian spirits Africans located in specific locations places where "secret cults" might develop.

Another attempt to challenge the White control of the slave population can be found in the slaves' practice of witchcraft, or *obeah*. There are, as in the case of the slaves' mortuary traditions, scattered references to the presence of *obeah* men who had obtained considerable power among other slaves within the plantations (Abrahams and Szwed 1983:181, 184). *Obeah* is mentioned in the letters of the Methodist missionaries who reported being employed by slave owners to help combat the evil. Although their references to it are very brief they leave the impression that *obeah* was, in fact, quite common, and that *obeah* men and women were rather fearless people who believed that the supernatural powers which they controlled through their art made them immune to others (C154:16 November, 1821; C241:11 November, 1825). They therefore could only be countered by those who had access to even stronger supernatural power, such as the missionaries who were convinced of the superiority of their own religion and therefore did not fear *obeah*.

Many aspects of slave culture were not directly oppositional in nature, but rather worked within the institutional frameworks established and recognized by the colonial society. This was particularly true for the performative culture. It was, for example, common for slaves to sing in the fields while they worked, a custom which was fully accepted by the White population. This singing was characterized by changes between lead singers and a chorus, and was rather admired by Rev. Smith, who described it as "harmoniously tuned" (1745:231). The slaves' right to sing while working does not seem to have been questioned by the planters and was also a common feature on other West Indian islands (Handler and Frisbie 1972:15; Olwig 1985a:36). According to Smith the slaves sang "merrily, i.e. two or three Men with large Voices, and a sort of Base Tone, sing three or four short lines, and then all the rest join at once, in a sort of Chorus, which I have often heard, and seemed to be, *La, Alla, La, La*" (1745:231). It is interesting that the slaves were able to perform their own form of music with lyrics that were not entirely understood by the White population right in the plantation fields in the presence of the planter or overseer. The field songs could be rather critical of the slave system, however, as apparent in some of the field songs which were recorded in the Virgin Islands (see for example Olwig 1985a:193).[14]

As during the early colonial period, much of the performative culture of the slaves continued to take place within a framework of traditions closely tied to the patriarchal society of early modern England and therefore of a more inclusive kind. James Tobin claimed that "mirth, festivity, music, and dancing, engross no small portion of their leisure: they have an ear for music, and a graceful activity in dancing, far beyond the dismal scrapings, an aukward caperings of an English May-day, or a country wake" (1785:96). Although Tobin's description of slavery was a rather rosy one, there is no reason to question his statement that music and dance occupied a great deal of the slaves' free time. It is, furthermore, of interest that Tobin described the slaves' music and dance in relation to seasonal folk festivals known from English rural society, such as those which were seen to have been brought to the island during the seventeenth century. The importance of English institutional frameworks for much of the slaves' music and dance is most apparent, however, in the Christmas celebrations.

By the eighteenth century, it was common practice throughout the British West Indies for the slaves to use especially the days granted at Christmas to dress up in costumes and stage dances for one another as well as for their owners, who gave them food and drink (Dirks 1987). It also remained a tradition for all the slaves to receive special allowance at Christmas, so that they were given beef instead of their customary herring (Gay 1964:172; SC:Bundle 13). This seems to have become so established that planters were willing to pay dearly for the meat, if it was difficult to obtain, and managers expressed a certain amount of apprehension, if the absentee plantation owners had not made arrangements to procure the special Christmas allowance for the slaves (BC:21 May, 1779). This was related to the strong expectation on the part of the slaves to receive special foods and drinks at Christmas. If the planters neglected this custom, the slaves were known to do mischief on estates, by, for example, setting fire to cane fields. Furthermore, the Christmas celebrations where groups of slaves toured the island dressed up in various costumes could not just lead to a general spirit of "drunkenness, quarrelling, fighting" among the slaves, but, it was feared, to general rebellion. For this reason the White population continued to patrol the island in special guards during the Christmas season (Watson 1835[1817]:502; Dirks 1987:167).

Detailed descriptions of the sort of singing, dancing and masquerading, which these Christmas celebrations entailed, only exist for later periods of history as far as Nevis is concerned; however they exist for other West Indian islands. In his extensive survey of the slaves' Christmas saturnalia in the British West Indies, Dirks thus presents several accounts of slaves waking up their master and mistress before dusk in order to dance for them accompanied to fiddles and drums, in return receiving presents as well as generous entertaining in the great house with food and drink. Other descriptions noted male mummers or female setgirls dressed up in various costumes, frequently with fancy headgear or masks, who walked around, often congregating in towns giving the market place "the atmosphere of a fair". Among the most popular were John Canoe, entertainers wearing grotesque masks and wooden swords, and Actor-Boys who wore white masks, gowns and fantastic headgear and toured the island in troupes (Dirks 1987:1-8; Bettelheim 1988:45-49). Traditions such as those described for other West Indian islands clearly were also present on Nevis during slavery, since they were well established during the postslavery period, judging from later accounts of the Christmas celebrations which flourished on Nevis. As shall be seen, they included John Canoe, Actor-Boys and mumming plays such as "St. George and the Dragon" and "The Christmas Bull Play" and a version of the

English morris termed the "Masquerade" (AW; Abrahams 1983:13; Bettelheim 1988:79–83).

During the eighteenth century, the slaves incorporated other European cultural traditions to their performative culture, as they were brought to the island by the White population. Masquerade dances, which became popular in England during the early eighteenth century had been adopted by the slaves on Nevis when Tobin wrote his work on slavery in 1785: "My readers will probably be tempted to smile, when I mention negro-masquerades, yet such amusements they have occasionally among them; and which are no bad burlesques on the insipid *I know you's*, and *You don't know me's* of the Pantheon, or the Hay-market" (1785:96). According to Tobin, the slaves' masquerades therefore were "takeoffs" on the masked balls held at popular theatres like Pantheon and Haymarket of London, where conversations among masked participants often were initiated by verbal exchanges like "I know you" or "Do you know me?" (Castle 1986:35). A court case from the early nineteenth century, which noted a dance being held in April 1817 at Mr. Jeffrey's "negro houses", probably referred to such a masquerade in that one slave, Richard, was described as having appeared as Bonaparte with "a sword by his side (made out of a stave)" while another, David was supposed to have been the Duke of Wellington. Apparently, these festivities continued the next afternoon, where the slaves danced the reel (*Case in Nevis* 1818:25).

The social implications of the slaves' "burlesques" on their owners' masquerade balls were rather different from those of the Christmas sports. Sports were held in the open and had a public character. In the West Indies they involved both slaves and their owners in common festivities. When masquerades began in England, on the other hand, they were rather exclusive affairs, held in private houses or ballrooms, where admission was only possible for those with a ticket (Castle 1986). The masquerades which were organized by the planters undoubtedly also had this private character, and judging from the above mentioned reference to their being held in "negro houses" they may well have begun in this fashion among the slaves. By the end of the nineteenth century, however, they had become incorporated into the public tradition of the community-based sports, such as those which took place at Christmas. They eventually became known as an important feature of these sports and were often combined with a local version of the quadrille dance.[15]

The slaves' Christmas sports represented a challenge to the whole plantation society, because they presented a formally accepted structure through which the slaves could display their own culture of music and dance, which otherwise had to be performed more or less under cover in the slave villages on the different estates. By boldly displaying this important aspect of their culture within the framework of English folk traditions right in the homes of the planters, the slaves thus challenged the planters on a cultural terrain which implicated the planters themselves. By making their culture public through traditions of the old English rural society, known by the planters, the slaves forced them to recognize the existence of a wider community which included slaves as social beings with certain rights. "Custom" was still at that time a force in English culture which was difficult to deny—as was seen by John Pinney's attempts to shuffle free time to prevent the slaves from attaining customary rights. Christmas celebrations therefore constituted another means of counteracting the slaves' marginalization in the plantation society as socially dead property.

GAINING PRIVILEGES WITHIN THE PLANTATION SOCIETY

A number of slaves succeeded in gaining privileges within the plantation societies by establishing strong ties of attachment to their masters. As already noted, the relationship of dependence upon a patriarchal master which the slave experienced during the seventeenth century would have been perceived by the Africans as an avenue of attachment and incorporation into the island society. An example was Frank, who succeeded in improving his social standing by cultivating an intimate relationship with his master. Frank was kept as a slave, however, and eventually chose to escape from the island. Another slave, Joseph Herbert[16] who belonged to an old woman, obtained his legal freedom when she decided to set "her faithful slave at liberty". He remained attached to his former owner, built her a house and provided her with part of the profits from his trade as a cooper, she having no means of supporting herself (Nisbet 1789:46). One of the reasons why this freed slave remained attached to his former owner may be found in his desire to retain the social visibility which he had in the colonial society by virtue of his tie to his former owner. The freedom, which he had gained through his emancipation, thus secured him no place of acceptance of his own within that society.

During the course of the eighteenth century many slaves had, in fact, experienced an improvement in their individual condition by being allocated to more desirable occupations in domestic service or the trades than the strenuous field work. In 1788 it was estimated that out of a working slave population of approximately 5500, 1500, or more than a quarter of the economically active slave group, were engaged as domestics, tradesmen and fishermen (Goveia 1965:146). In 1834, by the time of Emancipation, the proportion employed off the fields had increased to more than one third of the working slaves (Higman 1984:48).[17] Some of the tradesmen were allowed by their masters to hire themselves out, working on their own either full time or in their free time, paying a fixed sum of money to their owners for this right (Goveia 1965:140–41; Pares 1950:129). The domestic slaves worked directly for their masters, and were thus under their constant surveillance. Furthermore, they were not given a day free on Sundays, but were required to attend to their masters throughout the week. These disadvantages were somewhat compensated for by special privileges in terms of better clothing and food, which most of them enjoyed, and some of the domestics also developed a close relationship with their owners and their families.

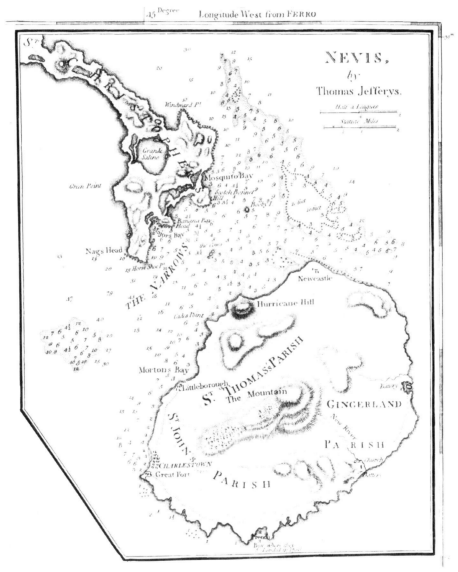

PLATE 4   *Map of Nevis. Thomas Jefferys'* The West Indian Atlas; or, a *General Description of the West Indies: Taken from Actual Surveys and Observations, Thomas Jefferys, Geographer to the King. London: Printed for Rbt. Soyer & John Bennet, 1775.*

This could mean that they gained their confidence, travelled with them, even to Europe, and a few of them even were taught to read (C25:21 May, 1802).[18] In some cases, the relationship between the slaves and the planter's children became so close that the children failed to adopt the English speech pattern and manners of their parents and instead emulated the slaves. This, apparently, was the case in 1780 when John Pinney decided to move his family to England with the first fleet the following year. He decided, however, that it was "advisable for the time I had to remain in this Island, to endeavor to place my Daughter in a situation as free from the conversation and company of negroes as the state of the Country would admit" for which reason he attempted to place her "under the tuition of Mrs. Robinson, a Gentlewoman of exceeding good character at St. Christopher" (PP:31 July, 1780).

For some domestic slaves, the relationship to their master could become rather too intimate, as when they were exploited sexually. Such relationships, however, bore the possibility of attaining further privileges and securing a better position for the offspring of such a union. Thus Colored slaves were, generally speaking, not used in the field, but employed as domestic or artisan slaves (SC:September, 1783; Goveia 1965:231). In some cases, sexual relations between White men and slave women developed into fairly permanent unions, which resulted in the birth of several children, and it has been estimated that around 1817 16.4% of the Creole slaves on Nevis (those who were born in the West Indies) were Colored, i.e. issue from unions involving at least one White ancestor (Higman 1984:148).[19]

Sexual relationships between Whites and slaves or the freed apparently became so common that in 1802 a Methodist missionary claimed "it is well known that more than half of the White men in the West Indies, cohabit with Negroe or coloured women" (B34:1 August, 1802). As a result of these practices, a free Colored population emerged.[20] In 1788, 120 free Colored were counted on Nevis, and this population grew rapidly. By 1820, the free Colored in most of the Leeward Islands were believed to constitute the majority of the free population (Goveia 1965:96). These free Colored, who lived mainly in the town, made a living huckstering, keeping small shops, fishing, and working in "sedentary trades", as for example writing clerks or tailors, or in artisan trades as carpenters, coopers and masons. Small farming did not constitute an attractive means of living, since the free, who had to rent land, could not compete with the provision farming of the slaves, who did not have to pay for the use of marginal estate land (ibid.:227–28).[21]

BELONGING IN A SLAVE SOCIETY

In their discussion of African slavery Kopytoff and Miers emphasize the importance of membership in a kin group as a criterion for holding full citizenship in

African societies. Attachment to a kin group via a patron therefore presented the best African strategy of negating a slave status. This is in contrast to modern Western thinking, where freedom, meaning personal autonomy unhindered by social bonds, is regarded as the opposite of slavery (1977:17). The Western conception of freedom has played an important role in many of the historical works on slavery in the New World, where rebellion and maroonage, involving the severing of all ties to the hated system of slavery, have been seen to constitute the main form of resistance (Heuman 1985). The African background suggests, however, that the negation of the slave status might have been sought via attempts at creating ties which generated for the slaves a position of belonging in the society.

While a significant minority of the slaves improved their condition through ties to their masters, or mistresses, the majority did not find such relationships particularly conducive to any sort of advancement and incorporation into the colonial society, but rather found themselves placed irrevocably in the bottom of the society working in large gangs on the sugar plantations. The social fields which the slaves established in connection with their music and dance, economic activities, kinship and family, religious beliefs and practices provided for these slaves the most important contexts within which they could develop ties and communities of belonging. Some of these fields, most notably the secretive *obeah* practices and the religious cults which invoked sources of power outside the control of their master, challenged the master's absolute position of authority and therefore posed a serious threat to the plantation system. Most of these spheres, however, initially developed in a sort of symbiotic relationship with the plantation system and were perceived by the masters to be harmless and perhaps even beneficial. Dance and music were regarded as a welcome release from the slaves' daily drudgery; economic activities were seen as providing a useful means of self-feeding; families were seen as necessary in the bearing and rearing of children, while religious practices in connection with death, for example, provided a convenient means of disposing of the dead. By creating several partly overlapping social fields, slaves established a multiplicity of ties which offered other possibilities of belonging. Since these ties were not controlled or formally recognized by the plantation society, they did not in and of themselves establish for the slaves a social and cultural identity in that society. The traditions and institutions of the early English colonial society which had been appropriated by the slaves during the course of the seventeenth century provided an avenue whereby they could display this identity and engage in a critical discourse on the dominant social order.

The interplay between African cultural principles and European institutions and traditions within a colonial society which has been delineated for Nevis finds parallels in other Caribbean slave societies. Different islands have, naturally, presented the slaves with different types of historical and geographical crevices, depending on a variety of factors such as the institutional framework of the colonial order; the productive system of the island societies, and the geographical condition of the islands. The networks of relations which the slaves developed therefore varied from island to island and can be regarded as variations over the basic theme of establishing a belonging in the New World. Generally speaking, the White-dominated colonial orders were alienated societies, however. Most of the large plantation owners preferred to live in Europe and run their estates via managers. The small White population which lived in the colonies remained oriented toward Europe and never regarded themselves as permanent settlers in the West Indies. The slaves' attempts to establish lasting ties of belonging in the West Indies therefore could only be seen as a threat to the fragile colonial order of the White minority, and planters, such as John Pinney, who found that their families were becoming too intimate with the slaves and too much influenced by them escaped to Europe, if possible.

The social order of the eighteenth century British Caribbean differed from that which emerged in the slave-based British colonies of North America. The northern continent was colonized by people who settled there and organized lasting local communities (Lemon 1984). This had important implications for cultural development there, as shown in Sobel's study of slave society in Virginia (1987). A substantial White population lived permanently as patriarchal plantation owners, and the slaves were incorporated into their society, albeit at the lower rungs of the social ladder. As a result, a merging of African and European cultural notions took place during the course of the eighteenth century which allowed for the development of coherent world views shared by the entire population. While some cultural merging may have occurred in the Caribbean in the early seventeenth century, with the rise of large scale sugar production, the White population became dominated by a small plantocracy, which attempted to separate itself from the cultural universe of the slaves. The slaves therefore developed their own culture in crevices of the plantation society and exploited the traditions and institutions of the White society to which they had already gained access to display this culture. In the process they formed a wide array of relations, which became for them an important basis for establishing a place of belonging within the colonial societies.

NOTES

[1] The slaves' working conditions during the latter part of the eighteenth century are described in more detail by James Ramsay (1784:69–77), who was an Anglican minister on St. Kitts for several years. He held strong abolitionist views, which no doubt colored his account of the general condition of the slaves. He was opposed by Nevisian planter James Tobin, who wrote several pamphlets and testified at British Parliament in support of slavery (Tobin 1785; see also Pares 1950:121, 353, 356–57).

[2] The parish of St. Paul, where Robertson was a rector, consisted mainly of relatively poor families and he had baptized a few slaves who attended church with their master. He did not, however, see the possibility of desirability of converting the slaves before they had given up such customs as "*Polygamy, Random-Divorce* and their Marketings and Merry-makings on the Lord's Day" which he found to be "repugnant to the frame and Purposes of Christian religion" (1730:21–22; Oliver 1914:322).

[3] Queely's critical attitude towards White women must be seen in the light of the fact that he himself had had a slave as a "wife". He regarded such a wife as quite useful, thus she had saved his life "by detecting some poison that had been prepared for me by our head boiler, who being a kinsman to our cook wench, from his influence with her caused her to prepare some potions of it in water gruel for me" (BC:5 August, 1774).

[4] Ironically, David Stalker had been sent out, originally as an indentured servant, in order to act as a spy on the manager (Gay 1964[1928–29]:152).

[5] During the American Revolution, when supplies of provisions from North America were cut off, 300–400 slaves died on Nevis; an equal number on St. Kitts; approximately 1000 on Antigua and close to 1200 on Montserrat (Goveia 1965:6). The feeding of the slaves was regulated in 1798 in the Leeward Islands slave law, which "prescribed weekly allowances of 9 pt of corn or equivalent quantities of beans, peas, wheat flour, rye flour, Indian corn meal, oatmeal, rice, cassava flour, biscuits, yams, potatoes, eddoes, tanias, plantains, or bananas, and 1.25 lb. of herring, shad, mackerel, or other salted provisions, or 2.5 lb. of fresh fish or provisions". These were also the allowances which were stipulated in the Nevis abolition act in 1834 (Higman 1984:207).

[6] In their study of the slaves' provision grounds on Jamaica, Mintz and Hall also found that the available descriptions were vague (1960:9).

[7] The large Jewish population in Charlestown, which in the 1730s comprised about a quarter of the inhabitants of the town, were alleged to deal with slaves who sold them stolen goods and thus to practice unfair trade. Similar accusations were made against Jews throughout the West Indies and seem to have been occasioned by the fact that they controlled a large part of the trade on several islands during the late seventeenth/early eighteenth century. On Nevis, the Jewish population had disappeared by the end of the eighteenth century (Oliver 1914:322; Pares 1950:24–25; Fortune 1984:160).

[8] Similar kin networks have been found by Craton in his study of the Jamaican plantation Worthy Park (1978:162, 166) and in my own study of slavery on St. John (1985a:66–68).

[9] The great significance of maroon societies in this context is that they afford a glimpse at the sort of social structure which the slaves might have developed, had they not been restrained by the plantation system (see for example Price 1973). Slave rebellions also presented occasions for the slaves to display more formalized social systems such as the leadership patterns which Gaspar (1985) has detected in the slave conspiracy to stage an islandwide revolt which was discovered on Antigua in 1736.

[10] A number of studies of the slave family have been based on lists of actual slave groups, which enumerate the slaves according to household or family, or baptismal records which list the parentage of the christened children (see for example Higman 1973, 1975, 1978; Craton 1978, 1979). The problem with these studies, as pointed out by Higman (1977) is that it is difficult to ascertain what the record keepers meant by "household" or "family", and whether their concept of these terms coincided with those of the slaves (see Olwig 1981).

[11] This was written in response to James Ramsay's statement that slaves had to steal the

materials necessary to build their houses (Tobin 1785:64).

[12] Some runaways were caught and brought back by slaves belonging to other estates, because they were awarded with money for this. In 1736, David Stalker, as manager of William Stapleton's plantation, paid "Smith's Negro Dick" for having captured a "Negro woman named Hanah" and "William Herbert's Negro Pompey for taking the same Negro Hanah, runaway" (SM5/2).

[13] The slaves' mortuary practices display strong African influence according to Handler and Lange's study of slavery on Barbados. Among the important African features they note are: "the emphasis that slaves placed on the funeral and the central role of the funeral in socioreligious life; the importance attached to ancestors, and the manifestation of this importance in interment and postinterment rites; sacrifices or offerings of food and drink at gravesites during these rites; goods interred with the corpse, the sacred nature of gravesites and the expression of this in ordeals and oaths; the apparent norm that interment and, especially, postinterment rites be performed, at the minimum by close kin or affines; the value attached to locating burial sites close to the houses of the living and interment under the houses; the prominent role of various forms of musical expression; the custom of 'carrying the corpse'; and such beliefs as the emphasis on witchcraft or sorcery as causes of death, the survival of the soul, and its migration to a spirit world where the dead reside and the ancestors are rejoined" (1978:210–11). Several of these African features were, as noted, present on Nevis.

[14] One of the songs referred to an incident where slaves were believed to have poisoned an unpopular manager and threatened the new manager with the same treatment if he did not treat the slaves better (Olwig 1985a:36, 193).

[15] For an interesting discussion of the scholarly literature on Caribbean dance, which also touches on the significance of the quadrille dance, see Maurer (1991).

[16] I do not know whether this Joseph Herbert was related to the Joseph Herbert who was the manager of William Stapleton's estate earlier in the century.

[17] The breakdown of the slaves working in the various job categories was: 64.1% field laborers, 3.9% head people, 16.8% domestics, 8.4% on wharves, 6.8% tradesmen (Higman 1984:48).

[18] One slave who gained the confidence of his master and his family was Thomas, who was a house slave for the planter Walter Nisbet. Apparently he, through his close association with the planter family, was taught to read and learned to speak "good English". Thomas was one of the slaves described in "Testimony of several Negroes living and dying in God":

> "He was a faithful and good servant and proved himself such on an instance I shall mention. He accompanied his Master to England who being in the company with some other Gentlemen from the West Indies observed their boys were not as attentive to them as in their own country and as they were in a land of liberty they feared they would take theirs if they corrected them. Mr. N. called Thomas and taking his whip broke his head telling him he might go about his business. Thomas made for answer no Master I wont leave you & He returned again with his Master to the West Indies and when his master was dead he was sent again to England with the children his fidelity herein procured him favour and at his return he was permitted to leave the Estate and live in the Town paying something weekly for his hire. Now it was that he began to attend Chapel regularly, joined Society and became a steady member always having something good to say of the Lord respecting his own soul. He could read the scriptures and spoke very good English" (C25:21 May, 1802).

[19] The color of the slaves on Nevis was listed as follows in 1817 (Higman 1984:154–56):

Black (entirely African descent): 8057

Yellow (uncertain, but possibly the same as Quadroon): 194
Red (uncertain): 2
Sambo (children of Mulatto-Black unions): 707
Mulatto (children of White-Black unions): 571
Quadroon (children of White-Mulatto unions): 1
Mustee (children of White-Quadroon unions): 64
Mongrel (uncertain, but possibly the same as Sambo): 5
Indian: 1

20 If the father did not free his Colored family before his death, their situation might deteriorate seriously, especially if he also had a White family. This was the case with the slave John, whose father Edward Huggins, one of the richest planters on Nevis, had died when he was thrown from his carriage (C380:3 August, 1829). John Huggins told a Methodist missionary about his difficult situation: "the present Mr. Peter Huggins, to whom the old man left the work of his property is my brother on my father's side, but I am his *slave!* My father always said that he would free me, my mother and the other children she had by him, but he was cut off so suddenly. A few days after his death I went to Mr. Peter Huggins, while he was talking to his brother Edward (both of them my brothers) and said 'I beg you will not be angry with me, sir, but you know the old gentleman was taken away so unlooked for, that he could not do with us as he intended. Will you be kind enough to let me purchase myself of you?' He said that 'There were many things to attend to at present, but he would think of it!' But from that time to this he has not named it. I have been working for him as master carpenter since July & had I been free I should for the work I have done [have received] nearly 100 pounds but he has only given me a shady (two shillings our way, or one shilling sterling). With the other slaves I get 6 pounds of cow meat a week & two shads, or herrings. I work on Sunday at my trade to make a little for myself & the other Sunday I attend the Chapel and the School!" The missionary added, "How horrible! Yet this gentle man is, in many respects, a kind man as much so indeed, as any planter I have known" (C64:2 November, 1829). In some cases, the father freed the children and their mother, such as occurred in the case of John Queely, the overseer who, as mentioned, had 6 children with his domestic servant (BC:6 December, 1774).

21 Relevant studies of the social conditions of the free Colored in the West Indies can be found in Handler 1974; Cox 1984 and Heuman 1981.

PART II

IN PURSUIT OF RESPECTABILITY

PLATE 5   *The Methodist Chapel in Charlestown, Nevis, from Thomas Coke's* A History of the West Indies, *vol. III. London: Printed for the Author, 1811.*

CHAPTER THREE

The Methodist Society

TOWARDS AN EGALITARIAN ORDER

The hierarchical order which had constituted the organizational principle of the plantation society had become seriously undermined by the end of the eighteenth century. As already noted, many of the planters who were the formal heads of the main socioeconomic units in the colonies resided in Europe and ran their West Indian estates through managers who had neither a personal nor a long-term interest in the plantations. The hierarchical units of the plantations therefore lacked effective heads, leaving the slaves both without the protection and the control usually associated with patriarchal relations.[1] At the same time, a growing number of slaves had been able to obtain their legal freedom and thus removed themselves from the authority of their former masters. They lived a sort of liminal existence in the plantation society having no formal position in it. They were "unappropriated people", as Handler has termed them in his discussion of freedmen in the slave society of Barbados (1974:71). This was because the hierarchical order failed to incorporate the rapidly expanding free segment of the population, just as it lacked the sort of leadership which was necessary to uphold the system of authority and deference which underlined this order.

When during the 1780s, the Methodist "Society" (the term which the Methodists preferred to the term "Church") initiated a mission in the West Indies, it introduced a new social order which came to fill some of the social void left by the old patriarchal order. This was an egalitarian order closely connected with the idea of respectability which had emerged within the growing middle classes of European society during the eighteenth century. Respectability was constituted through the establishment of " 'decent and correct' manners and morals" (Mosse 1985:1), in particular with regards to sexuality, and the achievement of respectability demanded complete control over sexual behavior, which became regarded as having procreation as its primary, if not its only legitimate purpose (Cominos 1963:21). If great restraint was required, as far as sexual behavior was concerned, much energy was expected in terms of economic activity. Idleness and the yielding to sexual temptation were seen to be closely related and, in turn, associated with poverty. Industry and sexual continence, on the other hand, were the virtues that led to the making of a citizen who held a respected position in society (ibid.:223, 227). The rowdy and licentious festivals and social pastimes of the lower classes which were held in crowded public settings were frowned upon and replaced by quiet relaxation within the family. The home became "a sanctuary and its 'fireside comforts' were the highest rewards" (Malcolmson 1973:155–56).

Respectability became an important means by which the rising middle classes first legitimized and demarcated themselves and later upheld their special status *vis-à-vis* both lower and upper classes. The very lifestyle of the middle class was seen by them to earn them a position of respect and social recognition in society; this, in turn, implied that respect and recognition were due only to those who adhered to the middle-class life style. The social order of respectability therefore was an exclusive one which rejected those who, in their eyes, did not live a respectable life. Later, in the nineteenth century, nationalistic movements adopted the middle-class ideal of respectability and made it an ideological foundation for modern European nationhood (Mosse 1985:9), and respectability came to provide an important moral and social underpinning for the new nationalism (see also Hobsbawm and Ranger 1983).

In England the Methodists, many of whom came from the upwardly mobile middle classes, were among the foremost advocates of respectability. They preached against the social diversions of the rural communities which took up much of the time of the lower classes and were associated with heavy drinking, gambling and sexual licence, and denounced any sort of secular activities on the Sabbath, including the Sunday market. In their place the Methodists sought to propagate relaxation within the family home and religious activities through church attendance and participation in Sunday school. From the late eighteenth century, they, along with other evangelically inclined individuals from various denominations, including the Anglican Church, organized a great number of Sunday schools for children and youngsters of the lower classes. Being active in the organization of Sunday schools, in fact, became an important aspect of the sort of respectability to which the middle classes aspired (Laqueur 1976:25). The Sunday schools offered religious instruction as well as secular education for the youth and, gradually, became one of the most pervasive institutions catering to the young people. Sunday schools also organized a number of more social activities, for example the celebration of various anniversaries (such as that of the Sunday school itself) which were intended as "counter-recreation designed to combat the evils of traditional festivals" (ibid.:177). These schools were particularly important among the working classes, who came to regard them as an opportunity to "display respectability and self-esteem" (ibid.:171). This lead some religious authorities to note with annoyance that parents went to great pains to dress their children properly for Sunday school and seemed relatively less concerned about the religious significance of the institution (ibid.:170–77; Malcolmson 1973:106, 156).

The Methodists began to missionize on Nevis in the late 1780s, shortly after they had initiated their West Indian slave mission on Antigua in 1786. They introduced to the plantation society an institutional framework associated with an egalitarian order, recognized by English society, which was open to the Black and Colored population. The basis of the mission was thus the principle that "all men, including slaves, were brothers in Christ" (Blackman 1988:4). This was certainly not generally accepted Christian dogma in the West Indies. In the Eastern Caribbean the Moravian and Methodist Churches were, in fact, unique in recognizing the "black slaves, the free and the coloured people as equal with whites in the sight of God" (ibid.:2).[2] It is important to recognize, however, that the brotherhood—or equality—that these missionaries offered the slaves, was not based upon a feeling of general, panhuman equality. They did not subscribe to the notion that all peoples and cultures, including all religions, must be respected as equal, nor did they challenge secular, this-worldly distinctions between master and slaves. In order to be admitted to the brotherhood of the Methodists, or Moravians, it was necessary to be converted to Christianity, which, to the Methodists, was closely connected with the notion of respectability.

This section will focus on the impact of the English culture of respectability on social and cultural processes in the mature colonial society. It will discuss how, in the period from the eighteenth to the middle of the twentieth century, notions of respectability and egalitarianism became firmly established in the plantation society, manifested primarily through religious and educational institutions and traditions. These cultural forms came to present an important means whereby the Afro-Caribbean population asserted a social presence in colonial society, both as approving members of the growing local middle class which embraced the English culture of respectability, and as protesting plantation laborers who sought to negate their continued social marginality by asserting their Afro-Caribbeanness within the institutions of respectability.

WORKING WITHIN THE PLANTATION SOCIETY

The Methodist mission on Nevis began in January 1787 when Dr. Thomas Coke and his entourage of missionaries visited the island from St. Kitts where they were establishing a missionary station (Coke 1811:12). Although the missionaries were received on Nevis with "the greatest civility and even with politeness", Coke found that "every door seemed to be completely shut against our ministry" and it appeared that the trip to the island had been in vain. Soon, however, one of the missionaries who had been stationed on St. Kitts began to receive invitations to preach on the estates of planters who "wished to have their slaves instructed in the principles and practice of Christianity", and when Thomas Coke returned to Nevis in 1789, a class of 21 catechumens was established and a missionary stayed on the island to continue the work. In 1790 when Coke paid his last visit to Nevis a chapel had been secured in Charlestown (ibid.:12–14). The Methodist Society grew rapidly to a membership of nearly 400 in 1793 (ibid.:16) and almost 1200 in 1803 (C1:8 March, 1803), more than 10% of the population (Higman 1984:417–18). Although the number of actual members in the Methodist Society continued to fluctuate at the level of about 1000, a much greater number was exposed to Methodism through the missionaries' preaching. Furthermore, there was a large number of people who had been expelled from the Society for having failed to live up to the strict rules of conduct required by the Methodists. The Methodists did not seem to be in want of people who desired to become members of the Society, but rather experienced great difficulty in finding members who were willing (or able) to become the sort of members that they found desirable.[3] During the early nineteenth century the Methodists erected two other chapels, in the Gingerland area and in Newcastle, and two missionaries were usually stationed on the island. Despite the growing importance of the chapels, the Methodists continued to go out to the slaves on those estates where planters were willing to allow this, in order to recruit new slaves for their faith. They generally came every two weeks, preaching either in the estate yard under a big tree or in the boiling house, which was fitted into a chapel for the occasion. Often the manager or planter was present during the service (C432:27 September, 1831).

Those who expressed a wish to join the Society, after having been "catechized" by the missionaries, were placed in classes (first on a trial basis) under a leader who spoke to each member individually every week and reported to the minister on the members' progress and problems. A White person acted as leader, or, if no Whites could be found, "an experienced mulatto or negro" was chosen "whose religious change and steady conduct had had full proof" (Watson 1835[1817]:465).[4] Apart from attendance at class meetings and the regular services in the chapels, the members also were expected to go to the quarterly "love feasts" where they could bear testimony to their conversion and to "watch nights" where the congregation also testified and prayed together in silence. These watch nights often were held on special occasions such as New Year's eve. A condition of membership was payment of class money and purchase of admission tickets. Those who failed to pay were expelled from the Church, particularly during the early years, when it was reported that "although of ever so exemplary lives, expulsion is the certain consequence of nonpayment" (Goveia 1965:292). Those who could afford it, paid extra for a pew (C166:24 April, 1822).[5] Membership in the Methodist Society therefore reflected a certain economic standing among the slaves, and those who were unable to pay for their admission ticket chose to stay home to avoid the shame of coming empty-handed to church. During hard times attendance at the chapel therefore declined markedly (C28:20 January, 1814).

The Methodists also established Sunday schools where children were instructed in the Bible. These Sunday schools later on developed into proper schools, thus in 1816 a missionary requested certain religious materials and "a few sets of letters for the instruction of the children of the Sunday School on the Lancastrian Plan" as well as "Bibles, Testaments & spelling Books, etc." (C49:28 August, 1816).[6] In 1817 a morning school was established in Charlestown where about 50 Methodist children were taught to read and spell, 12 of them also learned to write (C50:8 September, 1817). In 1818, this morning school was described as commencing every day after service at six o'clock lasting for one hour. The missionaries taught the children "to read, spell, sing and the catechism" with the assistance of "several of our young female friends", however, the school was in dire need of Testaments and spelling books (C66:30 April, 1818). Two years later, the school was reported to be open from six to eight in the morning, when the missionary and his wife taught the children, whose number had grown to about 100, 60–70 of whom attended regularly (C113:16 May, 1820). The Methodists gradually expanded this education system, and schools were established in other parts of the island, so that in 1833, the year before the Emancipation of the slaves, 600 scholars were reported to attend the Methodist schools (C28:20 January, 1814; C232:20 July, 1825; C267:12 January, 1826; C482:8 October, 1833).

The initial reaction on the part of the planters towards the Methodists' attempt to missionize among the slaves was, as noted, skepticism. On the neighboring island of Antigua, where the mission first began its activities, the upper class attempted to dismiss the mission with statements to the effect that the missionaries might as well "try to turn [...] mules and oxen into men as make Christians out of [...] slaves" (Gumbs 1986:39). Judging by the views expressed by the Anglican minister William Smith earlier in the eighteenth century, such ridicule no doubt disguised a real fear that Christian missionizing among slaves would disturb the delicate balance of the social order. This fear of the effects of christening slaves was clearly still prevalent when the Methodist missionaries arrived on Nevis, and this explains the hostility with which the missionaries were met on the part of some planters, who refused to let them preach on their estates. This hostility turned to persecution when the missionaries were suspected of being connected with the English abolitionists who had established an organization for the abolition of slavery in 1787, later known as the Anti-Slavery Society, and supported a parliamentary campaign against slavery led by William Wilberforce (Williams 1970:256). The adversaries of the missionaries sought to disrupt and break up the services. At one point they even attempted to burn down the chapel while the congregation was singing (Coke 1811:21–22; Goveia 1965:291, 295). This persecution ceased when the colonial authorities showed their willingness to support the missionaries, and in 1805 one of the missionaries could report: "the principal Inhabitants have treated me with respect", and there were even "some very respectable persons in Society" (C6:7 August, 1805).

One of the major reasons why the Methodists became accepted was that they succeeded in reassuring most of the White population that far from being agents of revolutionary change, they were a stabilizing force in the plantation society. The 1821 report of the Methodist Missionary Society thus makes clear that the Methodists were being accepted because they helped keep the increasingly restless slaves quiet by giving them a more divine purpose to live for. The report notes with great satisfaction that "open opposition to the efforts of the Missionaries has ceased" and goes on to state that "nothing but prudent and persevering exertions are necessary, under the divine blessing, to fix in the minds of the slaves generally the sanctifying truths of our holy religion, to bring their conduct under its salutary control, and thus at once to promote their present happiness, and to fix the peace and security of the colonies upon the surest foundations" (*Report* 1821:lxxxi). This role of the missionaries as keepers of the social order in the colonial society was made clear in a letter from 1823 by two missionaries on Nevis which stated, "truly religious Negroes become in general so much reconciled to their providential lot as to indulge but little anxiety respecting any great political change in their outward condition" (C203:20 October, 1823).

This does not mean that the missionaries were proslavery, or that they found the slaves' condition acceptable. Missionaries in their private correspondence expressed strong feelings against the institution of slavery and the general conditions under which the slaves lived:

> O how painful to our feelings of justice, humanity and religion are [...] the scenes, which are exhibited in this country. Here you behold a marshaled gang of Negroes wielding the hoe from break of day till sun set, beneath the scorching rays of the sun, urged by the whip to vigorous constant toil, with meager looks in tattered garments. Then you behold a multitude of diseased wretches which are doomed to linger out a miserable existence. A general gloom seems to hang over both persons and property. Indeed the whole system is every way repugnant to religion. My soul come not though into their secret? my honor, be not though built upon such a foundation (C123:2 October, 1820).

Such feelings could not be expressed in the local Nevisian society, however, and the missionary added, "Tho such are my views I know religion and prudence must govern any proceedings both in a private and public intercourse with all classes of the community" (ibid.). Whatever feelings that the missionaries held against slavery had to be suppressed in order to promote the greater missionary cause (see also Turner 1982:9).[7]

METHODIST AND AFRO-CARIBBEAN CULTURE

Since the basis of Methodist missionizing among the slaves was a belief in the equality of all human beings in the sight of God, one of the most important first steps for the Methodists was to bring the slaves within the sight of God by convincing them to give up their old heathen ways and become respectable Christians. The Methodists found that this was difficult because the slaves, who had not been exposed to any civilizing influence, had a very low level of understanding. One missionary writing in 1837, a few years after Emancipation of the slaves, thus noted that one could not expect as much of the "Negroes" as of the Englishmen with regard to understanding of religion, because they were "extremely ignorant, degraded almost to the level of beasts, oppressed and cruelly treated by their owners" (CA994:11 September, 1837). Apparently it did not occur to this missionary that the Black population might have a culture of their own with a different religious practice and understanding. This is related to the fact that the missionaries in their work with the slaves emphasized those cultural values and norms of behavior that would meet with respectability in the wider society which was oriented toward English culture. They therefore were not particularly eager to acquaint themselves with the Afro-Caribbean culture which had developed among the slaves, not to speak of making any attempt to reconcile Methodism with this culture.

The Methodists' lack of understanding of the slaves' religious practices and beliefs posed a significant obstacle to their endeavors. One fundamental difference in the missionaries' and the slaves' understanding of religion was to be found in their concept of humanity. To the slaves it seems that humanity was basically "good" and not, as the Methodists believed, sinful and in need of salvation by God (see also Turner 1982:71). One woman who refused to attend the missionaries' preaching just did not see any reason why they should bother to save her: "Massa me no muroter, no kill, me trouble nobody, me no sinner massa, me no used prayers massa" (C363:3 December, 1828). This failure to see human beings as basically sinners is also apparent in the following letter which expresses almost complete frustration on the part of the missionary at the impasse which he had reached in his missionizing efforts:

> I have been utter astonished at the darkness and ignorance which covered their minds. Many who have attended the house of God for numbers of years know no more of their state as Sinners, or of the plan of Salvation than the beasts which perish. And I find it exceeding difficult to get them to understand what they are by nature and what they must be by grace, before they can enter the kingdom of Heaven, however after giving them what instruction I can, I commend them to God who alone can enlighten the mind of man. And as to the pride of these people, it exceeds all I have seen before and appears to be increasing every day (C579:18 March, 1837).

Another aspect of the slaves' religious conviction which did not go well with

Methodism was their belief in witchraft, or *obeah*. In their fight against *obeah*, the missionaries found allies in the planters who disliked the fact that *obeah* practitioners held a position of power among the slaves, thereby creating an alternative structure of authority on the estates.[8] Since *obeah* was illegal, it was practiced in secret and not perceived by many Whites on the island. The missionaries were, however, sometimes called in to deal with those discovered to be associated with *obeah*. One cure was to make the offender kneel down and repeat the Lord's prayer. In one case an old *obeah* man was threatened with the switch when he refused to repeat "Thy Kingdom come", jumping up and shouting, "'*Me* no Kingdom come! no kingdom! Me no Kingdom come!'" (C241:11 November, 1825). Apparently this *obeah* man was in no doubt as to the position of power which he derived from *obeah*. The missionary characterized him as a most fearless man, and when he was asked by the missionary what he expected from "his master, the devil in the other world", he replied that "he would be employed by him as a *driver* or *hunter* after the runaway negroes!" (ibid.).

One of the aspects of the Afro-Caribbean culture that the missionaries did show a certain amount of recognition was the slaves' system of small farming, if for no other reason than that it provided an important economic basis for the Methodist Society. The missionaries, almost only referred to it, however, when it failed to provide adequate funds for the Society. This occurred most often when there was a serious drought on the island, which made it impossible for the slaves to grow sufficient crops in their provision grounds to feed their own families, let alone the missionaries (C96:20 July, 1819; C584:10 May, 1837). This lack of sufficient funds had, as noted, the further consequence that the slaves stopped attending the chapel, or even left the Methodist Society entirely (C28:20 January, 1814). The missionaries showed little understanding of the cultural importance of small farming and displayed a startling lack of awareness of any sort of skills and knowledge among the slaves. One missionary thus was shocked when he learned that the slaves knew as much as he did about the cycles of the moon and the weather believed to be associated with these cycles, important knowledge when farming. The missionary asked in disbelief the slave from whom he happened to learn about this how "it was that the negroes who cannot read, know as well as us who can, the exact changes of the moon?" to which he received the terse reply that "there was nothing they knew better" (C355:28 August, 1828).

The missionaries paid considerably more attention to the markets, where the slaves sold their agricultural produce, for the simple reason that the markets held as they were on Sundays, the only free time available to the slaves, presented a serious public break of the Sabbath.[9] While during earlier periods shops had been kept open on Sundays, by the nineteenth century those shops which were owned by the White population remained, for the most part, closed on Sundays (C1:7 May, 1803). In this way, the slaves' markets became stigmatized by the very fact that they were forced to take place on Sundays, even though they were sanctioned by law. Some of the missionaries sympathized with the slaves' lot and saw in the markets an opportunity to spread the gospel to those slaves who did not attend the chapel. They therefore went to the market place itself and preached for the people there:

> As the Negroes did not come to the chapel to hear us I have thought it my duty to go to them. Accordingly I went & preached in the Market after preaching in the forenoon in the chapel on the sabbath day which is nearly at an equal distance from church & chapel. When the Negroes saw me entering the Market with the Hymn Book in my hand they immediately cleared away all their provisions for the accommodation of the congregation & almost the whole of the negroes surrounded me like a swarm of Bees & heard with seriousness & attention. I ascended an old wall at the side of the Market which I made my Pulpit. In this situation I stood whilst a pious old negroe held an umbrella over me to keep my head from the effects of a vertical sun. It is impossible for me to tell you with what pleasure I made the trumpet sound forth the glad-tidings of great joy to my black & coloured brethren who summoned to receive the word with a smiling conveyance of gratitude to God & man. One of the negroes cried out when I began to sing 'O! Me never saw like! He be good Massa!—Me don't know where he be come from!—O! God bless good Massa!'—Another poor woman like the woman at Jacob's well forgot her provisions at the other end of the market and came & joined the congregation! (C261:24 March, 1825).

Other missionaries were not just against the market, because it took place on Sundays, but also because they saw in it an ungodly place where a sort of language and behavior was displayed which was entirely unsuitable for respectable adults and children:

> Slave children at c. six years old, or under, are employed picking grass for the cattle, vine for hogs and rabbits and this they do daily from light to dark. On the Sundays, their parents, or some other relations wash, and put a clean frock or shirt upon them and take them to market. Here they see and hear nothing good everything bad, for slaves without the fear of God, can use, when offended the most obscond language (C255:October 30, 1824).

The social life which took place among the slaves in the markets early on Sundays continued on the plantations where the slaves gathered in the afternoon to dance to the music of the fiddle and tambourine. This sort of entertainment was seen as completely incompatible with the Methodist faith, and one missionary noted with deep regret that "Sunday dancing is much more common than preaching, and the houses that are regularly open for this wicked and disgraceful purpose are more in number than places of worship" (C413:16 December, 1830). The Methodist reports are filled with descriptions of missionaries having entered dances held either in private houses or in the open in order to break them up (C363:4 December, 1828; C55:28 February, 1 May, 1820; C361:3 November, 1828).

Convinced that only evil would come from the slaves' own social intercourse, missionaries began to go to the slave houses on Sundays in order to demand that they attend the chapel. One missionary, who decided to visit the Negro huts in Newcastle, before he began his preaching there was quite shocked at the indifference toward the keeping of the Sabbath on the part of the slaves: "I found some *sowing*, others *cooking, lolling, sleeping, building* & *attending the sick* & others *walking about doing nothing*!! I asked them, was this right, thus spending their sabbath". Having thus roused them from "their *guilty slumbers*" he proceeded to "*compell* them" to come to his preaching (C232:20 July, 1825).

Despite the popularity of dancing and drumming among the slaves, the missionaries seemed to think that they made some headway with regard to the Christmas festivities which had been so popular among the slaves. Rev. Watson thus claimed in his *Defense of Methodism* published in 1817 that due to the beneficial effect of the Methodist mission it was no longer necessary to keep a guard on Nevis during the Christmas season (1835:502). He seems to have been rather optimistic, however, as a missionary report from 1825 noted that martial law was proclaimed during the Christmas holy days and referred to a militia (C258:4 January, 1825).

The one area of the slaves' culture which the missionaries were the most eager to reform, perhaps because it was the greatest blow to the sort of respectability which they promoted, was the slaves' practice of cohabiting without being married. In the early period of their missionizing activities, the Methodists confined themselves to "joining" slaves who were cohabiting.[10] This was an informal ceremony, which was not considered to constitute a real marriage, and apparently the slaves did not regard it as such, neither were the joined slaves recorded in a register. In 1819, the Methodists began performing official marriages of slaves (C203:20 October, 1823), and in 1822, it was made a requirement for cohabiting members of the Society to marry. The bans were published in the church, as was done for the White population in the Anglican Church, and as far as the Methodists were concerned these marriages were completely valid (C171:5 August, 1822; C175:10 October, 1822).[11]

In their eagerness to establish a "proper" marriage among members of their congregation, the Methodists seem to have ignored the fact that the slaves' family system perhaps was not so much based on the marital union as such, as on the wider, consanguineal family. The references which appear to this sort of family therefore are only indirect, such as the description of the father who called a son to his deathbed to give him his blessing, an incident which was referred to in the "testimonies of several Negroes living and dying in God" (C25:21 May, 1802). The importance of kinsmen is apparent in other descriptions of death scenes, where the missionaries admonished relatives gathered around the dying person about the "King of terrors" who awaited those who had lived in sin. In one instance, the sin was caused by the fact that the dying had shown greater loyalty to his family than to the Methodist Society, having felt obliged to attend a dance held by his father (C363:4 December, 1828; C380:3 August, 1829).[12]

RESPECTABILITY IN THE PLANTATION SOCIETY

In view of the fact that the Methodists condemned virtually all aspects of Afro-Caribbean culture, it may seem strange that they managed to attract any members to their congregation among the Black population. Several reasons have been suggested for the success of the missionaries in converting the slaves in the West Indies. In her study of the Methodist mission on Jamaica, Turner sees the Sunday service itself as a significant source of attraction for the slaves, in that it offered ritual and religious fervor; the personal attention of the missionary and contact with friends gathered there, as well as the opportunity to spend time "away from the plantation, clean and neatly dressed, to contemplate a better life and pray for strength in this one" (1982:84). The importance of the personal ties between slaves and missionaries is emphasized by Rooke in her overview of missionary education among British West Indian slaves during the nineteenth century. She also mentions factors such as the importance of a new religion at a time when the African religious structures no longer were intact; the "self-identity, social cohesion, and group identification", which the slaves found in the missions, and the role of the missions in providing a means of leadership "for slaves among themselves". Finally she suggests the "possibility that social approval from significant others could be obtained by emulating white religions and adopting white values" (1979:62–63). Price, in his work on the Moravian mission among the Saramakas, descendants of runaway slaves in Suriname, has pointed to the possibility of the converts seeing missionaries as important links to power, being Whites with close connection with the colonial government. Furthermore, he notes, since the missionaries mastered reading and writing they have presented an opportunity for the people to learn these skills which were also associated with power (1990:67).

As shall be seen, the Nevisian material suggests that the overall importance of the Methodist mission should be found in the fact that it provided the slaves with a public locus for the development of cross-racial ties, a social and symbolic resource of great relevance in the colonial society, as well as a socially recognized framework for cultural display, which might help establish a social presence for the slaves in the island society. The mere fact that the Methodists' mission allowed the slaves to seek a sort of recognition which had been denied them was of fundamental importance. Baptized slaves thus had to be recognized at least as Christians by the colonial society, which was, if nothing else, nominally of the Christian persuasion. The recognition which the Methodist slaves could demand, however, was greater. The

Methodist mission, by advocating sexual restraint, a decent family life, proper manners and decorum among the Black and Colored population, was seeking to institute a kind of life which was highly valued among influential segments of English society at the time and therefore had to be accorded a certain amount of respect by the White population in the English colony.[13]

The concern in the mother country with the moral standards of the lower segments of society was apparent in a bill to ameliorate the condition of the slaves which the House of Commons forced the assembly on Nevis to consider. The instructions for the bill which were sent to Nevis during the 1820s included such suggestions as the right of Christian slaves to marry without interference of the master; the institution of Sunday as a day of devotion and the abolishing of the Sunday market; the right of slaves to purchase their own freedom; the abandonment of the cart whip as a means of punishment by drivers, henceforth to be called leaders; the outlawing of the separation of families at sales; the acceptance of testimony on the part of Christian slaves; the securing of slaves' property by law; the outlawing of the punishment of females by cart whipping and the indecent exposure of them during punishments (*Nevis Assembly Minutes* 1823–27:15 May, 1824). The assembly delayed deliberations as long as possible, and it was not before they, along with the legislatures of St. Kitts and Tortola, had received a reprimand from Downing Street for their "dilatory proceedings" that they passed a much reduced ameliorative Act "to legalize the marriages of slaves in the Island of Nevis, to declare their property secured to them by Law, to render them competent witnesses under certain restrictions, to regulate proceedings at Law respecting them in civil and criminal cases, and further to ameliorate their condition" (ibid.:30 March, 1826). The planters of the old school who attempted to continue their old practices in their treatment of the slaves were, however, in danger of losing their own position of respect in the society.[14] Visitors to the island, such as Henry Nelson Coleridge, thus were horrified at the slaves' situation and expressed disgust at the planters who let their slaves work naked in the field, when it was quite clear, also to the slaves, that this was shameful (Coleridge 1832:189).

For the planters, who did not wish to substantially alter the status quo, but who desired to keep their social position, the inviting of preachers to their estates in order to missionize for the slaves became a welcome means of achieving local respectability without altering the socioeconomic situation. The popularity of this practice increased when the Anglican Church began to missionize actively among the slaves. The Anglican mission was spearheaded by the rector of St. Paul's Anglican Church in Charlestown, Daniel Gateward Davis. Born on St. Kitts in 1787, he came under the influence of antislavery views while he studied in England. In 1812 he returned to the West Indies to become a rector in Charlestown having been appointed as a missionary among the slaves by "The Society for the Conversion and

Religious Instruction and Education of the Negro Slaves on the West Indian Islands" which had been established in 1792. Rev. Davis was an ideal apostle of religious and educational improvement among slaves within the framework of the plantation society, in that he knew it from the inside, being the son of a planter and Anglican minister on St. Kitts and having married into one of the large planter families on Nevis. During the twelve years he worked on the island he managed to convert a great number of slaves and also instituted free schools of instruction for slaves (Walker n.d.; C60:9 October, 1817; C91:11 May, 1819; C413:16 December, 1830; C472:28 February, 1833; C267:12 January, 1826).

During Rev. Davis' tenure as Anglican rector on Nevis, religious and educational instruction of slaves appears to have become somewhat fashionable, as illustrated by the opening of a chapel which the planter Thomas Cottle had built for his slaves in 1824. The affair was attended by all the Anglican clergymen and many ladies and gentlemen of the island and concluded with a dinner and dance on the estate, which went on so late that some of the guests did not return to Charlestown before four o'clock in the morning, if we are to trust the account of the Methodist missionary (C251:4 September, 1824).[15] The sincerity of the planters' engagement in missionary work among the slaves was questioned by Coleridge, who thought that as long as the planters were not bothered to clothe their slaves they could not be true Christians and gentlemen. He wrote, "I suspect the man who talks to me about preaching and teaching and baptizing, when he, at least for his own part, should be measuring and sewing and building; for until you have taught a man or a woman to respect themselves, it is vain for you to attempt to teach them to respect anything else" (Coleridge 1832:189).

While the Methodist (and later the Anglican) missionaries could not remove the shame which they felt the slaves experienced toiling as brute labor in the fields, they did, nevertheless, admit the slaves to an institution whose respectability was recognized by colonial society. In this way, the Methodist Society was able to extend to the slaves a few hours of respectability, when they went to the chapel fully and properly dressed in order to attend the service. Some were even able to increase this respect by becoming classleaders in the Society, a measure of high moral standing (C25:21 May, 1802; C154:16 Novemnber, 1821), or by occupying a pew in the chapel, a measure of financial achievement (C55:13 June, 1820; C166:24 April, 1822). Furthermore, the Methodist Society offered a growing number of Church-related institutions to the slaves, which allowed them to expand the sphere of respectability associated with the Methodist Society to other aspects of their lives.

As already noted, one of the social institutions of respect which the missionaries presented to the slaves was marriage. During the earlier period of slavery, the slaves had not been able to legalize their informal marital relations and apparently the common impression among slaves was that marriage was only "for buckra" (i.e. Whites) (C92:11 May, 1819). This was also the general feeling among the free Colored and Blacks, who by and large practiced cohabitation without marriage (C60:9 October, 1817). The Methodists did, however, convince several of the free members of the Society to marry, in particular the women, who were active as leaders or Sunday school teachers (C154:16 November, 1821). Marriage therefore had become associated with a certain social standing in colonial as well as Methodist Society, and apparently it was a general impression that a slave by marrying became free and that the marriage of slaves therefore was illegal (C92:11 May, 1819). This belief was shared by most of the slaves, many of whom apparently also disliked the irrevocable tie which marriage invoked and preferred the informal joining ceremony which the Methodists had performed (ibid.; C104:3 January, 1820). This changed when in 1817 the right of the slaves to marry, even without the consent of their masters, was made public in a statement by the Bishop of London (C60:9 October, 1817).[16] This led the Methodists to actively work for marriage among slaves, and they succeeded in performing a great number of marriages, partly by persuading the slaves of the importance of accepting this "Divine Institution", partly by threatening with expulsion of those who refused to marry.

A primary reason for the slaves' interest in marriage was apparently that it involved the publication of banns in the church (C171:5 August, 1822) which implied a public recognition of the union, even if the slaves obtained no legal rights thereby. The performing of marriages thus had the effect of "stamping the institution with its original sanctity, and imparting to religion itself a dignity and importance which in their [the slaves'] eyes it had not before" (C203:20 October, 1823). In this way, the Methodist marriage became a way in which the slaves were able to institutionalize an aspect of their family and gain an increased position of respect within the community.

This raising of the slaves' marital unions to an official level of respectability on a par with the Whites clearly was a provocation to the White population. Some planters attempted to prevent their slaves, or persons who had been freed by them, from getting married, and in 1823 a marriage bill which would prohibit the Methodists from performing marriages was rumored. This bill was feared by the Methodists who felt that they would be "lowered in our public's eyes" and the slaves placed in the hands of the Anglican clergy (C203:20 October, 1823). In 1828 the marriage act was passed in the Nevis legislature which granted only the clergy of the Church of England and Ireland permission to perform marriages, and made illegal the marriages which the Methodists already had performed. The Anglican clergy reacted by remarrying several persons who were married in the Methodist chapel, to others (C357:9 October, 1828). The marriage act was kept in effect until 1842, several years after the abolishment of slavery, clearly as a means of keeping the ambitious Methodists in check. As the Methodist missionary noted with regret: "Some of our respectable people who have a house to live in—a horse to ride and other property are looked in the face by some of the opponents and then told by them that the Marriage in the chapel is not good and if they did they cannot make a will and leave their property to their wives because they are nothing more than concubines and their children bastards" (CA1013:September, 1814).

If the people of respect, to whom the missionary referred, were not able to become married by the Methodist missionary, there was nothing to prevent them from having their homes blessed by the Methodist missionaries, and during the late 1820s it became common to consecrate a new house, or a house which had been enlarged or rebuilt, by holding a social gathering where the Methodist missionary was invited to say "a word of God and prayer" in it. By opening a new house, a mark of upward mobility, with a religious ceremony instead of "a fiddle and a dance", as had been common, the occupants thereby used the missionaries to make a public display of their position of increased respectability in the colonial society. One member of the Methodist Society certainly succeeded in this when her consecration ceremony was reported to have been attended by "persons of all colours" including some "persons of respectability" (C330:7 January, 1828).

The Sunday schools and the day schools which grew out of them also became important institutions which served as a means whereby the slaves and the freed could further their position in the colonial society. The schools were not just important as seats of learning, but also as means of gaining social recognition. This was quite apparent when in 1820 a public exam was organized in Charlestown where all the students "who were not detained by sickness, slavery and disallowed for improper behaviour" were able to demonstrate in public their superior knowledge through the recitation of hymns, psalms and sections of the catechism. The missionary noted with satisfaction that the boys and girls performed "in such a way as would have delighted the committee in London almost to ecstasy had they heard them". The children were rewarded with a dinner, which they ate using a knife, fork and spoon, which they had brought in anticipation of the meal. After the dinner the students walked in a group through Charlestown, where all the inhabitants came out to look at them, and then gathered again at the chapel for prayer (B55:13 June, 1820). While the Methodist missionaries were eager to make a public display of their great civilizing influence by orchestrating this exam, the Black population certainly seemed equally eager to participate in this event and enjoyed the respect shown the young scholars by the residents of the capital. The importance of education as a means of social mobility is also apparent in the case of a slave, who took advantage of the education which he received from the Methodists to establish himself as a teacher on the plantation to which he belonged. Here he gave instruction in his own hut on how to read the Bible, keeping school by candlelight (C265:12 January, 1826).

Some of the main beneficiaries of this usage of the Methodist institution for the worldly purpose of gaining greater respectability in the colonial society were the freed who possessed property and whose children were able to attend the morning schools. On Nevis the free seem to have been concentrated in Charlestown and in Bath, a fishing village near Charlestown (C203:10 October, 1823). The only formal institution which distinguished them from the slaves was the Colored militia, in which all free had to enroll. According to Goveia, the Colored militia was a burden to the free, since it marked their inferior position in relation to the Whites, who were organized in their own militia (Goveia 1965:219). To some freedmen, however, the militia seems to have been regarded as a privilege, because it marked their superior position vis-à-vis the slaves. This superiority received recognition in the Methodist chapel, when the free Colored militia were allowed to march at Christmas "with their music" to the gates of the Methodist chapel, and from "thence with a silent march into the chapel" where they were treated to a Christmas sermon along with the rest of the congregation. This consisted almost only of free persons and urban slaves, however, because the estate slaves were detained on their estates, where they received their special Christmas allowance (C258:4 January, 1825). In this way, the ability to celebrate Christmas in the chapel marked a certain position of privilege in the plantation society.

It was not uncommon for those among the free who were well-to-do to display their affluence by donating generous sums to the Society. Thus a "pious consistent member" who inherited property from his father in England not only purchased his own and his family's freedom with the money, but also contributed a significant amount when the chapel in Charlestown was enlarged (C189:12 May, 1823; C475:10 May, 1833). In other cases, the freed demonstrated their superior means through the orchestration of grandiose ceremonies, such as the funeral of a Colored woman in the Anglican Church, which very much impressed the Methodist minister because of its "respectability and solemnity". At this affair the clergy of the Anglican and Methodist Churches headed the funeral train, walking in front of the corpse which was carried by six men and followed by "thirteen mourners in white hoods" who were accompanied by several servants who "walked bearing candles in gloss canteens" (B55:5 May, 1820).

If the upwardly mobile members of the religious communities tended to use the religious institutions for the worldly purpose of gaining greater respectability in the colonial society, many slaves lived in a social and economic situation of a nature that did not allow them to engage in any public expressions of achievement. For them the mere fact of attending service and class meeting, and thus maintaining membership in the Methodist Society, was a major effort, as is apparent in the appeals of a slave woman to avoid expulsion due to irregular attendance at class meetings: "Ma got, said she weeping, six little children dat much wat and me attend to dem. After me no ting to eat for myself nor me children but me bless Jesus tank him for his goodness to me, poor soul. Me happy at night when me go to bed expecting naked hunger kill me before morning. Blessed Jesus heavenly Massa" she explained lifting up her eyes to heaven and the big tears running down her cheeks and then turning to us she begged not to be excluded, explaining "me no comfort but what me get from dis house" (B55:21 February, 1820).

These slaves seem to have regarded the Methodist Society not just as a place of religious comfort, but also as a forum where they, along with their fellow sufferers, could make their plight as slaves public. The slave testimonies which were brought forward at the watch nights and love feasts, where the members of the congregation were encouraged to bear witness to their conversion to Methodism, were not just characterized by praises of the "glorious liberation" from the "power of Satan". Rather the slaves used the opportunity to present a testimony in public to bear witness to the ill treatment which they received as slaves. The missionaries were clearly rather uncomfortable about this turn of events:

> It is the first West Indian love feast that I have attended and I am really almost at a loss to say what I think of them. The violence of the speakers—their singular gestures and ideas with an inability on my part fully to understand them produced on my mind at first an unfavourable impression however this [...] declined after I had heard the testimony of several of them (B55:9 April, 1820).
>
> I held my head down and wept over the affecting description that some of them gave of their condition for it was impossible to prevent them from talking about their trials though I sat in fear every time they spoke upon that subject (ibid.).

Although the missionary's unhappiness with the situation was mainly caused by the fact that the testimonies could be interpreted as rather political in character and therefore posed a threat to the mission's continued acceptance in the colonial society, he also seemed to be apprehensive about the whole manner of speaking of the testifiers. The reason was probably that the slaves were expressing themselves within an oratory tradition, which emphasized forceful speaking and gestures of such a character that they were quite foreign to the missionary. This tradition apparently also included strong responses to the testifiers on the part of the listeners, which was also noted by some of missionaries (C25:21 May, 1802; C50:2 January, 1817; C227:10 May, 1825). The employment of religious ceremonies to make public protests against slavery and to engage in Afro-Caribbean verbal performances and exchanges, which these love feasts and watch nights reflect, represents an early example of the appropriation of a Methodist institution by the Afro-Caribbean community in order to serve their own social and cultural interests. They clearly show that the adoption of the Methodist institutions of respectability on the part of the slaves did not necessary imply an adoption of the English values of respectability which the Methodists identified with them.[17]

MAKING A SOCIAL PRESENCE THROUGH THE METHODIST MISSION

The way in which the Methodist Society was used by the Black and Colored population suggests that its importance lay in the fact that it provided a publicly recognized institution in which people who were socially marginalized could display an identity as upwardly mobile members of the colonial society, as religious leaders, as pious Christians, as human beings protesting the degradation and oppression to which they were exposed as slaves, or as Afro-Caribbeans appreciating oratory talents. Furthermore, it made it possible for the slaves to become initiated into the mysteries of reading and writing, which had been perceived by the slaves as an important, almost supernatural, source of the position of power which the White masters had in relation to their slaves.

For the Methodist missionaries, conversion to Christianity and the adoption of a respectable way of life represented a complete break with former ways of thinking and acting. In their social order equality and respectability were so closely linked that failure to live a respectable life meant exclusion both from human society on earth and from God's heavenly kingdom in the eternal life promised in the great yonder. Most of the Afro-Caribbean slave and free population of Nevis did not perceive the mission as representing such an exclusive social order, but rather as the offering of another, significant context within which they could develop new social relations and make their plight and/or achievements visible in a society which had sought to marginalize them entirely. Furthermore, the mission, through its preaching of the White man's religion and learning, presented an opportunity to uncover the secrets of White power, which had been feared and respected by the slaves from early times. In other words, the Methodist mission became incorporated into the inclusive and multi-associational framework of the Afro-Caribbean population.

NOTES

[1] A first step to ameliorate the condition of the slaves was taken when the Leeward Islands Act was passed in 1798. This act gives some indication of the severity of the slaves' treatment. Among the improvements to the slaves' position were regulations which required that the killing or maiming of slaves should be dealt with as if they were free; that slaves dying suddenly had to be examined at a coroner's inquest; that disabled slaves could not be manumitted and thus lose their maintenance by their owners at a time when they ceased to be of economic value. Furthermore, the act made legal the customary working hours of the slaves which were to begin not before 5 a.m. and to stop not after 7 p.m. with half an hour's break for breakfast and two hours for dinner. These working hours could, however, be extended in crop time and under special circumstances. Certain food and clothing allowances for the salves also were fixed by law. Marriage in church was seen to

be "unnecessary and even improper" for slaves, but they were to be encouraged to have only one spouse (Goveia 1965:191-96). Even though this act instituted certain duties towards the slaves on the part of the planter, its execution was not safeguarded, largely because slaves were not allowed to testify against Whites and thus to bring a legal complaint against their maltreatment (ibid.:197). This was not remedied before 1826 when the Nevis assembly was forced by England to pass a law which granted the slaves certain rights, including the right to testify under particular conditions (*Nevis Assembly Minutes* 1823-27). Another important act was instituted with the cessation of the transatlantic slave trade in 1808, which made it impossible for planters to import new slaves from Africa and forced them to rely on the slaves' own reproductive abilities. Higman's demographic study of the slave population of the British West Indies shows that "the improvement in fertility was most significant in the old sugar colonies, particularly Barbados and Montserrat, though Nevis barely managed to maintain its level" (1984:355).

[2] The Moravian mission among the West Indian slaves began in 1733, when the Brethren arrived on St. Thomas in the Danish West Indies. The Moravian missionary activities in the Eastern Caribbean, particularly the Danish West Indies, are described in Oldendorp 1987[1777]; Lawaetz 1902; and Maynard 1968.

[3] One missionary reported, for example, that he had "been under the painful necessity of excluding 2 for adultery; 7 for fornication, 4 for encouraging their Daughters in fornication, 1 for sabbath breaking (a free woman), one slave for ditto by dancing and party making, 1 for lying, 1 for swearing" (C64:11 November, 1829).

[4] Henry Nelson Coleridge, who accompanied his uncle, Wm. H. Coleridge, the first Anglican bishop of Barbados, on his first visitation through his dioceses in 1825 (Ragatz 1932:221), scornfully characterized the system of classes supervised by leaders as "a completely organized espionage" whereby "the secrets of every family are at their command; parent and child are watches on each other; sister is set against sister, and brother against brother; each is on his guard against all, and all against each. In this manner these sectarians possess an army of dependents already lodged within every house, and fixed in the heart of every plantation. Their dominion over these poor people is as absolute as was ever that of Jesuits over Jesuits. The fear of being turned out of their class operates like the dread of losing the caste in Hindostan, and the negros know that this formidable power rests entirely with their ministers" (Coleridge 1832:171-72).

[5] According to Goveia (1965:292), Whites paid 16/6 per year for "their seats in chapel" indicating that the pews, at least initially, were intended primarily for the White population. The Society attracted few Whites, however. In 1803 when the Methodist Society numbered 1200 only a dozen were White, four of them men (C1:8 March, 1803).

[6] The Lancaster system whereby the more experienced students helped teach the younger ones was quite common in English Sunday schools and was also employed in the West Indian colonies (see for example Cox 1984:129). It fit in well with the Sunday school culture of self-help, self-improvement and respectability (Laqueur 1976:102, 155).

[7] The impact of the missionaries on the slave societies has been criticized by Goveia (1965:305), who found that by preaching submission, the missionaries created a feeling of consent among the slaves that helped maintain the slave system and thereby the slave society. Rooke (1979:54) has seen the missionaries as not merely introducing a sophisticated system of control, but also as presenting a new social and intellectual milieu to the slaves. Nevertheless, the fact that the missionaries were on a moral, not a political, crusade meant

that they "saw their role as that of preaching the gospel and saving the 'poor heathen' from the slavery of sin and not the sin of slavery" (ibid.).

8   The planters probably also feared the *obeah* men, who, as noted, were believed to have knowledge about the preparation of potions of various sorts, including poisonous ones. It was well known that slaves knew the properties of the local plants better than did most planters (Rymer 1775:24–25), and on some estates this knowledge was put to good use (Pares 1950:128). On other estates, the slaves, herbal knowledge rather seems to have been employed to harm the planter or overseer, as in the case of the overseer John Queely referred to above. Smith (1745:230) also mentioned fear of poisoning by slaves. The *obeah* practitioners' position of power probably was increased by the fact that they were able to collect a fair amount of money from their customers (C154:16 November, 1821; C241:11 November, 1825).

9   Provision cultivation also occurred on Sundays, but since it took place in marginal areas, hidden from view of most White people, it did not provoke the missionaries to the extent that the markets did.

10   A description of the special marriage ceremony which was offered to the slaves is found in Watson (1835:441), who relates how one missionary performed the ceremony: he told the slaves that they must "confine themselves to each other till death should separate them; and when they have submitted to this, I have appointed them to attend me. I then explain to them the nature of the marriage covenant, and the blessings resulting from its observance. They then kneel down; I took their hands, and united them together, and desired them to repeat after me, 'I, Quamina, take thee, Quasheba, to be my wife; and I promise to leave all others, and cleave to thee alone as long as it shall please God we both shall live.' I then loosened their hands, joined them again, and the woman plighted her faith. We concluded the service with prayer."

11   These marriages did not in any way change the slaves' situation as the property of their owners and therefore did not, for example, confer on the married slaves any rights of cohabitation in case the slaves belonged to different plantations. In their propagation of marriage, the missionaries therefore tended to emphasize "the importance of matrimony and monogamy, rather than co-residence" (Higman 1984:369), or the importance of the formal appearance, rather than the everyday practical implications of the marital relationship.

12   The references to the family that are found in the Methodist records indicate that the Methodist "espionage" system did not penetrate the families, as Coleridge (1832:171–72) believed, but rather operated between families.

13   The Methodist Mission was aware that a position of respectability in the White population also depended on a certain socioeconomic standing in the local society and therefore made sure that the West Indian missionaries received sufficient economic support to "come under the cognisance of white stewards of respectability" (Watson 1835:466–67), which included such musts as the service of a proper number of servants in the homes and horses for transportation purposes (Turner 1982:26).

14   The planters on Nevis were in particular need of improving their public image due to a case involving a severe public whipping of several slaves administered by one of the wealthy planters, which led to the death of one slave. The planter was charged with cruelty and murder of his slaves, but was acquitted (Pares 1950:154–55). This case which took place in 1810 received a great deal of publicity in England and the fact that the planter was tried on

Nevis, but failed to be convicted, was an embarrassment to the planter community on the island (*Case in Nevis* 1818; Walker n.d.:4–5).

15 The Methodist missionary was, understandably, upset about the opening ceremony. The Methodists had been the first to preach on the estate, however, when the chapel had been erected. Mr. Cottle, who himself was an Anglican, invited the clergy of the Church of England to preach there. This reflected a general turn of events. Thus as the Anglican ministers began to missionize among the slaves, several planters preferred inviting them to their estates, and during the 1820s, the Methodists were "deprived of some Estates in order that the catechist belonging to the church might attend them" (C294:22 December, 1826). According to a pamphlet about the building of Cottle Church, Rev. Davis reported the opening of the chapel to Dr. Barret, the secretary of the Conversion Society in England in this way: "Mr. Cottle's chapel was opened for the first time on Wednesday, May 5th, on which occasion we had a solemn service in place of consecration. It was an exceedingly interesting day. Mr. Cottle made it a holiday for all his slaves: they consequently attended as did many of the ladies and gentlemen of the island" (Walker n.d.:7). Although, generally speaking, the Methodist and Anglican ministers did not seem to cooperate, but rather boycotted each other in the missionizing activities, Rev. Davis appeared to get along with at least some of the Methodists, thus one of them reported having gone to Charlestown, where he "had a very beneficial interview with the Rector of this Town" (C412:7 November, 1820).

16 The right to marry slaves with or without their owners' consent was declared by the bishop of London, because the Anglican priest, Rev. Davis, had complained to him about having been prevented from publishing the marriage banns in a case where he wished to wed a slave to a free person (C60:9 October, 1817; C91:11 May, 1819).

17 In their employment of respectable forms for other purposes, the slaves, ironically enough, were not unlike the planters whose interest in institutions of respectability did not always extend to the values of respectability which they were meant to embody.

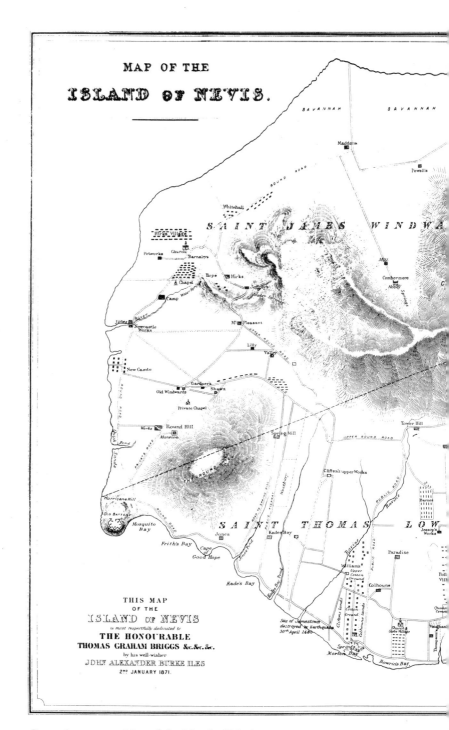

PLATE 6   *Map of the Island of Nevis, 1871.*

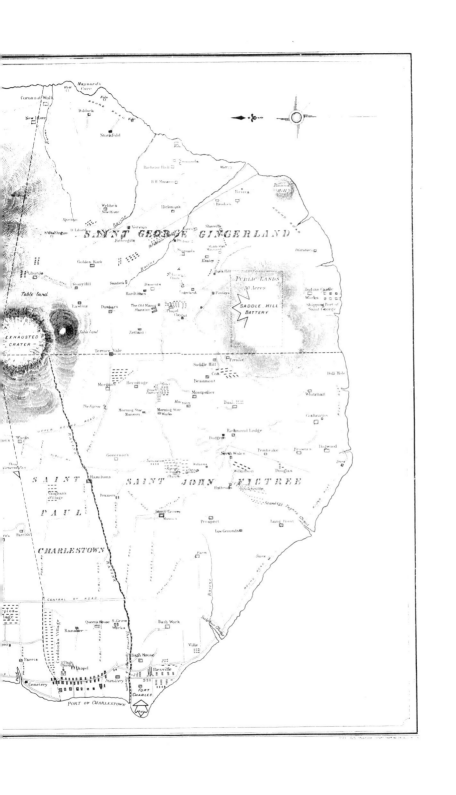

CHAPTER FOUR

In a Free Society

T he multitude of socioeconomic relations which the Afro-Caribbeans developed from the early period of slavery were seen to establish for them a place of belonging which negated their social marginalization. In accordance with their concepts of freedom, the legal redefinition as autonomous human beings which they underwent with Emancipation therefore was less important in some ways than the possibility to consolidate and further develop some of the socioeconomic fields which they had created during slavery and which had attained cultural significance for them. During slavery the Afro-Caribbean population could be seen to have followed three main avenues of belonging: 1) attachment to a patriarchal owner, or manager, who offered special privileges which gave access to a variety of resources and might lead to obtainment of legal freedom; 2) establishment of networks among slaves revolving around provision cultivation, marketing, family and procreation as well as religious practices, generating Afro-Caribbean communities which were, to a great extent, self-reliant and increasingly independent from the planters; 3) membership in the Methodist Society which offered a religious and social community outside the sphere of the plantation regime as well as the teaching of useful skills such as reading, writing and knowledge of the influential English culture of respectability.

These avenues, as shall be seen, presented the freed with a great deal of difficulty during the post-Emancipation era. The economic foundation of the plantation system was crumbling, and the planters did not offer the freed much more than the continued exploitation of their labor power. They therefore saw no future in staying on the estates and many wished to settle as small farmers in their own communities. The planters saw the possible emergence of a relatively autonomous Afro-Caribbean community as a threat to the patriarchal relations of authority and deference which had tied the laborers to the planters and did everything in their power to prevent this. Since they controlled virtually all land on the island, they succeeded in this until well into the twentieth century, when the plantation system finally collapsed. The modern egalitarian order of respectability was also initially seen by the planters to pose a threat to the old hierarchical order and countered by all means possible. This order was, as noted, closely associated with an "English" respectable life style which was not easily combined with life in the Afro-Caribbean community, and it was only an attractive, and realistic, opportunity for the small middle class which emerged at the time of Emancipation. Most of the freed were largely frustrated in their attempts to create an economically viable life and a place of social recognition and cultural identity for themselves in the island society.

Due to the crucial role of the missionaries in the administering and upholding of the cultural models of respectability necessary for social acceptability, whether within the upwardly mobile group of civil servants and managers or in a more stationary lower class of small farmers, they came to hold a central position in the socioeconomic developments of the nineteenth and early twentieth centuries. For this reason, they constitute an important focus in this discussion of economic, political and cultural developments in post-Emancipation society on Nevis.

"DEPARTED GLORIES"

The post-Emancipation period was one of great changes in most of the West Indies. On the Leeward Islands of St. Kitts, Antigua and Montserrat, there were frequent and large-scale transfers of property as part of a process of economic polarization which reduced dependence upon estate labor. Montserrat saw the collapse of sugar cultivation and the rise of independent small farmers, while Antigua and St. Kitts saw the modernization of the sugar industry with the help of the plough, harrows and steam mills, and the establishment of "free" villages for the workers (Hall 1971:43, 44, 50, 112). On Nevis, however, few changes occurred. The stony soil of Nevis made mechanization of cultivation difficult, and the poverty of the planters prevented the erection of steam mills on most estates. Despite the low profitability of sugar production, the planter families were relatively secure on their old estates and held on to their property. They just "tightened their belts", paid the laborers subsistence level wages or instituted a sharecrop system on their plantations, and attempted to prevent the workers from leaving the estates (ibid.:114). In this way most of the planters managed to maintain their position on the island until the early part of the twentieth century.

The social and economic conditions which were presented to the newly emancipated Nevisians were not substantially changed from the conditions under which they had lived formerly. The Emancipation act which was instituted in 1834 essentially prolonged slavery with six years of apprenticeship for the field laborers, four years for other workers. Children below the age of six, however, were emancipated immediately. The apprentices were obliged to work for their owners 40½ hours a week, for which they received such necessities of life as food, clothing, housing and medical care, in accordance with the privileges which had been instituted by the Leeward Islands slave law. Apprentices could not be sold, unless the entire estate was sold, and they could not be punished by their owner, in that all disputes between laborers and masters were to be settled at a special magistrates court. Finally, all apprentices had the right to purchase their freedom at a price agreed upon by the worker, his owner and the magistrates (Hall 1971:16).

When this act became known among the slaves in July 1834, they expressed great dissatisfaction with their terms of freedom. To them an Emancipation beginning with a six year apprenticeship period under conditions which were almost indistinguishable from those of slavery was no freedom at all. One of the Methodist missionaries spent much of the month of July visiting the slaves on various estates explaining the act to them and attempting to convince them that it really was "the king's law" that most of them should be apprentices for six years. He was met with disbelief and disappointment reflected in statements such as "we neber believe de king gee a'we free, & then take em back from us again", making the missionary conclude that it "would have puzzled a philosopher of the first order to make them understand how they were to be free on the 1st of Aug^t 'to all intents & purposes', & yet be made apprentices for 6 years!" (C515:2 July, 1834). Many slaves refused to receive the address, which he had prepared on the matter, believing that if they did so, it would "bind" them to their estate (C515:7 July, 1834).

When the apprenticeship system was initiated on August 1, 1834, a few of the freed did not show up for work, but the situation on Nevis generally remained calm, and the planters did not experience the massive work refusals which characterized St. Kitts, where martial law had to be instituted (C487:5 August, 1834; Hall 1971:25; Frucht 1977:384-86). One of the Methodist missionaries found that the laborers behaved "very properly", but that the same could not be said about the planters, who pursued "a wretched policy" not making the slightest effort "to conciliate the minds of the people, but the very opposite line of conduct appears to be studied. Whenever a nook in the law admits of anything in the shape of imposition or hardship, the apprentice is sure to feel it" (C511:4 October, 1834). Most planters made little effort to communicate "information to the apprentices relative to the privileges the law secures for them", and they did not even seem to be bothered too much about the law, knowing that the magistrates court was controlled by planters, who would not be favorably inclined toward any complaints on the part of the freed. This was quite unsettling to the free: "I have you to judge of the effects upon the minds of the labourers, to see their masters driving about the magistrate in their carriages to hear complaints against themselves" (ibid.).[1]

As a result of this close connection between the planters and the magistrates, many planters continued to use the whip liberally and demanded extra work of the laborers for the slightest wrongs. One of the missionaries thus reported having met a young man who had severe wounds, but who was prevented from bringing a complaint to the court, because the planter had taken his clothes, so that he could not go there, being completely naked. He probably would not have found much justice at the court, however, the magistrate being the brother of his master. In another incident the whole gang on an estate had been sentenced to work 6 days a week for some offence, forcing them to do their domestic chores on Sundays and thus preventing them from going to church. Not only were the freed treated with the same sort of brutality and exploitation as during slavery, but many of them were faced with starvation, as the planters used a clause in the local act which allowed them to give one free day a week instead of food allowances. Many apprentices therefore were allocated a piece of land overgrown with bush and "fit for nothing" to grow their provisions, the planters disregarding the problems the workers would have feeding themselves until their provisions were ready for harvest (C512:31 October, 1834; C511:4 October, 1834; C573:31 December, 1836).[2]

When during the year after the institution of apprenticeship, agents of Demerara planters arrived on Nevis, offering to buy up the apprenticeship of those who were willing to bind themselves there for a limited period of time during which they were to be provided with houses, gardens, provisions, clothing and wages, many accepted (C566:23 September, 1836), and in the period from 1835 to 1842, 294 Nevisians emigrated for Demerara (Richardson 1983:88).

When the complete Emancipation of the slaves was instituted on Nevis on August 1, 1838, after the apprenticeship system had been entirely abolished two years earlier than originally planned, few of the gentry chose to participate in the Emancipation services, which were held in the island's churches and chapels. According to a missionary, the workers were offered one shilling per day as well as the privilege of a house (which usually was "the Negroe's own house"), a plot of land to cultivate and medical care (CA1000:15 August, 1838). The wage level of one shilling a day was not maintained, however; thus the Nevis workers were reported to have received 6d a day in 1839 and 1842, 10d in 1845 and only 5d in 1848 (Hall 1971:55). In 1850, wages as low as 4d, paid mainly in provisions such as cornmeal, were reported by a Methodist missionary, who noted that the mass of people were very poor with some dying of starvation (CA:14 October, 1850). Many emigrated to St. Kitts, Demerara and Trinidad, where better wages were offered (CA1013:September, 1840; CA1022: 21 April, 23 June, 22 August, 1842), and by 1846, 2609 Nevisians had emigrated to Trinidad alone (Hall 1971:41).

The Nevis planters could not afford to pay even the subsistence level wages, which were offered to the freed, and in the early 1840s, they began to employ the laborers on a sharecropping basis, by which workers were given two acres of land to cultivate in sugar, receiving one-third to one-half of the crops instead of wages (Hall 1971:114). This practice became very prevalent on Nevis, and in 1866, for example, 40 of the island's 80 estates were reported to be wholly or partially using the "metairie system" (*Nevis Blue Book* 1866:274). With this system, the planters had effectively shifted most of the economic loss experienced during bad years to the laborers. The laborers had the burden of planting, weeding and harvesting the canes, often being forced to pay for help with the harvesting, regardless of the profits derived from the crop, while the planters had no direct expenses and were sure to benefit from gains during good years. The sharecroppers apparently found it difficult to manage when harvests were poor, and in the early 1850s many of the cultivators were forced to abandon their farming, not being able to make ends meet due to a poor crop (CA1068:13 March, 1852). Such problems continued to plague the sharecroppers' farming.

The introduction of the sharecrop system was, as one English resident in the West Indies around 1850, John Davy, wrote concerning Nevis, "rather a conservative measure than one adopted for improvement—one of submission to adverse circumstances rather than of enterprising struggle to overcome them". With the sharecrop system no improvement in the agricultural production had taken place, the "hoe and the hand being the chief implement and power employed" (Davy 1971 [1854]:485). While agriculture was mechanized on the neighboring plantation islands of St. Kitts and Antigua, on Nevis, only four steam mills had been erected by the 1840s of which two dated back to the 1820s (Coleridge 1832:183).[3] Only one of them was still functioning when Davy visited the island, the others being "out of repair" with no one skilled enough to get them in working order (Davy 1971:487). Agricultural production on Nevis was not appreciably mechanized before the 1860s, when a Barbados proprietor purchased approximately 15 of the estates on Nevis, on which he invested heavily in labor-saving equipment such as steam mills, setting in motion the mechanization of sugar production on several other estates, and by the middle of the 1870s, 30 steam mills were reported for the island. This period also saw the introduction of cotton cultivation which took place as the market for the crop improved as a consequence of the American civil war during the 1860s (*Nevis Blue Books* 1866, 1875; Hall 1971:145). While cotton cultivation did not become important at this time, it became the main crop on the island beginning with the 1920s, when the market for the muscovado sugar which was produced on Nevis collapsed (Frucht 1966:42). In 1940, only six steam sugar mills were still in operation (*Leeward Islands Blue Book* 1940).

The planters were not able to prevent the laborers from emigrating to places which presented better economic opportunities than the poorly paid estate work and the unattractive sharecropping which constituted virtually the only means of making a living on Nevis. They attempted, however, to prevent the development of a class of independent small farmers, which could cause the estates to loose their labor force entirely. The planters therefore strictly enforced the law against trespassing in order to make squatting impossible (*Nevis Blue Book* 1876:246), and this effectively prevented any sort of squatting, because Nevis, unlike many other British West Indian islands, had no crown land where the population could settle (Davy 1971:482;

Kingsley 1871:52–53). An old Jewish burial ground in Charlestown, which had been abandoned for more than a century, offered the only opportunity for squatting and several houses were built on it during the 1830s (*Nevis Blue Book* 1863:283). This policy against squatting, according to some, not only prevented the development of the free villages, which emerged on many other West Indian islands during the post-Emancipation period, it also ensured that the laborers did not return "to their original savagery" and that they were kept "well-ordered and peaceable, industrious, and well-taught" (Kingsley 1871:52–53).

Despite their successful suppression of squatting, the planters did not manage to keep all the workers who remained on Nevis on the estates. This is largely because a few planters decided to parcel out their estates as a means of facilitating their sale at a favorable price. In 1848, for example, lots were offered for sale at a price of 20 pounds sterling per acre, at the plantation owned by George Pollard. Many apparently wished to acquire land, and 36 Nevisians paid for deeds to land, and 3 obtained 900-year leases.[4] They never received proper deeds for the land, however, and most of the money they paid to the local agent selling the land was never forwarded to the owner (PM:23 February, 1863). During the latter part of the nineteenth century, a fair number of freeholders were noted in the *Nevis Blue Book*; most of them, however, possessed lots which were below two acres. In 1863, 800 freeholders were reported, a number which in 1865 had increased to 940, 45 of whom were living in villages that had been built since Emancipation. In 1871, the Blue Book noted that there were "no less than 900 freeholders" explaining the uncertain estimate by the difficulty of documenting the number, there being "no means of obtaining exact information, as property deeds are not always recorded". In 1876, when an act was instituted to tax land, 2,135 persons (out of a population of 11,864 in 1881) were listed as freeholders, but only 129 of them owned more than two acres (*Nevis Blue Books* 1863:193–94, 1865:194, 1871:108, 1876:126, 1881:171). Approximately half of the freeholders lived in St. Paul's parish, which was dominated by Charlestown and the fishing village of Bath (*Nevis Blue Book* 1865:194), leaving about 1000 small freeholders who lived in agricultural districts.[5]

This acquisition of land was also noted in an account of Nevis from 1871, where the working classes were described as "a proprietary body—their cottages are comfortable, and their homesteads per family extend from one-fourth of an acre to three acres, at an average value of £75 per acre" (Iles 1958 [1871]:11). According to a later report by a Methodist missionary, many of the people who belonged to the Society's Gingerland Chapel were described as living in the small villages of Fig Tree, Brown Pasture, Cox, Zetland, Rawlins and New River, as peasant proprietors possessing small holdings consisting of "three acres and a cow" (CR749: Report from Nevis Circuit 1907; see also Burdon 1920: 188, 217).

This picture of the small holders seems to be rather too optimistic, however.

Many, if not most of the small holders owned merely house spots, which were located in gullies or in dry areas, where agriculture was difficult (Frucht 1966:71). In general, the landholdings which the small farmers were able to acquire at this time were small, and did not present a basis for the development of a landed peasantry. For the Black Nevisians migration from the island to destinations in the Caribbean, North, South and Middle America therefore continued to provide the most attractive alternative to plantation labor (Frucht 1966; Richardson 1983). Due to the loss of laborers caused by this emigration, several hundred East Indians, called "coolies", were imported to work on the sugar estates during the 1870s (CA1232:11 November, 1874; CA1236:9 August, 1875).[6]

The plantation economy was seriously threatened during the 1890s, when the sugar planters were faced with "ruinous prices", which led to a general economic depression on the island. The diaries of Rev. John Jones, who was an Anglican minister on Nevis from 1887-98, reflect a society in decline. The burning of cane fields by desperate estate workers was becoming increasingly common, making the institution of martial law and the stationing of marines in Charlestown necessary in February 1896. The growing poverty of the people was reflected in the increasing numbers who attended the annual Christmas dinner given to the poor by the Anglican church (John Jones' Diaries: 28 January, 25 December, 1895, 20, 21 February, 1896, 25 December, 1897).

The general depression which the West Indian colonies experienced at this time led to an investigation of the Caribbean islands by a Royal Commission in 1897, which found the need for "urgent action [...] to improve the lot of the people of Nevis" and recommended such measures as the erection of a sugar factory on the island and a land settlement scheme, which would replace sharecropping. It was to be based on mixed farming with sugar as the main crop and cotton as another important cash crop (quoted in Merrill 1958:98). None of these recommendations were followed, however, and the island continued to be characterized by the disintegrating plantation economy. When the English woman Antonia Williams visited Nevis in 1908-09, she described estate houses which had been abandoned by their owners and were turning into ruins as they were invaded by tropical plants and animals (AW:43). A decade later *A Handbook of St. Kitts-Nevis* described Nevis as a place characterized by "worn-outedness" with the capital Charlestown "as a town of departed glories" (Burdon 1920:188, 212). As the old English planter families finally gave up on their plantations, the White population on Nevis decreased. The White population of approximately 400 at the time of Emancipation in 1834 thus had declined to 260 in 1861; 180 in 1891, and 90 in 1921 (Hall 1971:8; *Nevis Blue Books* 1862:197-98; *Leeward Islands Blue Book* 1891:142, 1923).

During the early twentieth century, a number of estates were acquired by the growing local middle classes, who purchased them either through the courts, or directly from the English owners who at that time were keen to sell their estates (Maynard 1987:2; Frucht 1966:74). Some of the new owners attempted to farm the land, others divided it up and resold most of it in smaller lots, letting out unsold portions on sharecropping terms. The social significance of this acquisition of estates on the part of non-Whites was quite apparent to the upwardly mobile middle class. As noted by the Nevisian Eulalie Byron in one of her two pamphlets on prominent White and Black families of Nevis, "A new page in history was being turned in Nevis. Black men were now becoming estate proprietors, producing on a large scale, and exporting, muscovado sugar, cultivating sea island cotton, and controlling a sizeable labour force" (1981:17). While the social incentive for a man of color to acquire a plantation was great, the economic benefits to be derived from being an estate owner at this time were not appreciable, particularly when the inflated prices that had been commanded by sugar and cotton during the first world war decreased. A son of one of the Nevisians who purchased an estate during the First World War, has written with a certain amount of bitterness, "After the war these prices did not last and most of the money from the good prices had gone to England and [there were] some who were left with plenty of land and no money to work it" (Maynard 1987:2).

By 1930, most estates had stopped production and the Crown began purchasing estate land some of which was sold in smaller lots or rented as small holdings as part of a major land settlement program (Frucht 1966:42, 85). When the geographer Gordon Merrill did his research on St. Kitts and Nevis in the 1950s, he found only a handful of estates which were still operating, having converted to livestock raising and the production of coconuts. Much land which had been cultivated formerly was now abandoned and in scrub pasture with "scrawny beasts in scanty number competing with each other for food" (1958:107-08). Most agricultural production at this time was done by peasant farmers, and the government now actively encouraged the establishment of a population of small farmers growing foodstuffs for sale on Nevis and neighboring islands, particularly St. Kitts, where there was a ready market.

Little development of this sort took place, however, despite the fact that there was a large available labor force on the island during the early 1950s. This attempt to establish a society of small farmers had come too late. The Nevisian population might have responded favorably, when the establishment of a landed peasantry was recommended by the Royal Commission in 1897. By the middle of the twentieth century, small farming on the old estate land, which had degenerated after centuries of monocrop cultivation, was not an attractive proposition. The governmental efforts to institute small farming on the "worn out land on the lowland of Nevis", in Merrill's opinion, had "little to recommend it" (1958:112). More was needed to re-habilitate small farming, which for so long had been associated with a socially marginal population and had been confined to areas only marginally suited to agriculture.

THE CULTURAL MISSION OF THE CHURCHES AND SCHOOLS

The modern egalitarian order of respectability came to play a central role in the colonial society, as the economic foundation of the plantation society crumbled. This was even more the case, when the old plantocracy lost its political control over the island, as an increasing number of non-White Nevisians gained the right to vote, and as the island lost its political independence. As early as 1852, Black and Colored members of the local assembly surpassed the number of White members (CA1068:13 March, 1852). In 1866, all legislative powers were passed to the Crown, and in 1871 colonial administration was removed from the island with the formation of the Federation of the Leeward Islands (Frucht 1966:43; Hall 1971:175-79). With the removal of the political and economic underpinnings of the hierarchical order, the cultural basis of the modern egalitarian order became much more important as a bulwark against the collapse of the colonial system.

The ministers of the Methodist and Anglican Churches remained vital in this cultural mission, working through the schools as well as the churches. As one Methodist missionary noted, "*Freedom Sanctified* must civilize, and guided by a missionary they will be safe, but if left alone, they will [...] go back instead of forward" (CA1019:15 September, 1841). In their cultural efforts, the Methodists, in particular, attempted to establish a population of upright citizens, who could become the backbone of the culture of respectability which they advocated for the island society. As this culture became entirely dominant in the Victorian era of the later nineteenth century and early twentieth century, Anglican ministers also became active cultural missionaries. Since only a relatively small middle class acquired the economic and social basis for adopting the English culture of respectability, the result of this English cultural mission, in effect, was to provide a solid ideological foundation for the establishment of a small local Black (and Colored) upper class and the exclusion from the social order of the vast majority of the population.

During the turbulent Emancipation period, the Methodists saw one of their most important roles as that of helping to maintain public order in the plantation society. Thus, when the apprenticeship system was instituted in August 1834, those who were members of the Methodist Society were told that they would be expelled, if they did not show up for work as expected (C503:4 August, 1834). Virtually all obliged under this threat, and a few weeks into August, the Methodist ministers could report proudly that many of their members had been chosen to be constables on the estates, a position which was given to "one of the most moral & respectable among every 50 Negroes on an Estate" (C506:22 August, 1834). This did not mean that they endorsed the plantation regime with its heavy usage of unskilled, underpaid laborers, but signified perhaps rather that they regarded any disruption of the social order as a threat to the temperate and modest life required by respectable citizens. Any improvement in the position of the freed was to take place in a peaceful and orderly fashion, well within the boundaries of the law.[7]

One missionary hoped that a way to initiate this peaceful change had been found, when he heard a few weeks after Emancipation that some of the apprentices were talking about purchasing a piece of land "under the new system" in order to settle there with their family:

> My expectations are large. The liberated Negro will yet become a fond of industry, good order, and domestic comforts, as the peasantry of Britain. Then Isaiah 32 16–18 will be fulfilled & God glorified. What altho some of these lands should become the property of the rising generation should it not be pleasing to the one who is now a child, taking his children by the hand, & exclaiming 'O what a change! On yonder field my F[ather] and M[other] toiling, sweating, and trembling under the lash of the Driver, laboured as slaves; now it is *mine* & I can leave it to you.' When I hazard a conjecture respecting N[egroes] in the twentieth century: religion seated on the throne of intellect; shedding its mild and hallowing influence over the common concerns of life; changing the face of society [...] & sweetening the comforts of the humblest cottage. Britain has raised the children of Africa to a level with her own (C506:22 August, 1834).

Such missionary dreams were far from the slave-like conditions which the planters sought to maintain during the apprenticeship period.

When the sharecropping system was introduced about a decade later, the missionaries again saw in this an opportunity for the industrious to help themselves in that they would become "respectable tenants" and, "if the Land Owners were only generally willing", the island could see the rise of "a class of Middle Men who would be what the Farmer is in England" (CA1032:16 January, 1844). Again the missionaries' high expectations were disappointed. The uncertain income from the crops did not allow the sharecroppers to help themselves, and landowners were not "generally willing" to see the sharecroppers become independent farmers.

During the latter part of the century the missionaries seemed to have rather given up seeing any substantial improvements in the material condition of the vast majority of Nevisian people, regarding poverty and migration as a general fact of life on the island. Thus one minister, when reporting the loss of 25 members due to the inability of some people to pay their dues and the emigration of others from the island, counted himself lucky: "considering the circumstances against which we have to contend we feel there is cause for gratitude that matters are not worse" (CA1238:25 January, 1876).

If the Methodists had rather given up on any major social and economic improvements on the island, they worked diligently for moral improvement on the island society. This occurred at religious teaching at the chapel services and Sunday schools as well as at more social events such as Sunday school anniversaries and picnics, and at tea meetings, fund raising events, where a soft drink and sweets were served and people could enjoy "the pleasures of Religion and Sociality together" (CA1019:15 September, 1841).

The importance of the modest lifestyle which was associated with English respectability was strongly impressed upon the Nevisian congregations at such events as the celebration of Emancipation Day, which was organized in Charlestown in 1839 by the missionary in collaboration with the classleaders. The freed population apparently regarded Emancipation Day on the first of August as their "Christmas", and in order to prevent them from engaging in the drinking and carousing usually associated with Christmas, a Society meeting was called at 2 o'clock in the afternoon on Emancipation Day. 1400 showed up for the event, which probably was as different from Christmas carousing as possible:

> The arrangement was that all must have Society tickets to get admission and upon their admission they were to go to the part of the chapel and take their seats just in the same order as when they are met in class. This was done. Each leader was then at the direction of the preacher to wait upon his or her members and present to each one two cakes and a little water. This was done in a quiet and orderly manner after I had addressed our people on about fifteen virtues such as [...] piety, prayer, Love, Honesty, Faithfulness to their engagements etc. etc. After we had done this, we then in a very solemn imposing and respectable manner renewed our covenant with God in much the same manner as at the close of the year (CA1006:2 August, 1839).

It is little wonder that the missionary later in his report, which described this celebration, could relate "it has been said by many of the gentlemen in this colony that Methodism is the principal cause of that good order which has prevailed" (ibid.).

The teaching of a virtuous life of respectability was, perhaps, even more forcefully carried out at the schools and Sunday schools, which were run by the Anglican and Methodist Churches in the post-Emancipation period. In 1845–46, a total of 690 children were registered at the Methodist and Anglican day schools, 1020 at Sunday schools, according to magistrates' reports (Hall 1971:49). During the post-Emancipation era, a body of professional teachers began to be trained at teachers' colleges located on other West Indian islands such as Antigua and Jamaica, and in 1843, the Methodists reported that the first group of 5 teachers were returning to Nevis where they were to be stationed at different schools on the island.[8] In order to pay these teachers adequate salaries, a weekly tuition of 2–6d per child was collected in the Methodist schools, depending on the child's grade (CA1028:18 May, 1843; CA1029:10 August, 1843), and a few years later these schools were reported to be "effective & successful" (CA1047:12 November, 1846).

These teachers were expected to teach the children not just such basic skills as reading and writing and, for the girls, needlework, but also proper manners, including how to make a "decent appearance". Thus at the boys school in Charlestown, probably the most ambitious of the Methodist schools, the rule that children were obligated to wear "a jacket and trousers" was strictly adhered to (CA1021:16 April, 1842; CA1020:1 January, 1842; CA1029:10 August, 1843). That the attempt at "civilizing" the Nevisians had made some impact on the children is apparent from a visit to Charlestown Boys School during the early 1850s by an Englishman, who described the students as happy and well behaved, "neatly dressed" and clean. When they passed him on their way out of the school, they impressed him by touching their cap, many of them shaking hands with "a 'How do you do, Sir?' said in an innocent, cheerful way" (Davy 1971:483).

The Sunday schools played perhaps an even greater role in imparting notions of respectability to the rising generation of Nevisians in that they reached a much larger group of people. The Sunday schools, like the day schools, were important as places of cultural, as well as religious instruction as is apparent in the following description of a procession, which was held by the Methodist Sunday school in Charlestown:[9]

> they were arranged in order for walking under the care of their teacher. I then took my place at the head of them and immediately followed the biggest boy belonging to the day school with a large Flag with the following motto "Wesleyan Infant School—Fear God and Honour the Queen". Among the Boys were two more small flags with the following words "Loyalty" and "Modesty". Then at a given distance there were two similar flags with these words "Temperance" & "Honesty" inscribed on them. I suppose there were nearly 400 children. Boys and girls all smartly clothed. The boys had caps and straw hats, Jackets and Trousers. Shoes and stockings almost without an exception. The girls were all in white, many with bonnet and almost every one with shoes and stockings. I can assure you it was a lovely solemn attractive sight (CA1012:7 August, 1840).

Despite these several attempts at molding the islanders to become good Christians as well as loyal and upright citizens, the missionaries were often disappointed with the results. This was largely because the majority of the population regarded being part of the Afro-Caribbean community as more important and vital to daily living on the island, than membership in the Methodist Society. Ties to blood relatives were, for example, valued more than ties to the spiritual brethren and sisters of the mission, when forced to make a choice by the missionaries. One missionary thus complained that several members of the Society had daughters in their home "large with child" and was "all but determined to put the whole of our young people from our Sunday schools." He found that the expelling of people did not have much effect, because those who left the Methodists just went to the Anglicans who did not "discipline the members" and were more than happy to receive new members, their churches being badly attended (CA1068:13 March, 1852). A cholera epidemic, which raged on the island during the following year, killing about 10% of the population, came to his help in that several hundred people joined the Society and scores of people decided to get married in order to escape from God's wrath. While the missionaries rejoiced in this increased interest in religion and morality on the part of the islanders, they feared that few of these conversions were "sound" (CA1081:26 April, 1854).

Social and economic relations within the Afro-Caribbean community were also seen to be more fundamental than those allowed and offered by the godly community of the Methodists. The severe restrictions placed on sexual relations often led to conflicts. In 1861, for example, expulsions from the Society due to fornication included a chapel keeper, "by whom two young women are with child", three Sunday school teachers and several adult scholars, one of them a married man "who had left his lawful wife to cohabit with a widow within a week after the death of her husband." One female leader in the Society was expelled for having rented housing to three couples "living in fornication," because she refused to stop renting out her rooms to these people explaining that she "wouldn't give it up, as it was all she had to live by" (CA1132:10 September, 1861).

The people seem to have employed their own forms of social sanction, when needed, whether or not they were acceptable to respectable society. The missionary was shocked to hear that "a respectable looking woman who for some years had met in the Minister's Wife's class" had been fighting with another woman on her way to church, and that two women "in a mixed company of old & young men & women, and within hearing of the family of the Manager of the Estate [where they had sought shelter from the rain in the wind mill] began to curse each other with the unclean lips with which they had but just ceased to 'bless God'". He added that while the "communications" of each were "filthy" enough, one of these poured forth such a torrent of "Hell's horrid language" as it must be impossible to exceed. In other cases members resorted to obeah, and one was reported to be "one of the most notorious Obeah men in the Island" who had been involved in a murder charge (CA1130:8 June, 1861). Most of these instances of "bad" behavior were discovered quite late by the Methodist ministers, if they were discovered at all, and in several cases the ministers only learned all the details when they contacted the superintendent of police or attended the court, where some of the cases were heard, such as those dealing with obeah, which was illegal (ibid.) The reluctance to report on relatives and neighbors clearly was related to the central importance of the Afro-Caribbean community as the most immediate context of socioeconomic relations for the majority of the islanders.

The economic deprivation which most of the Black population suffered made it very difficult for them to take advantage of the education, which the Anglican and Methodist schools offered. On Nevis, the government did not pay grants to the schools, as it did on several other West Indian islands (CA1016:2 April, 1841; CA1052:9 June, 1848). Many parents were unable to pay the school fees, and many children were kept at home in order to work for the family under the sharecropping system. In 1850, a missionary reported that many parents in Charlestown were unable to pay the debts which they owed to the schools for their children's education there; in Gingerland, where the children were taught "for a trifle", the salary of the school master had to be reduced due to the small income derived from teaching and he probably would have to be replaced by a female teacher, who would command a smaller salary;[10] At Clifton the attendance at school was very small and declining; and at Combermere the school was on the verge of closing, as children, who could be hired to do estate work for smaller wages than their parents, were employed on the estates, leaving many adults with no work. The teacher there had to contend with working for half the salary promised. This apparent lack of interest in the education, or welfare, of the children on the part of the planters, who seemed to see in children only a source of inexpensive labor to be exploited, was regarded by one missionary as a clear sign of their lack of social dignity, and they were characterized by him as "simple and cheap" (CA1063:14 October, 1850).

Perhaps due to the important economic role played by children in the plantations' faltering economy, the government offered little help to the schools. In 1861, as a measure of their good will, the local legislature voted to pay 30 pounds for educational purposes to be divided equally among the Anglicans and Methodists over several years, a sum which was to provide education for a reported school population of 987 (CA1154:27 February, 1864; *Nevis Blue Book* 1862:209–12). The Anglican schools also were faced with severe economic problems, and the educational situation on the island did not change much until an act of the newly formed Federation of Leeward Islands in 1871 instituted government grants for the schools. At that time, there were 6 Anglican schools with 292 students and 4 Methodist schools with 387 students. One Methodist missionary described the situation in the schools as disastrous, stating "Worse schools I never saw than the generality of denominational schools in these islands". He wondered whether the government would "establish a system of efficient general education with well paid Teachers & properly furnished schools or whether the denominations shall go on spending English mission funds and getting small grants from government to support miserably paid & furnished schools" (CA1223:26 December, 1872).

The latter course was taken. The general condition of the schools remained poor, the grants being characterized as "absurdly small" and some schools were "utterly destitute of all the modern necessaries of school keeping" (*Nevis Blue Book* 1872:132–37, 1872:n.p.). When in 1890, another act made school attendance compulsory and the employment of children below 9 years of age illegal, the number of scholars on roll increased to 2,152, however the average attendance was only 990

(Crosse 1962–63:n.p.; *Leeward Islands Blue Book* 1891:n.p.). Even though the many parents who kept their children at home were fined (John Jones' Diaries: 20 March, 1895), school attendance remained low and the performance of those children who went to school and took the annual examinations was often unsatisfactory, (John Jones' Diaries: 19 January, 1894, 20 March, 1895, 19, 25 March, 1896).

Whereas the Anglican Church seems to have played a rather passive role during the post-Emancipation period, being poorly attended and having only one Sunday school (in Charlestown) by 1860 (CA1068:13 March, 1852; *Nevis Blue Book* 1862:209–12), it took an active interest in the welfare of the Black population during John Jones' tenure as minister on Nevis. Jones was, like the Methodists, quite concerned with matters of respectability and found certain aspects of the White upper class culture, such as women's clothing that exposed a great deal of breast, to be "highly vulgar" (John Jones' Diaries: 4 January, 1887). He held services in the villages in order to reach those who did not attend church and made valiant efforts to convince those members of his congregation who lived "improper lives" to marry, "marriage being altogether an afterthought with these people" (see for example John Jones' Diaries: 4 March, 7 March, 18, 21 April, 24 June, 22 August, 7 September, 1887).

Rev. Jones also organized a number of more social activities and his diaries thus mention, besides the ordinary services held on Sunday in the church, tea meetings (John Jones' Diaries: 4 April, 1893, 8 November, 1894); special lectures, often with "Magic Lantern" displays[11] on for example views of London or "some old Testament scenes" (ibid.: 12 November, 1893, 11 October, 1894); harvest festivals (ibid.: 21 June, 10 July, 1887, 26 July, 1896); Christmas trees with fancy fairs (ibid.: 20 December, 1894), as well as picnics for Sunday and day school children and Sunday school processions (ibid.: 21 June, 1887, 25 May, 1896). Also, Jones actively promoted the organization of voluntary Friendly Societies in the different parishes (ibid.: 26, 30 August, 2, 27 September, 7, 8 November 1887) and published a magazine (ibid.: 15 January, 1894).

Unlike the Methodist missionaries, Jones maintained close contact with the White upper class and participated actively in their cultural events. Thus he kept a small private school for the children of an estate owner as well as his own children (John Jones' Diaries: 1 March, 1887, 15 July, 1895); he was active in the Odd Fellows' lodge in Charlestown, presiding at their meetings and preaching at their marches (ibid.: 23 August, 26 September, 1893, 11 September, 17 October, 1894), and he also attended Masonic concerts on St. Kitts (ibid.: 27 March, 1894) and preached when the Nevis Freemasons had their procession to St. George's church (ibid.: 27 December, 1895). He played tennis at the government house (ibid.: 11 January, 1893) and attended interisland cricket matches (ibid.:6 August, 1894). While the church offered a Christmas dinner for the poor, Rev. Jones and his family usually had their

Christmas dinner at an estate (ibid.: 25 December, 1894, 25 December, 1895, 25 December, 1897).

The Methodists did not appreciate this sudden competition on the part of the Anglican Church and tried to convince the Nevisians that " 'prayers read from a book' were of no avail" and that only prayers by a "Wesleyan Leader" could save "a dying churchman". The Friendly Societies were referred to in "disparaging terms" by one of the Methodist ministers, who also attempted to prevent the holding of Anglican mission meetings in the villages (John Jones' Diaries: 3, 5 September, 5 October, 1 November, 1887). While the two denominations never achieved a stage of cooperation during the nineteenth century, which might have furthered their common cause among the Black population, they must have learned to accept one another. Thus in 1895, John Jones recorded having paid the Methodist minister a visit, adding "the first time that I have ever done such a thing" (ibid.: 15 February, 1895). The Anglican and Methodist Churches did not really join forces on the island before well into the twentieth century, when other denominations, such as the Seventh Day Adventists and the Pilgrim Holiness Church had begun to assert themselves, and the Methodist Society had become one of the established Churches on the island.

The educational role of the Anglican and Methodist Churches was finally taken over by the colonial government in 1915, when public schools began to provide education for children from 5–16 years of age. As formerly, the schools continued to teach reading, writing and arithmetic, religious instruction, as well as needlework for the girls, but some geography, history, hygiene and moral instruction were also offered. The schools kept the tradition of basing their curriculum on the teaching of British culture, and thus the students continued to concentrate most of their energy on learning about a distant part of the world that had little to do with the island society in which they lived.[12] The problems generated by this approach have been vividly described by a former Nevisian school teacher:

> Many of the lessons taught in the school were based upon foreign material that had no relation to the lives and environment of the pupils, although it proved to expand their ideas further afield, they were left ignorant or with little knowledge of their immediate surroundings. The geography lessons were on the mountains, bays, rivers, and towns of various continents; while history lessons were on the Wars of Roses, the Indian Mutiny and the Battle of Hastings, forgetting that Nevis among the other West Indian Islands were of strategic importance during the many later battles between England, France and Spain. The lessons for moral teaching were on such topics as good-manners, honesty, thrift, truthfulness and many more which were of no real worth to the normal development of the pupils, for the difficulty of presenting them to the pupil with the examinations in view resulted in a question and answer system, quite unsuitable for moral training. The physical exercises

were a chief subject on the curriculum and were done in a military way—long marches and drills performed to number with precision and a certain measure of rigidness which created much dislike to the lesson [. . .]. Music took the form of vocal singing which was done by Tonic-Solfa, which meant that the teacher must have a good knowledge of the rudiments of this form of music to be able to teach the pupils by so laborious a way. The rudiments of music were not taught to the pupils (Crosse 1962–63:n.p.).

Teachers often were rewarded financially according to the grades obtained by the students at exams, leading to even greater emphasis on rote learning. The primary schools provided a seventh standard examination, which remained the highest degree granted by the public schools until a secondary school was opened in Charlestown in 1950.

The seventh standard examination qualified the successful to become a student teacher in the classroom, at that time the main avenue of upward mobility within island society.[13] Most children never reached the seventh standard, but dropped out in the lower grades. The attendance rate remained low, because many children had to work in the cotton fields or help care for younger siblings while their parents worked. In the school year 1916–17, the 3007 students who were enrolled in the public schools had an average attendance rate of 45.9% (Burdon 1920:198). Although this rate had improved by the middle of the century, the educational situation in the 10 schools which were operating on the island at that time still was unsatisfactory. A colonial annual report from 1948 thus noted that little effort had been made during the year to enforce the law compelling children to attend the schools because "school places are not as yet available for all of the children" (*Colonial Annual Report* 1948:22).

The educational system which was to have been an important means of helping the Nevisians improve their condition in the free society instead became, as an institution closely connected with the culture of respectability, the means whereby the exclusion of most Nevisians from the upper levels of society was effected and justified. Education was only available for those children who could be spared in the depressed rural economy. Furthermore, the education which was offered in the schools did not equip the children with any knowledge or skills which were useful for them as agricultural workers, but rather emphasized the history, geography, literature and language of the distant colonial power which governed the island. The main practical value of mastering English culture was that this allowed entrance to the island's middle class through positions as teachers or low echelon employees in the colonial administration. This was not a practicable or realistic possibility for the vast majority of the students, however, and the schools therefore, far from being avenues of enlightenment and improvement for the Nevisian population in general, came to be seen for what they were: fortresses of the English culture associated with the dominant classes, and thus as one of the main reasons why the lower classes could not advance in local society.

While it might be impossible for most Nevisians to become proficient in "proper" English or acquire a sufficient knowledge in the subjects which were required at the schools, it was everybody's privilege to become a pious Christian, who could command the respect of the religious community, which included the upper as well as the lower classes. Even though the Methodist Society of the first half of the nineteenth century was a rather stratified one, where the "aristocratic" also tended to be the "influential of the church", even the most "poor & humble" were able to become classleaders, if they displayed deep religiosity and devotion (CA1259:24 May, 1880). The Methodist Society therefore continued to provide an institutional framework within which everybody could assume positions of leadership, regardless of their background, even though such positions no doubt were assumed more easily by those of the right cultural and thereby social and economic background.

By convincing Nevisians of their worth as Christians and of their right to lead others, as long as they were worthy Christians, the Methodist Society can be said, paradoxically, to have opened the door for other religious denominations on the island. This is because the tendency of the more "cultured" upper classes to control most of the positions of leadership in the Methodist Society led many of the ambitious members of the Society, who were frustrated in their attempts to become leaders, to turn to other Churches which began to missionize on the island during the twentieth century.

ADAPTATION TO UNDERDEVELOPMENT

Like other West Indian societies, Nevis underwent a period of social and economic adjustments during the century after Emancipation. On Nevis, the planters held on to their properties, and their adjustments involved few attempts to tackle the problems associated with the declining plantation economy. They entailed rather adaptations to the poor performance of this economy through, for example, sharecropping arrangements, and the prolonged demise of the plantation economy prevented any internal economic development from taking place. Post-Emancipation society on Nevis therefore became characterized by its ability to adjust to poverty and increasing underdevelopment, rather than its ability to initiate new economic development. This was particularly the case with regard to the lower class of plantation laborers whose aspirations to become independent small farmers were stifled by the plantocracy, which saw in this a threat to their dominance on the island.

The notion of respectability had been important, in English society, in providing a cultural value system which could be associated with the new socioeconomic order which emerged in England, as it changed from a communally based rural social order to a more individualistic, industrial order. Respectability similarly gained significance in West Indian society as the old hierarchical order lost its hold on the colonial society, offering a new order to replace the old. Only the small middle class of people who were educated or trained in the trades was able to gain admittance to the "egalitarian" social order of respectability. As the White employees in the management of plantations or in civil service in the colonial administration disappeared, a vacuum was left which this class of people was able to fill due to their special educational and vocational skills. The culture of respectability became an important mark of distinction for this local middle class, which therefore became preoccupied with guarding and refining this culture to a point where it was quite beyond the grasp of the lower classes. The socially degraded, poverty stricken existence as plantation laborers or sharecroppers, which was offered to the bulk of the Nevisian population, was not compatible with the English notion of a position of respectability. Neither was the Afro-Caribbean community which was an important context of life for this group of people. The importance of the culture of respectability, to them, was that they had access to many of its institutions or traditions and were able to appropriate many of these cultural forms of respectability as frameworks within which to give the appearance of respectability to their own Afro-Caribbean culture.

NOTES

[1] The magistrates were supposed to be appointed in England and therefore independent of planter interests. Since a magistrate's salary was very small—a "mere pittance" according to one missionary—magistrates became dependent upon favors from the planters and therefore failed to maintain a disinterested position in the island society. The planters were rather displeased about the active role taken by the Methodist missionaries in informing the freed about their rights under the law (C511:4 October, 1834).

[2] The problem was exacerbated by the fact that no extra allowance was provided for children who were below six years of age in 1834 and therefore became free immediately, or for those children who were born after 1834. In this way, mothers barely received sufficient allowances for themselves to live on (C573:31 December, 1836).

[3] One of the mills was located at Stoney Grove, where it was erected by the Pinney family who owned the estate in the 1820s, the other was located at Mount Travers, which was owned by Peter Huggins (Pares 1950:301, 312).

[4] Some of the papers state that the leases ran over 99 years.

[5] These figures seem excessively high, and it is difficult to reconcile them with statistics on landownership from the early twentieth century. Thus in 1929, when the *Blue Books* began to report on the acreage owned by small holders, only 384 landowners were listed, 76% of whom held less than 10 acres (Frucht 1966:78). The difficulty of documenting the development of landownership among small holders is related to development of family

land, which took place, as the small landholdings were passed on to the heirs of the original owners. Such family land is not legally recognized "as joint tenure, or even as tenure in common" (Frucht 1966:173), and it is therefore difficult to know how it may have been accounted for in the records of landownership. The development of family land is discussed in more detail in the following chapter.

6 According to Richardson (1983:96), 315 East Indians arrived on Nevis on March 30, 1874, in order to work there on 5 year contracts. Some of them broke their contracts in order to emigrate to Trinidad, which attracted a large Indian population during the nineteenth century. Those who chose to remain on Nevis refused to renew their contracts, when they expired after 5 years, but used the money which they received upon expiration of their indenture, to invest in shops or to purchase land (Byron 1981:11).

7 That Methodist missionaries genuinely wished to see the social and economic conditions of the Black population improved is apparent from an enthusiastic description of the Emancipation service which was held in the Methodist chapel in Charlestown in 1834, where the missionary baptized his daughter Libertina, and commenced the service with a hymn he had composed himself, which began:

> Hail happy, happy day
> which bless the Lord we see!
> When in thy house O God we pay
> our debt of praise to thee.
>
> Thou Lord our chains has broken!
> and set the captive free
> No more we wear the oppressive yoke
> Hail sacred liberty.
>
> Once ev'ry human heart
> seem'd stul'd against our care;
> Yet there was *one* who took our part
> and heard the negroe's prayer
> (C487:1 August, 1834).

8 Education was provided at the Coke College in Antigua, which was run by the Methodists (Byron 1987:2); the Spring Garden Teacher's Training College in Antigua, which was run by the Moravians (*The Beacon* 1958:7; Sargeant 1988), and at the Mico, a Teacher's Training College in Jamaica (Byron n.d.a:16).

9 Such Sunday school processions also were quite common in England and were seen as "occasions to display respectability and self-esteem" (Laqueur 1976:171, 177).

10 While the Methodists, generally speaking, thought that women could be quite competent as teachers, they did not think that they were as qualified to lead a school as were male teachers. This was partly because they were not believed to be able to take on the responsibility of such leadership, partly because they were not seen to be able to "look after absentees in the different Estates in the neighborhood" (C577:20 February, 1837).

11 "Magic Lantern" shows also were popular in England, where they became an important "counter-recreational activity" intended to draw the attention of the working classes from their traditional leisure activities connected with the public house (Laqueur 1976:176, 236).

12 These educational problems were not unique to Nevis. See, for example Seaga 1973[1955]; M.G. Smith 1973[1960]; and Williams 1973[1951].

13 The fact that teaching presented virtually the only possibility of upward mobility meant that many were teachers, not out of occupational preference, but out of necessity. While

this may have attracted a number of "gifted and dedicated young people" to the schools (Byron 1981:24–25), the fact that teaching was not "their first love" must have made their teaching less than enthusiastic, just as it must have led to a great turnover in the teaching staff, as those fortunate enough to find a better position elsewhere left the schools.

CHAPTER FIVE

The Struggle for Recognition

Christmas mummers at Russell's Rest, Nevis, photographed by Antonia Williams, December 25, 1908. Courtesy of the University of the West Indies Library (Mona).

The Methodist missionaries had been disappointed in their hope to establish, through the English culture of respectability, an orderly and independent free society of hard-working and pious people. As social and economic conditions deteriorated on Nevis during the nineteenth century, this came nevertheless to provide the primary framework within which the local, Nevisian struggle for social mobility and recognition took place. Rather, however, than providing an alternative to the colonial order, it became the embodiment of a new version of that order. On the one hand, the small minority of Black and Colored people who belonged to the merging middle class adopted the culture of respectability as their own and sought thereby to consolidate their claim to be the heirs of the colonial order. On the other hand, the vast majority of the people who were part of the lower class further developed and made visible their Afro-Caribbean culture by displaying it within the framework of the many institutions and traditions associated with the culture of respectability. In the process they engaged in a critical dialogue with the local middle class which, through its exclusive affiliation with the culture of respectability, can be seen to have furthered its own cause by alienating the lower ranks from the colonial society. Respectability therefore became, in a colonial context, the center of an intense cultural struggle which highlighted class divisions within the Afro-Caribbean population after Emancipation.

THE LOCAL ELITE OF THE MIDDLE CLASS

The main beneficiaries of the newfound freedom had been the small group of "most respectable" people, emerging at the time of Emancipation, who had "a house to live in—a horse to ride and other property". For these people, the Methodist Society in particular represented an institution in which they could assume leadership as "classleaders", local preachers, and later in the century, fully ordained preachers. Since they had been among the first to take advantage of Methodist school education, a number of them were able to become schoolteachers, when the educational system expanded as the demand for education burgeoned after Emancipation. Others became estate managers or civil servants in the colonial administration. One of the first and most successful families to emerge within the ranks of the Colored elite was the Bridgewater family, which for many years set an example for others aspiring to rise in society.

The account which the family gives of its beginnings is interesting both because the factual content can be corroborated, and because of the way it links the origins of Methodism on the island to the origins of the family. The Bridgewaters descend, according to family history, from a slave woman who belonged to an estate owner, Mr. Brazier, with whom she cohabited and had two children. When Reverend Coke arrived on Nevis to missionize among the slaves (Mr. Brazier was the first planter on Nevis to invite the Methodists to preach for his slaves (Coke 1811:13)) Coke told this slave woman that she was living in sin, and she therefore left the house, and presumably also Brazier. As punishment for this she was made to work in the field and not being accustomed to this, she soon died. The son John Podd Bridgewater managed to purchase his own freedom and acquired some property in Charlestown, possibly from money earned from carpentry. Later he became the first Black postmaster on Nevis, and he was a member of the Nevis Local Assembly for many years. He married a woman who was the daughter of a White plantation owner and a brown skinned woman, and they had a number of children, whom they educated in their home. The most prominent among them was John Henry

Bridgewater, who was the first Nevisian to become fully ordained as a Methodist minister. One of his daughters, in turn, was to found a private secondary school in Nevis at the end of the nineteenth century.[1]

If the Bridgewater family was somewhat unique in its successful rise in society, it nevertheless demonstrates some of the important features in the development of the local elite. Like the Bridgewaters, many of those who assumed prominent positions in local society were the offspring of Black-White unions, who had been taught to read and write and who were skilled in the trades. They were able to take advantage of the opportunities in teaching and colonial administration offered after Emancipation. Much as John Podd Bridgewater held a civil service position heading the colonial postal service, his wife Anna Maria worked as a schoolteacher for a period of years. She was aided in her successful efforts to work her way through the Methodist Sabbath school, graduating "from scholarship to the office of first class teacher", by the fact that she, as a child, had received private education—having been placed by her parents "under the tuition and care" of a woman who was a Methodist classleader (CA1259:24 May, 1880).[2] Like his wife, John Podd Bridgewater was active in the Methodist Society and at the time of his wife's death, during the cholera epidemic of 1853, he was characterized as one of the Society's "most useful men, as a Local Preacher and Class Leader" (CA1078:29 December, 1853). Some years later he was indisputably the "senior male leader" and his name was met with "respect among all classes" in the Methodist Society (CA1132:10 September, 1861).

Just as Anna Maria Bridgewater had received care and tuition from a respected lady, the Bridgewater family itself had its children educated privately. This pattern of providing private education for children became an important mark of distinction for the middle class. Middle class children were taught at small often female-run schools in private homes, or, if the parents could not afford to pay for others to do this, the children were educated by the parents themselves. The popularity of the private schools was related to the low quality of the teaching that was identified with the denominational schools. A Methodist missionary thus complained in 1861 about one of their schoolmasters, who had held his position for 20 years and no longer had the "physical and moral qualifications for his place" for which reason he did not "command the respect of the people". The result was that his school was poorly attended, while "Dame Schools", private schools run by women, were "numerous & flourishing in the parish", one of them, ironically, being run by the teacher's wife and daughter in the teacher's cottage (CA1130:8 June, 1861).[3]

Since many of the members of this middle class, in particular the women, had worked as pupil teachers at a certain point in their lives, they were quite capable of providing education for children in their home. Some of them had even received education at teacher's colleges. Furthermore, as women were expected to resign from their teaching positions in the schools upon marriage, or at least when they became pregnant (Sargeant 1988), many of the middle-class women were able to make good use of their education and still maintain a respectable appearance as housewives if they kept school in the home. In this way they also were able to help supplement the income which the breadwinner earned, something important for the many middle-class families who had to manage on the meager wages that could be obtained from civil service jobs. The "breadwinner", according to the English mores of "respect-ability", had to be the male "patriarch", but this collided with the Afro-Caribbean family organization, where women often shared this responsibility. In the context of education, the male head teachers often failed to maintain the standards of respectability within the schools, causing the leading Methodist families to send their children to private schools run by women and thereby disavow the male led schools run by the advocate of respectability par excellence, the Methodist Church.

The main object of educating the children privately was not just that of securing for them the best possible schooling, but also that of making sure that they were not exposed to the children of the lower orders, whose social conduct and language were markedly Afro-Caribbean, and identifiable with the culture of the field slaves. The importance attached to the suppression of Afro-Caribbean behavior and attitudes, if one were to rise in society, was quite apparent when John Podd Bridgewater's son John Henry, who worked as a school teacher, was recommended for training to become a fully ordained minister in the Methodist Society in 1868. The missionary's nomination reads: "He is black—but of very superior ability. He is a thorough student, shrewd & acute, possesses good preaching talent. There is no negroism about him either in speech or manners. He has command of excellent English" (CA1189:10 July 1868).

In providing private education for their children, the middle class was basically following the pattern which had been set by the White population, whose children were educated by a private teacher, until they could be sent abroad to further their education. While the Black middle class was able to furnish elementary schooling for their children locally, secondary education had to be sought abroad, a rather expensive venture even for the children of the White planters who were experiencing increasing difficulties holding on to their estates. In the late nineteenth century, grammar schools were established on St. Kitts and Antigua to fill the need for further education in the islands, and in 1897 the foundation for a secondary school on Nevis was made, when the daughter of John Henry Bridgewater, Helen Bridgewater, began teaching a small group of White children who "came to keep up their studies till it should be convenient [for them] to return to their regular school" (*The Excelsior School Quarterly Magazine* c.1928). They stayed on, and gradually other students joined, including some from the Black and Colored middle class, and within a few years the Excelsior School was established. This school prepared the students for the Cambridge Examinations, and taught such subjects as religious knowledge, English language, English literature, English history, geography, hygiene, bookkeeping, arithmetic, algebra, geometry, French, Latin and drawing (ibid.). The school clearly attached great importance to teaching the students the fine art of the English culture of respectability.

The selection of students was not just based on their scholarly ability, but also on their family background. When the school was established, according to a former student at the school, Rev. Bridgewater worried about the sort of behavior patterns and outlooks that would prevail as the twentieth century brought "the people of Nevis as well as those of other West Indian islands completely out of the shadow of slavery into a free age". He therefore "made his daughter promise to hold on to, and carry forward in her school, a few of those standards of the past [the Victorian era] for as long as she could". He admonished her to be careful about accepting the right students: "no students of unwed parents, no children of doubtful background, or any who cannot, for one reason or another, maintain the rules that you will lay down regarding dress and conduct".[4] The students' English had to be "flawless and their manners impeccable!"[5] Boys were expected to jump "to their feet when a lady entered the room", and to vie "as to who would be the first to pick up her fallen handkerchief", while girls were taught that "if they remembered their dignity, the boys would remember their distance!" (Byron 1987:2-3).

Even though the school had students who belonged to the Anglican as well as the Methodist Churches, it was closely associated with the Methodist Society, and the Methodist students were naturally expected to attend the chapel and its Sunday school every Sabbath and to participate in the church choir, which was conducted by Helen Bridgewater, who was a choirmistress and organist in Charlestown Methodist Church. In this way, the school educated many of those who became leaders and local preachers in the Methodist Society. The Excelsior School also emphasized the English culture of respectability through sports such as tennis for both boys and girls, which was played on private tennis lawns through the school's tennis club, and later netball, which had been developed as a respectable sport for middle-class women in England. Furthermore most of the Excelsior boys joined the Boy Scouts, when they were organized on the island (*The Excelsior School Quarterly Magazine* c.1828, 1929; Olwig 1987c).

The close association of the Excelsior students with the culture of the British Empire was displayed prominently at the school graduations, which were celebrated in the court house and presided over by the warden of Nevis and his wife. According to *The Excelsior School Quarterly Magazine* the graduation ceremony took this form in 1929:

> As the Hon. Warden and Mrs. Tibbits entered, the National Anthem was played and the programme commenced with the scene in the Forum after Cæsar's Murder, from Shakespeare's Julius Cæsar.

> After an introductory speech by the Headmistress, came the distribution of school prizes by Mrs. Tibbits.
>
> After these prizes were delivered and the recipients all cheered, the Hon. Warden presented the Cambridge Certificates for the 1928 Examination results and the Examination prize which was Hunn's *The Makers of the Empire*.
>
> In the same room directly after our prize-giving a piano playing test was conducted among the pupils of Miss M.I. Bridgewater. (*The Excelsior School Quarterly Magazine*, December Quarter 1929:2-3).

During the first half of the twentieth century, Helen Bridgewater's Excelsior School taught a large number of children to appreciate and master the English culture of the old empire and to carry on the "old mores and manners of the Victorian era". As a reward, the graduates of the school found positions in the colony's civil service as teachers and clerks, some of them gradually rising to prominence as they transferred within the colonial administration of the Leeward Islands, finishing their careers in top positions as treasurers, magistrates or wardens, as the English transferred the colonial government to the West Indian population. In this way, the Excelsior graduates dominated the local elite for more than half a century.

Even though the Bridgewater family's White-Black background was rather typical for the early middle class which emerged in the post-Emancipation period, many of the local families that were to rise to prominence later on were only "White" from a cultural point of view, in that they had no known English ancestors. Some of them rose to middle-class status through the schools by doing well at the seventh standard examination, thus qualifying to become pupil teachers and to compete for a scholarship at a Teacher's Training College. Others improved their status by emigrating for a number of years, returning with enough funds to enable them to purchase property or to start their own business (for examples, see Byron n.d.a, 1981).

Because the established Colored elite did not maintain its numbers, these upwardly mobile people provided a welcome addition to the elite, as long as they adopted the English culture of that class.[6] It is characteristic of the prominent Nevis families, described by Byron in her two pamphlets (n.d.a, 1981), that they tended to diminish in number on Nevis, once they had achieved prominence. This is partly because highly ambitious male offspring often left the island to further their careers abroad, and partly because many of the female family members preferred spinsterhood to marrying "down" in a situation where there were few eligible males on the island. This tendency for the upper class to fail to reproduce itself has also been noted by Lowes in her study of the development of a middle class in Antigua during the nineteenth century, where she has demonstrated that the Colored elite of the Emancipation period virtually disappeared from the island during the following century. They were replaced by the select few from the Black population who succeeded in obtaining middle-class status (Lowes 1987).

The upwardly mobile were quite keen to validate their middle-class status by demonstrating their orientation toward "English" culture. Those families who could afford it acquired pianos, or organs, so that the children, in particular the girls, could learn to play, and girls also were taught to sew dresses, to embroider and to crochet. Dressmaking became, along with private teaching, another respectable occupation for many women of the middle class. The middle-class families displayed a strict sexual division of labor whereby the father, as head of the family, was supposed to be the provider, whereas the mother was expected to confine herself to housewifely duties inside the house. Furthermore, no self-respecting middle-class family was to be found working the land with a fork and hoe; if they wished to cultivate land of their own they were expected to use hired help. The most prosperous families also hired maids to do the heavier work in the household.

The middle class displayed a strong commitment to marriage and the sanctity of the home, which was an important aspect of the culture of respectability, which they cultivated. This led to a close association between marriage and the lifestyle of the middle class. Thus even though the marital union constituted the only publicly sanctioned family form, it was seen as being incompatible with living in the parental house or under uncertain conditions in a rented house. Marriage required a proper dwelling and a certain amount of economic security, and it therefore came to be confined to members of the middle class and those, often older persons of the lower class, who had accumulated enough funds to obtain the requisites necessary for marriage.

Despite this orientation towards the English culture of respectability, the middle class seems to have developed specifically local patterns as far as relations between the sexes were concerned. Whereas women were expected to spend most of their time in the home, men had considerably more leeway in their social relationships, including sexual ones, and it was quite common for a male of the middle class to have a number of "outside" children as well as children with his wife.[7]

This difference between the lifestyle expected of men and women meant that for married as well as unmarried women the church and chapel provided the only respectable public arena, where they could meet and socialize and escape from the confinement of the home. Middle-class women, generally speaking, were not just active churchgoers, but also Sunday school teachers, organists, choirmembers and organizers of concerts and tea meetings through the Churches. Men, on the other hand, tended to be less active in the Church and were at liberty to develop a more varied social life, which included seeing other middle-class men in private clubs and lodges, as well as men of the lower class in the rum shops. One woman from a solid middle-class background described the situation to me in this way:

> I was in school during the day, and at home during the balance of the time. [. . .]
> When I was inside I did my homework, read, or I did nothing [. . .] I had to go

to church Sunday morning and night, and I had to go to choir practices. This was a duty, [...] I was never asked whether I wanted to go. A child was to be seen, not heard.

I worked as a teacher after obtaining the Cambridge senior exam, but when I married I had to quit my job. There was no law that said that married women could not work, but it was understood that with marriage, they must stop work to keep the home, while the husband supported the home. [...] The women stayed in the home, tending to their business there, and they sent a servant if they had to make purchases at the market.

Boys also had to be home at certain times, but married men had a lot of freedom. My husband went out whenever he felt like it, I had to stay home with the children. This was quite common. He would be out in the rumshop that was considered okay, it was like a meeting place for men. The men also sometimes could sit on benches at the end of the wharf and discuss world topics. There was a mixing among men of different classes then, but not among the women who stayed home most of the time.

Many men had outside children, especially before marriage. These children were with women from the lower class, it was less common afterwards. The outside children never associated with the children born in wedlock and didn't come to the home.

The married women had to accept if their husbands saw other women, they had to keep the home and stay there. [...] In rare cases did women from the middle class get pregnant without being married. The women might then get married, or they would be put to one side—they would get meals, but they were not accepted.

This tolerance with regard to male sexual relations outside marriage was not shared, however, by the Methodist Society. It expelled wayward members from their classes and from the choir, at least temporarily, and demanded their resignation if they were Sunday school teachers and leaders. In order to avoid this, some men chose not to acknowledge paternity of an outside child and broke off a relationship, as soon as the woman became pregnant. Others paid support to the child, but did not openly acknowledge paternity until many years later. One woman who was an illegitimate daughter of a Black estate owner thus told me that she, as an infant, had been placed by her father in a respectable home of a women who was a dressmaker. He paid for her upkeep, until he was able to manage for her to emigrate to North America.

Despite this local variant in the practice of the English culture of respectability, the middle class on the whole attempted to conform to English values and behavior patterns. Members of the middle class therefore accepted without question the superiority of this culture, which had been brought to them by the churches and the schools, and the need to maintain certain "standards" of behavior, as was one of the foremost missions of the Excelsior School. They did this, not just because they had come to identify with English culture, but because this culture constituted an important means by which they legitimated their privileges as a superior class *vis-à-*

vis the lower classes. The close association of English middle-class culture with a privileged life, which sharply demarcated the local elite from the lower classes, was noted by the chairman of Methodist West Indian Districts in a report from 1922, where he discussed the question of the recruitment of local persons for the ministry:

> it is a fact that very few of our ministers are drawn from "the people" [...]. Certainly today the majority of our "local" men never have lived in such lowly dwellings and on such simple fare as the peasant and artisan classes. Their upbringing has approximated much, *much* more closely to the European's than to that of the "people", and in many instances has been in the Middle-class, European level, but always, I think, without the care, responsibility and the touch of discipline that mark English middle-class life (CR776:30 March, 1922).

The Methodist missionaries had succeeded in inculcating English manners of respectability among the middle class of the Nevisian society; however, this class constituted a small, select segment of the population, and its local social position was more similar to that of the upper, than to that of the middle classes in British society.

THE LOWER CLASS

The eagerness on the part of the newly emancipated Afro-Caribbean population to manifest themselves as respectable citizens was exemplified by their willingness to move the market day from Sunday to Saturday. On the first Saturday after Emancipation, on the second of August 1834, hundreds of people crowded Charlestown in order to attend the market and walk the streets, showing off their "cheerful, happy countenance" (C487:2–3 August, 1834; C506:22 August, 1834). By holding their markets on Saturdays instead of on Sundays, the Black population made a clear statement of the fact that they now were free to celebrate the Sabbath, as they wished. At the same time they raised their market to a more respectable position in the local society because it now no longer constituted a break of the Sabbath.

The fact that 1400 chose to show up for the first Emancipation anniversary service in the Methodist chapel in Charlestown on August 1, 1839, is also evidence of the ex-slaves' wish to assert their freedom in a respectable manner. In 1840, the local assembly declared August 1st a public holiday—not in memory of the abolishment of slavery, but as a day of "thanksgiving for the escape of her Majesty and Prince Albert from Assassination" (*Nevis Blue Book* 1840:58). The result nevertheless was that a public holiday was declared, and it remained the day, where the Black population celebrated their freedom.

Other evidence of the assertion of respectability were the large numbers of children who were sent to school and the many people who attended the Methodist chapels during the post-Emancipation period. This was also a factor, when the sizeable Charlestown congregation during the 1840s erected a large new impressive chapel, which was so unlike the modest meeting houses known from English Methodism that one English visitor mistook it for the Anglican Church (Davy 1971[1854]:482). The parishioners are reported to have been proud to retort, when visitors made such an error, "No! it is *our* Church the Wesleyan Church" (CR749:Report from Nevis Circuit, 1907). The wish on the part of the Black population to assert their presence outside the context of plantation field labor was also apparent in the clothing which they wore. While they were described "as slovenly in their dress and careless of it even to a fault" on working days, they were "in the other extreme, on Sundays and holidays" (Davy 1971[1854]:482).

The vast majority of the Afro-Caribbean population living in "lowly dwellings", on the "simple fare of the peasant and artisan classes", never made the culture of respectability their own. Rather than pretending to abandon their Afro-Caribbean culture, they appear to have attempted to remove this culture, or at least certain aspects of it, from its marginalized, "immoralized" position in society to one of social recognition. Their attempts at becoming respectable citizens in the free society took two forms. One involved the adaption of certain aspects of Afro-Caribbean culture to conventions of respectability within the colonial society. As examples of this strategy have been noted the holding of the market on Saturdays instead of on Sundays, and the celebration of Emancipation in the Methodist church. They also, however, attempted to appropriate institutions of the colonial society as frameworks within which to promote Afro-Caribbean culture as such. This attempt at cultural recognition involved rather the adaptation of colonial institutions, including those of respectability associated with the Methodist Society, to Afro-Caribbean culture.

The Churches, particularly the Methodist Society, provided some of the most important institutional frameworks for displaying Afro-Caribbean culture. An example is found in the Noahite movement, which emerged in 1839, the year after the abolishment of the apprentice system. It was started by a newly freed man, Mr. Brown, from the village of Barnes Ghut. He called himself Noah and proclaimed that he was a "Prophet" and "Comforter". He started preaching and holding meetings "till a late hour", attracting congregations of several hundred persons (CA1003:8 April, 1839; CA1004:10 June, 1839; CA1016:2 April, 1841; John Jones' Diaries:10 February, 1887). At these services, or meetings, which were held every Sunday, quotations from the Scriptures, the Apostles' Creed and verses of John Wesley's hymns were important elements along with dreams, prophesies, various declamations as well as "extravagant dance in which the body is violently tilted and tossed till violent convulsions ensue". The culmination of the service was "one tumultuous roaring from the vehement mass of devotees; men, women and children writhing and rocking in wonderful confusion" (CA1172:11 May, 1866; CA1220:26 February, 1872).

Leaders of the Methodist Society, who witnessed some of the services, were shocked by the trances and "indecent exposure" on the part of some women. They became increasingly concerned by this movement, which apparently drew participants from all over the island, including some members of the Methodist Society. While some of the English missionaries dismissed the religion as "absurd and laughable" and thought it curious that "people should be found in this state in the midst of a civilized community" (CA1220:26 February, 1872), the local preachers were more uneasy about this "grossly ignorant perversion of Christianity" and wrote to the Methodist Missionary Society in London in order to make it take a more aggressive stand against the evil (CA1172:11 May, 1866). To these local preachers, leading members of the respectable community on the island, such a bold display of Afro-Caribbean culture through the appropriation and transformation of the Methodist service was apparently a threat to the established order of respectability in the society. During the 1870s, the Methodists succeeded in wiping out the Noahite movement through concerted preaching efforts in the Barnes Ghut area.[8] This resulted, however, only in a brief respite for the Methodists.

Early in the twentieth century, religious organizations which were willing to incorporate elements of Afro-Caribbean culture into their services began missionizing on the island. They came to offer important institutional frameworks where people from the lower class could aspire to religious leadership on the basis of Afro-Caribbean performative traditions. One of the most important was the Pilgrim Holiness Church, an American offshoot of Methodism, which had begun preaching on the island as early as 1910. The missionaries from this Church attracted a large following by holding services with forceful preaching and lively singing accompanied by tambourines—one of the Afro-Caribbean instruments that the Methodist missionaries had expended great energy to condemn as sinful. One of the Methodist ministers found that these " 'Free' Gospel missionaries" merely succeeded in attracting some of the more "emotional" members of the Methodist Society because of their "emotional and sensational methods" (CL2718:28 October, 1910). Interviews with early converts to the Pilgrim Holiness Church indicated, however, that this Church attracted many from the lower strata of society, who did not feel at home in the increasingly formalist Methodist Church, which had become dominated by the upper levels of society. Furthermore, the Pilgrim Holiness Church, by making donations of clothing collected in North America among members of the parent church there, made it possible for the poorest, who had been ashamed to show up at the Anglican and Methodist Churches in their working clothes, to become active in the Church.[9]

The first missionaries from the Pilgrim Holiness Church were two women, one of them from the Dutch West Indian island of Saba, who was described as a "vibrant evangelist" who was able to "blaze up the people" so that they could be saved. The willingness of the Pilgrim Holiness Church to grant women positions of leadership as preachers in the church appealed to the many women who had difficulty reconciling their socially and economically active life with the subordinate, deferential role model of respectability advocated for women by the Methodists. One Nevisian in her eighties related how her mother, who had been a Methodist, had gone in her plain clothes to watch the services from the outside. As she stood there, she felt that the minister was preaching to her personally, and the following night she put on her church clothes, went into the building and was saved. This did not sit well with the Methodist church and the woman's classleader admonished her husband that he, as the head of the house, ought not to allow his wife to attend the Pilgrim Holiness Church. He, apparently realizing that there were limits to his position of authority in the household, replied that he had not married a child, but a woman, and that she brought no disgrace on the home and family and could do as she pleased.[10]

The early missionizing services, which attracted so many, were undoubtedly more emotional than the Methodist services, which by then were quite sedate with the congregation remaining quietly in their seats while they prayed, sang to the organ and listened to the minister's sermon from the pulpit, after which they were dismissed. The Pilgrim services, in contrast to this, expected more participation on the part of the congregation, as persons went to the altar to pray, crying out and asking the holy spirit for forgiveness. Their services therefore did not last a set period of time, but continued until well into the night when the people were filled with the holy spirit. In their acceptance and encouragement of testimonies during the services, as members of the congregation were moved by the spirit, and in their usage of instruments associated with Afro-Caribbean music to accompany the spontaneous chorus singing, which erupted as participants in the service felt the urge, the Pilgrim Holiness Church in a sense sanctified important aspects of the Afro-Caribbean culture which hitherto had been condemned as sinful and heathen. This did not mean, however, that the Pilgrims accepted all aspects of the Afro-Caribbean culture. In their teaching, a Christian life according to the Bible meant not just spiritual participation in the services held at church, but also a strict life outside church, which precluded such evils as drinking or dancing, sexual relations outside marriage and excessive adornments such as jewelry. The rules, which the members of the Pilgrim Holiness Church were expected to abide by, in fact, staked out a secular life style which was even stricter than that advocated by the Methodists. While the members of the Pilgrim Holiness Church tended to be drawn from the lower classes, they therefore could, through their godly life, make claims to an equal, if not higher status, as far as their spiritual life was concerned.

A few years before the Pilgrims arrived on Nevis, the Seventh Day Adventists began missionizing. They were spearheaded by a Nevisian woman Eveline Walwyn, who returned from St. Lucia, where she had been converted to this religion. Her daughter, Olive, who became a schoolteacher, missionized in the "upper strata of society" as well as in the lower, and managed to convince some in the upper classes of the soundness of her religion. They did not join the Church, because "in a class-conscious society that was not eager to change, it was not convenient for them to become Seventh-Day Adventists" (Sargeant 1988:17). This denomination therefore also found most of its members in the lower classes, particularly in the rather isolated Butler village area, where the other Churches had not been strongly represented. The Seventh Day Adventists promoted a Christian life similar to that of the Pilgrims, but with their observance of the Sabbath on Saturdays and their prohibition of the eating of pork, they preached a life style which set them apart even more clearly than was the case with the Pilgrims.

With the coming of these new denominations, the poorest and least educated Nevisians could not only seek positions of leadership as Sunday school teachers, proselytizers, even preachers, but they could also, through the special life-style which marked their membership in the Church aspire to religious superiority in relation to the members of the older, more established Churches.[11] In this way, they could achieve a respected position in the new spiritual hierarchy which was in the process of establishing itself on the island. The Methodists—the dissenters, who throughout the nineteenth century had been rather critical of the Anglican Church—now had to see themselves heavily exposed to "narrow and uncharitable criticism" on the part of the other missionaries in whose eyes they were one of the "established Churches" (CL2718:28 September, 1910).

The aspiration for a position of respect within the new spiritual hierarchy remained the only avenue of progress on the island for most Nevisians, and during the course of the twentieth century a large number of denominations became established in the island society in this struggle to assume a position of religious leadership and achieve the highest form of respect in the divine order of life. The significance of this elevated spiritual position is apparent in the special clothing which was reserved for the church. Church attendance was thus a means of becoming removed from the mundane world, with all its social and economic problems, to a divine world of blessings. Church attendance was particularly important for the women, for whom involvement in church affairs presented the main possibility of obtaining a position of respect in the local community. The necessity of their continued involvement in the hard physical labor connected with sharecrop farming clearly precluded any aspirations, on their part, to become well tended housewives. Furthermore, the close association of marriage with the establishment of a proper home meant that many women with children did not marry, or only married at a relatively late age, when they were able to afford to establish themselves in a family house. For these women whose everyday life-style branded them as anything but respectable, the Church provided a means of seeking salvation from their earthly "sins".

DISPLAYING AFRO-CARIBBEAN CULTURE

The Churches not only offered important institutions where a sort of spiritual respectability could be sought which was impossible to achieve in the secular Nevisian society. They also provided frameworks for the assertion of aspects of Afro-Caribbean culture, which were quite different from the culture of the upper classes. As shall be seen, they, along with other colonial institutions of the time, enabled the lower class to present a critical, Afro-Caribbean perspective on the dominant culture of respectability. One of the clearest examples of this is the Nevisian tea meeting. It became an important secular framework within which some of the oratorial traditions were carried on, which had developed in connection with the early love feasts and watch nights, where members of the Methodist Society had been encouraged to give testimonials.

After Emancipation, missionaries began to organize tea meetings, which combined spiritual uplifting and social togetherness with the raising of church funds. During the 1840s a number of tea meetings were held to collect money for the new chapel in Charlestown. They became tremendously popular, apparently because they presented opportunities for participants to display their oratory talents. By the latter part of the nineteenth century, this oratory ebullience had gotten out of hand, according to one of the missionaries, because the meetings had become occasions for the display of great speeches, the flourishes of which bore little resemblance to the modest and temperate life advocated by the Methodists. Furthermore, the great professions of godliness had little relation to the kind of life which some of these speakers were known to lead. One orator, who liked to frequent the tea meetings, thus was described as having an "appearance equal to deceiving the most elect deputation that ever touched and glanced on every land!" The Afro-Caribbean performative talents were clearly taking over the scene, in the process changing it to something that the missionary did not wish to be associated with. He therefore desired that the meetings be "rigidly and thoroughly revised" so that they would be "properly understood" and attended by a more select group of participants (CA1132:10 September, 1861).

At the same time as the missionary attempted to revise the tea meetings held by the Methodist Society, an entirely different sort of tea meeting organized and held by the Black population itself emerged on Nevis as well as in many other West Indian societies (Abrahams and Szwed 1983:41). These profane tea meetings were studied

on Nevis and St. Vincent by Roger Abrahams during the 1960s, when they appeared
to be dying out. According to Abrahams, the meetings were held in local
communities and were headed by a court of a king and queen and their attendants
who were carefully outfitted with royal clothing, and called a meeting in a hired
meeting hall by a fife and drum. Having arrived at the hall, which was already
crowded with members of the community, they were placed on a stage, and people
from the audience made various performances of "prepared routine" such as
speeches, dialogues, poems or dances, while dressed in appropriate costumes. In the
middle of the meeting, tea (or another hot drink) was served, and "some ceremonial
cakes, fruit [...] and kisses from the King and Queen were ceremoniously auctioned".
This was followed by "elaborate and ironic speeches" on the part of the royalty and
their attendants sitting on the stage, after which more performances were made by
people from the floor. The meeting was supervised by two toastmasters, who held
long speeches, which included Latin phrases, riddles and plays on words, and it was
their task to keep control over the audience, which participated actively in the event,
laughing, joking, and jeering, when mistakes were made on the stage (Abrahams
1983:16–18).

Many of the "prepared routines", which were performed by people from the
audience, must have been quite similar to the routines which were taught and
presented in the schools and Sunday schools, except that at the tea meetings, loud
comments on these acts were expected from the audience, in particular from the
hecklers in the back of the room, who attempted to create as much confusion and
noise at the meetings as possible. The toastmasters were to see to it that the meeting
did not end in chaos. They did this through their displays of superior performatory
talent, by which they were expected to hold the attention of the audience. In their
performances they, in effect, parodied the culture of respectability with its obsession
with proper manners, as is the case in the following excerpt from a speech cited by
Abrahams:

> Ladies and gentlemen, this afternoon we stand here to accompany this
> company here, ladies and gentlemen, and I want to here, this afternoon, have
> decorum. Decorum. Remember the alphabet, ladies and gentlemen: A is for
> attention, B is for behavior, C is for conduct, and D is for DECORUM. And
> ladies and gentlemen, as we march on further, we go to J is for justice and P is
> for peace that is Heaven for the flocks. I ask you to remember those few letters
> in the alphabet: A, B, C, D, P and J. Ladies and gentlemen, I won't
> procrastinate much more of the valuable time while I ask—to provide me with
> a piece (1983:17).

As the noise and heckling from the back of the hall increased, such niceties
might not be able to keep the attention of the people gathered, however, and the
toastmasters had to resort to insults or even obscenity in order to resume control at

the meeting. One toastmaster thus saw no other way out than to "grab his wife and to begin to do a highly obscene dance" in order to attract the attention of the audience (Abrahams 1983:18).

Throughout this age of respectability, the old Christmas sports, which were associated with quite another, and older, English era, also presented a vital cultural form where Afro-Caribbean culture was displayed—despite the valiant efforts of the Methodists to wipe them out. A description of the Christmas sports by Antonia Williams, an English woman, who spent the Christmas of 1908 at the Nevisian estate of Russell's Rest, gives a fine impression of the great ability of this tradition to incorporate new cultural elements within an old form of traditional expression. Throughout Christmas day, Russell's Rest was visited by "all sorts of mummers" who did various acts:

> the boatmen danced on stilts on the uneven stone floor very cleverly. One man came dressed either as a devil or a monkey led by a chain, and some other men in white masks and head dresses of peacocks' feathers about three feet high, and their clothes sewn all over with penny glasses and post cards, and any other tinsel. The dance was a mixture of quadrille, lancer and war dance—very funny! The singing was discordant—the instruments, a drum and various [other instruments] they had made themselves (AW:52).

Later in the Christmas week, several groups showed up from the Gingerland village area, who:

> ... came with a tambourine and a sort of flute made out of Bamboo. Another rattled a round tin. They brought a Maypole and danced round it very slowly—the dresses were an odd mixture of European skirt and apron, and sort of war dress—all had white muslin masks with funny smug expressions. [...] It was not at all good dancing—the clothes were home made, a sort of fringe and paper frills on their head, picture postcads were also sewn on their garments. The same clothes came up several different gangs of men. They are most tiresome begging, they are very poor (AW:54).

When she arrived in Charlestown on New Year's Day, she found that the entire town was one big party:

> we were deafened all day with bands, of which drums were the feature and natives dancing cake walks and waltzing very inferior to their own dances. Some of the men had paper cake frills as their headgear, all very tawdry, and paper frills sewn on their clothes. Then came representations of David and Goliath, they repeated long passages of scripture and a few quotations from Shakespere—a small child was David and a tall boy with a drum 2 feet high of sheepskin did Goliath—he was finally carried off, and his head gear carried in triumph whilst he joined in the dancing as a minor character (AW:58).[12]

Christmas sports were still performed when Roger Abrahams did his research on Nevis in the 1960s, and he found that such old English mumming plays as *St. George and the Dragon*, the Christmas Bull play as well as a version of the English morris, called *The Masquerade*, had persisted. Furthermore, new acts had been added to the old repertoire such as Cowboys and Indians, inspired by Western films, and Giant Despair, an act using text from *The Pilgrim's Progress* by John Bunyan. The plays tended to be either farcical "wooing plays", involving a fair amount of sexual play and dialogue in Creole language on the part of "cross-dressed players", or combat plays done by beautifully dressed players speaking in elaborate language employing "stentorian tones and stately movements" and using Shakespeare texts such as *Richard III* and *Julius Caesar* (Abrahams 1983:13–16). The Shakespeare text recorded by Abrahams involved the dialogue surrounding the murder of Julius Caesar, virtually the same scene with which the graduation ceremony of the Excelsior School was begun in 1928. The sporting groups were led by "captains", men who were respected for their performatory talents and were able to attract a number of younger players, eager to learn the art. This was becoming increasingly difficult, however, due to the heavy migration from the island, which led to a certain breakdown of the local community and to the loss of players.[13]

If English traditions had provided ample opportunity for the Black population to display its particular culture of music, dance and oration and thus gain some measure of respect for it, it was much more difficult to assert and win recognition for other aspects of the Afro-Caribbean culture. This was true for the small farming and the extended family networks which had emerged during slavery and provided a vital basis of the development of an Afro-Caribbean community among the slaves. As discussed in Chapter Four, it proved impossible for most Nevisians to acquire sizeable plots of land on which they could establish the Afro-Caribbean tradition of small farming which they had developed during slavery. Instead they had to content themselves with becoming sharecroppers, a continuation of the hated toil in the plantation fields, except that the sharecroppers now gave the estate owners their labor in exchange for a share of the uncertain crop.

The Methodist Church had been very eager to establish marriage and the nuclear family among the slaves, as well as among the freed, and regarded a married couple and their common children as the only divine form of family. This family form had become associated with the middle-class life style, and therefore was regarded by most of the Black population as beyond their means. To Methodists, as well as most others of the middle class, the lack of a nuclear family sanctioned by marriage simply signified the lack of a proper family. Thus as far as the Methodists were concerned, parents, who let their daughters stay in their homes with children they had begotten out of wedlock, were evincing gross immorality, not compassion towards a close relative in need.

Whereas the social and economic basis of the Afro-Caribbean community in the tradition of small farming and the family networks was all but ignored by the colonial society, the Nevisian lower class apparently did manage to establish some sort of small farming on the smaller lots which they acquired during the latter part of the nineteenth century. The small farmers, who had acquired their own lots of land by the 1870s, were thus reported to supply the markets of Nevis and St. Kitts with all the butcher's meat consumed (Iles 1958[1871]11). The local marketing system, which sold mostly goods produced by the small farmers, was extensive enough to sustain its own monetary system in dollars, which was different from that of the colonial administration, the merchants, shopkeepers and tradesmen, who used pounds, shilling and pence (*Nevis Blue Book* 1879:56).[14] The market was of enough economic significance to warrant the opening of a new Nevis market in 1887 (John Jones' Diaries:9 May, 1887). Throughout the nineteenth and early twentieth century, the availability of small lots of land helped maintain the Afro-Caribbean system of small farming, though this farming never was a primary source of existence, but a second economy, which provided necessary subsistence goods to the impoverished share-croppers and wage laborers (Frucht 1966:130).

Ownership of land never became extensive enough to provide a basis for a community of farmers. Nevertheless it became important as a means of consolidating and, in some instances, codifying the Afro-Caribbean family through the institution of family land.[15] As land was inherited upon the death of the person who had acquired it, it usually became family land, held in common by all descendants of the original owner with the understanding that the land could not be alienated from his family through sale. Most of the family land was not recorded as such. A few of the owners, however, codified this transformation through officially notified wills. The basic principles in family land and its close association with the extended family is apparent in the following will, where one piece of land was left to seven children:

> All the lands which I have herein advised to my children are positively not for sale, given away (neither can any be rented to a stranger, without the concent of the other) they are merely life interest and are to be handed down from generation to generation equally.
> The children are to work in harmony and if anyone becomes unreasonable, his inheritance will be forfeited until he becomes united with the others (Records of Nevis, Wills 1880–).

The importance of blood descendants in relation to affinal relatives in the Afro-Caribbean family is made clear in another will, which specifies that none of the nine children were allowed to "take to the family residence herein bequeathed any friends, Husband, Wife or any other relation to the discomfort or annoyance of any other portion of the family or without the consent of all" (Records of Nevis, Wills 1880–).

Through family land the Afro-Caribbean family was therefore made visible and given an official status, not just in the local Black community, but also, in some instances, in official colonial society through the recording of wills. The significance of this usage of official recordings as a means of codifying a family form, which otherwise was not recognized in the colonial society, is apparent in one will which stipulated that "the deed of title should always remain in the Family as a symbol as an evidence of their Faith to carry out what I have demanded", and that the land *"MUST NOT BE SOLD* but must remain as their family Emblem and Trust" (Probate Register B.2).

REPUTATION AND SOCIABILITY

The importance of patterns of respectability in West Indian society was first discussed by Peter Wilson in his seminal analysis of Caribbean cultural values based on a case study of the English-speaking island of Providencia (Wilson 1969, 1973). In this work he suggests that West Indian societies contain two juxtaposed ideas of "respectability" and "reputation" which correspond, on the one hand, to the values of the official, legal society, and, on the other, to those of the local peasant communities. He sees women and men as identifying differently with these values so that the female sphere, which is associated mainly with the domestic unit and the church, is most concerned with respectability, whereas the male sphere, located in the public arena of the rum shops and informal street corner gatherings, can be seen to be oriented toward reputation.

In a reinterpretation of Wilson, Abrahams has suggested that the relationship between respectability and reputation is brought to the fore through an interplay between English, or colonial, form and Afro-Caribbean cultural content. Afro-Caribbean cultural expression therefore should be seen as revealing of "the polarities of conflicting attitudes and alternative lifestyles" (Abrahams 1983:108) which in the course of the post-Emancipation period came to characterize Nevis, as well as many other West Indian societies. Abrahams views the tea meetings as an encounter between Afro-Caribbean and Euro-Caribbean culture, or as a struggle between reputation in the local Afro-Caribbean community and respectability in the wider society, oriented towards European culture. The most successful tea meetings therefore were those where the toastmasters managed to keep a delicate balance between the two. The toastmasters, with their masterly combination of elements of respectability and license, rote learning and improvisation, were therefore the central figures at the tea meetings.

My historical anthropological analysis of Nevisian culture leads to the somewhat different conclusion, however, that the meetings represent more than a confrontation between two cultures, where neither is supposed to gain the upper hand. They provided a socially acceptable framework within which Afro-Caribbean performative culture could be counterposed to a foreign, higher-class culture.

In this way, one of the institutions of the culture of respectability was appropriated by a tradition which had become associated with the display of Afro-Caribbean culture. Thereby it became, itself, a forum for the display of Afro-Caribbean culture, and the resolution of the tensions between it and the European cultural elements then being introduced. The tea meeting therefore should also be seen as a manifestation of the attempt on the part of the Afro-Caribbean population to assert its own identity in a colonial society dominated by a foreign culture. This is born out by the historical connection of the tea meetings with the Methodist Church, and the great importance which is attached to maintaining an outward European appearance at the meetings which indicates that they functioned in much the same way as the pre-respectability institution of the Christmas sports. This is borne out by Antonia Williams' description.

Antonia Williams clearly found most of the elements in the Christmas celebrations recognizable—the characters depicted in the acts; the literary citations employed; the European dances performed, and the material culture used. The way in which these elements were used and combined by the mummers, however, clearly was novel to her. By counterposing Afro-Caribbean music and dance within the ancient pre-respectability framework of Christmas mumming (and maypole festivities), to White cultural elements, drawn from as disparate spheres of European culture as the Church (the biblical story of David and Goliath); English literature (Shakespeare); and European upper-class culture (the lancer and quadrille), the Nevisian mummers managed to both jokingly parody, and appropriate, the culture of respectability within an encompassing Afro-Caribbean culture.

In the Christmas mumming, the order of the dominant White culture was challenged by being taken apart, and incorporated in unusual ways within Afro-Caribbean patterns of performance. The challenge to the dominant order created by such joking, states Abrahams, does not institute a social transformation, but merely creates a brief relief of shared laughter, or "a ratification of common feeling" (1983:5). I would argue, however, that this, in fact, represented something of a cultural transformation, in which the culture of respectability was, on the one hand, incorporated into a pre-existing framework dealing with cultural opposition, and, on the other, provided a means through which Afro-Caribbean culture could be displayed and given recognition. Though this might not entail social change, it nevertheless represented a form of recognition of Afro-Caribbean culture on the part of White colonial society, which was not displayed in other contexts of social life. The sports therefore constituted a way in which the Afro-Caribbean people could institutionalize and make public certain aspects of their culture, or as noted by Bettelheim, Nunley and Bridges in their analysis of Caribbean street festivals, like those of the Christmas sports on Nevis, a means by which the Black people were able to "codify and package vibrant areas of cultural productions" (Bettelheim et al. 1988:36).[16]

The social implications of the sports were accentuated by the nature of the English framework which was used in order to display Afro-Caribbean culture. By employing a tradition which was associated with the English rural society of the late middle ages, the Nevisians, reminded the estate owners of the mutual rights and obligations which exist between the privileged estate owners and the poor rural population. This must have been an embarrassing reminder for many of the estate owners, who did not appear to have taken such moral considerations *vis-à-vis* the estate laborers in the post-Emancipation era. In keeping with this less personal relationship with their workers, the estate owners do not seem to have treated the Christmas mummers to food and drink in their homes, but instead preferred to pay them off with money. The Afro-Caribbean Nevisians on their part, apparently exploited this possibility of collecting money from the White population for all it was worth, leading Antonia Williams to complain about the "most tiresome begging" on the part of the mummers (AW:54). This does not mean that the Christmas sports had degenerated to institutionalized begging at the homes of the better off. Antonia Williams' descriptions of the Christmas sports clearly show that Nevisians displayed great enthusiasm and ingenuity in their acts, and they were encountered throughout the island, not just at the residences of White people.[17]

This analysis of Nevisian culture questions Wilson's discussion of reputation and respectability. His juxtaposition of respectability and reputation which views respectability as a foreign element being imposed from the larger, external society and reputation as an authentic concept generated locally in peasant communities which have been relatively isolated from the wider society (Wilson 1969:83) thus does not hold up to closer historical scrutiny. Reputation, cultivated in such public arenas as the rum shops or the street festivals of the Christmas sports, can be seen to be closely related to the traditions which were brought by the English small farmers to the early colonial society of the seventeenth century. Respectability, which is sought in the schools, the churches and the home, is tied to the institutions which English missionaries established on the island in the late eighteenth century. Both cultural values therefore are closely related to institutions connected with the English colonial society. Furthermore, both sets of institutions have been appropriated by the Afro-Caribbean population as a means to negate their position of social marginality in the English colonial society and have, in the process, become infused with Afro-Caribbean culture. Far from being a particularly local cultural value, reputation therefore can be seen to be tied to seventeenth century concepts of sociability. Like its eighteenth century counterpart of respectability it was appropriated, transformed and given new meaning and life in the Afro-Caribbean communities of the West Indian colonial societies.

The close association of respectability with colonial society derives from the importance which it attained after Emancipation. At this time the old English traditions came to be associated primarily with the lower classes of poverty-stricken plantation laborers, who were not able to patronize the schools and the churches to the extent that the upper classes were, and who did not have the economic resources to marry and settle in the proper homes which provided the necessary framework for respectable family life. The institutions of respectability, on the other hand, became connected with the emerging middle class of those who were educated or trained in the trades and who saw in the culture of respectability a means of rising from the rest of the Black population. Furthermore, since high social status in plantation society was associated with the ability to keep women idle and well-tended in the home—a value which, at least partially, coincided with the tenant of respectability that women were the guardians of the sanctity of the home—women became more closely tied to the culture of respectability than did men. This is because the women's success at maintaining an appearance of respectability became an important measure of the social status of the home. This different involvement in the traditions and institutions on the part of the upper and lower classes, and on the part of men and women reflects a situation where the complex of values of island society has developed in close association with a colonial power structure over which the Afro-Caribbean population has had little control but which it has sought to exploit to its best advantage.

I have chosen to retain the term "respectability" because it is one which was used by the Methodist missionaries and adopted by the Nevisian population. The concept of reputation has not been found to be equally emic, however; nor does it seem to connote the ethos of inclusiveness involving the bridging of different social groups and the sharing and performing, which is associated with the complex of traditions which can be seen to derive, in part, from English late medieval society. For this reason I have prefered, partly for the lack of a better term, the concept of sociability.

The colonial origin of the cultural traditions and institutions employed by the enslaved, and later freed, population should not lead to the conclusion that Afro-Caribbean culture is a colonial byproduct of basically European orientation. The European-like appearance of many of the cultural forms in the West Indies only points to the structural dominance of European controlled colonial societies, where Afro-Caribbean culture through centuries of marginalization was delegated to an existence in the shadow of the European-oriented culture of the upper classes. In this context it was impossible to establish a visible cultural identity through Afro-Caribbean institutions and it was necessary to display Afro-Caribbean cultural identity within traditions or institutions associated with the upper class, which were visible in the colonial society. In the process of doing so the lower class of Nevisians not only found a way of manifesting their social and cultural presence in the island society, but also a way of questioning the established social order. West Indian cultural traditions therefore should not be regarded as pale attempts at imitating European culture, but as forms of communication with, and critique of, a dominant European social order.

NOTES

[1] A slightly different version of this family history is found in Byron (n.d.a:5–8).

[2] The parents were apparently not Methodists, nor particularly friendly towards Methodism, and had not expected the teacher to have had this religious influence on their daughter. She joined the Methodist Society at the age of 16.

[3] The Methodist missionaries had attempted to prevent this school from being held in the teacher's cottage, but appear to have found this difficult, probably because most of the parents of schoolchildren were influential members of the Methodist Society.

[4] In the late 1920s the admission requirements were liberalized somewhat, according to *The Excelsior School Quarterly Magazine*, which reported that "It has been decided to admit, on certain conditions, any pupils from the Elementary Schools desirous of joining us. To gain admittance these pupils must furnish, signed by a Minister of Religion, a guarantee not only of their general conduct but of their satisfactory home connections and surroundings. Accompanying this should be a certificate from the Head Teacher of their School with regard to behaviour and general progress" (c.1928).

[5] If the students' English had to be "flawless" apparently it was good form to joke in the more flawed Nevis dialect. Thus *The Excelsior School Quarterly Magazine* included several "letters" written in the local dialect supposedly by a Nevisian travelling abroad.

[6] The cultural finesse to be learned by those from relatively poor homes who attended the Excelsior school is illustrated by the following anecdote in Eulalie Byron's portrait of her sister Millicent Theodora Byron: "Plans were afoot for a school picnic—there were a delightful number of these for all sorts of reasons one recalls—and happy voices were listing the delicacies to be brought saying, 'I will bring this! I will bring that!' Millicent knew the leanness of the family purse and listened keenly to hear some item she thought could be afforded. 'O, we must have tea for the afternoon' some prudish voice said. In a flash, up went Millicent's hand, 'We will bring the bush!' she burst out quickly before anyone else could seize on this inexpensive piece. All heads swivelled round to her in shocked surprise and 'Not bush tea Millicent!' said one of her White form mates witheringly. His tone, however, was mild and intimated that in the great house where he lived he was quite well acquainted with good old West Indian bush tea himself—on suitable occasions of course!" (Byron n.d.b:7).

[7] One man whom I interviewed saw this practice as merely another sign of emulation of English culture. He explained the practice as caused by the adoption on the part of the local population of the habit which White overseers had of engaging in extramarital sexual relations with Black women. This line of thought is also found in the work of some social scientists. See, for example, R.T. Smith (1987).

[8] Rev. John Jones noted in his diary having met Mr. Brown who "was once the leader of a sect which went under the name of Norites. Dancing was the chief feature in their worship" (John Jones' Diaries:10 February, 1887). One Nevisian whom I interviewed in 1989

remembered his father talking about Brother Noah and his religious meetings, where people would go into a trance. Although he was uncertain whether his father actually had met Noah, stories were told about how he had gone to the mountain to fast for 40 days, but only stayed there for 3 days.

9   The English woman Antonia Williams who visited Nevis in 1908–09 was surprised to find that "all the natives wore European clothes" to church and described the transformation which the local people underwent by putting on such clothes, which made it difficult for her to recognize them (AW:29, 44).

10   The husband respected his wife so much that they apparently agreed that the husband, who wished to remain in the Methodist Society, would bring the boys with him there, while the wife would take the daughters to the Pilgrim Holiness Church.

11   The defiance which the followers of the Pilgrim Holiness Church dared show members of the established congregations is illustrated in the story told by a Nevisian whose father was a schoolteacher and lay preacher in the Anglican Church: "My father was very annoyed about the Wesleyans coming to Barnes Ghut to hold meetings there in their tent. I think, that my father was jealous of the great following they were getting. My father always went to bed early and was mad at the late services that they held, and at a certain point he could not take it any longer and yelled out, 'Don't you think it is time to go to bed!' After a short silence, the people at the meeting then began to yell, 'Satan is mad, we are glad'. This made my father furious—being compared to Satan, when he was a respectable lay reader in the Anglican Church."

12   The folklorist Alfred M. Williams, who visited the neighboring island of St. Kitts in the 1890s, described similar Christmas sports for that island. He also recorded the dialogue of the play of David and Goliath (1896:117–20).

13   The Christmas sports which were performed on St. Kitts and Nevis during the 1950s and 1960s have been described in Mills and Jones-Hendrickson (n.d.)

14   In the Nevisian usage of the dollar system, 96 cents were counted to a dollar, rather than 100 cents (Nevis Blue Book 1879:56).

15   For a comparative analysis of family land in the Caribbean see Besson (1987).

16   In this publication Judith Bettelheim discusses Christmas sports on different Caribbean islands and prints two pictures taken by Antonia Williams of the Christmas mummers on Nevis (1988).

17   A similar change in the attitudes towards the Christmas sports had occurred in England during the eighteenth century (Malcolmson 1973).

Part III

HOME IS WHERE YOU LEAVE IT: PARADOXES OF IDENTITY

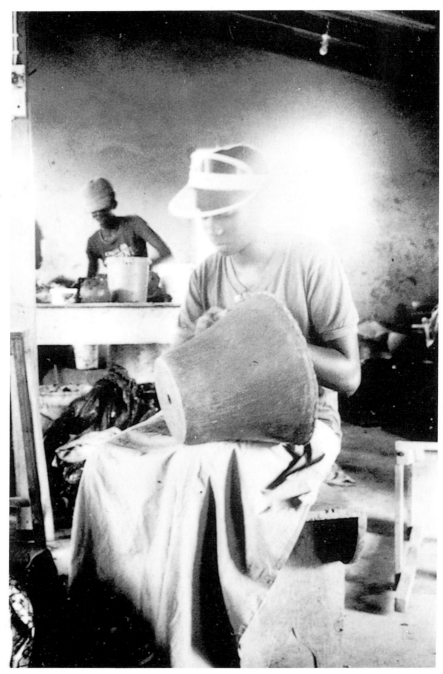

PLATE 8   *Newcastle Pottery, Nevis. Photo, Karen Fog Olwig, 1984.*

CHAPTER SIX

The Demise of the Local: the background for a global community

During the more than 300 years of colonial rule, institutions and traditions connected with the old imperial power have come to constitute central frameworks of life in Nevisian society. For the Afro-Caribbean population, cultural forms connected with the notions of sociability and respectability have been seen to provide different possibilities for cultural display and the establishment of a social presence in the local society. They also have presented rather restrictive and mutually exclusive possibilities for social and economic development within the Afro-Caribbean community. For this reason, the Afro-Caribbean people have increasingly looked for opportunities outside the island through emigration. This section discusses the almost complete reorientation of the Nevisian population to a global community which today has become the primary context of life. Within this global community it has become possible to institutionalize an Afro-Caribbean cultural identity, grounded in Nevis.

The demise of the local society which took place in the decades following the Second World War is discussed in this chapter. The Nevisian economy, which had declined steadily during the century following Emancipation, is seen to have come to a near nadir with the cessation of commercial sugar production, the virtual disappearance of cotton cultivation, and a drastic reduction in the cultivation of food crops. The attempt to introduce a tourist industry on the island has had only limited success. This collapse of the local economy has both been exacerbated by and contributed to the large-scale emigration, which has deprived the island of the core of its laboring population. Migration has not only depopulated village communities, it has directly affected virtually every family, so that close relatives, upon whom one once relied for help in daily life, are now settled permanently in distant migration destinations. Yet, despite all this, the average Nevisian has probably never had a higher standard of living, and in some respects traditional Afro-Caribbean family ties have never been stronger. Most of the migrants have thus remained in close contact with their parental home on Nevis leading to the emergence of a new transnational Nevisian community. Although the Afro-Caribbean culture based on small farming and rural life in the villages may be disappearing as a foundation of life on the island, it provides an increasingly important cultural basis for the new, global Nevisian community.

THE UNDOING OF THE LOCAL SOCIETY

During the 1950s the last two sugar estates to produce sugar were closed down because the government, which owned them, failed to maintain the aging machinery. After the last sugar had been ground at New River in 1957, the 540 farmers on Nevis who still cultivated sugar were forced to ship their cane to St. Kitts for processing at the central factory there. Transportation to St. Kitts was uncertain, and for several years it was not possible to harvest the entire sugar crop on Nevis because of shipping problems. This led, understandably, to a declining interest in sugar cultivation, and during the 1960s the acreage in sugar decreased steadily until 1969 when the last commercial sugar crop was harvested on Nevis (*Report for the Years 1955 and 1956* 1958:21; *Report for the Years 1957 and 1958* 1961:20, 22; *Report for the Years 1959–62* 1966:25, 27; Starkey 1961:7; Richardson 1983:164–66).

After the collapse of sugar cultivation, cotton growing constituted the main agricultural activity among small farmers, but the harvest was irregular because the crops were ruined by calamities ranging from drought and hurricanes to insect infestations. The 3042 acres which were harvested in 1951–52 declined to 1173 acres in 1961 and to 67 acres in 1971. The production of food crops also showed an overall decrease and the harvest of root crops, for example, was cut by almost half during the period from 1961 to 1975. Much of the land was turned into pasture to be roamed by herds of goats, sheep and cattle or abandoned to be overgrown by acacia. Many of the animals were raised by persons possessing less than an acre of land, and a survey in 1968 showed most farmers to own "stock equivalent to approximately 5 times the maximum carrying capacity of their grazing land". The result was overgrazing leading to serious soil erosion (Abbott 1964:163; Ferneyhough 1974:35; *Summary Report on the Census of Agriculture* 1975:xxiii–xxiv; Lowery n.d.:n.p.; Barker 1981:8, 10).

This practice of overgrazing was a sign of the increasingly "non-productive" relationship which Nevisians had been developing to the land during the twentieth century. A study of agriculture on Nevis reported upon in 1982 thus showed that the great increase in the number of animals on the island did not reflect an interest in commercial animal husbandry, because more than 40% of the farmers studied had not disposed of any of their animals during the 12 month period prior to the study, but merely kept them grazing. The animals were held as "walking banks" which largely represented the savings of emigrants who had invested in livestock on the island. A parallel development was represented by the growing number of Nevisians who purchased land during the 1950s and 60s, despite the fact that they had no real intention of farming it, or, often, even of living on it. The purchase of land was not just regarded as a good investment, but also as an indicator of rise in social status, reflected in statements such as "If you buy land, you someone" (Frucht 1966:7, 178; CARDI 1982:8, 12; Richardson 1983).

Until the 1970s, the only new economic activity on Nevis was tourism. This was strongly encouraged by the government through the granting of tax incentives and the completion of an airstrip at Newcastle in 1958. Most tourism involved visitors who stayed for about one week at one of the several hotels, which were constructed by expatriate Britons and Americans on abandoned sugar plantations, often out of the ruins from the old great house and sugar works.[1] These hotels, which catered for well-to-do visitors primarily from North America and Europe, had rather limited success. The average room occupancy rate on Nevis remained well below 20% throughout the 1970s. Tourism therefore offered little opportunity for Nevisians except for some seasonal employment, mainly in domestic service, which paid low wages (*Reports for the Years 1957 and 1958* 1961:3; Ferneyhough 1974:42; *Annual Digest of Statistics for 1981* 1982:33).

The economic collapse was seen, by the Nevisians, to be an effect of their political affiliation with St. Kitts. This island had been the seat of government since the three islands of St. Kitts, Nevis and Anguilla had become a separate colony in 1956. The government was dominated by the Labor Party, elected by sugar workers on St. Kitts, and Nevisians believed that it ignored the economic and social problems of the small farmers on Nevis by, for example, neglecting to build up, or even to maintain, an adequate infrastructure there. The Nevisians' sense of hopelessness was only heightened when the three islands obtained associated statehood in 1967 because independence, though only partial, strengthened Labor's rule. The platform of the major political party on Nevis during the 1970s was thus secession from St. Kitts. This political movement was fuelled by the successful Anguillean rebellion against St. Kitts, which resulted in the island resuming its status as a British crown colony (*An Agricultural Development Plan for Nevis* 1957:1; Richardson 1983: 166–69).[2]

If the island seemed to have come to a standstill as far as economic development was concerned, an important change in the island's educational system took place, when Charlestown Secondary School was opened in 1950. This school offered, for the first time, secondary education to all qualified students. Education at this school was based on the English system, just as had been the case with the Excelsior School, which closed when the public secondary school was established. The curriculum therefore was almost "completely divorced from the local environment", as one English observer described it. Furthermore, there was little emphasis on education in areas such as agriculture and tourism which could be of use in the local rural community. In this emphasis on an English curriculum, the school was like other contemporary West Indian secondary schools, which, because of the lack of a Caribbean examination system, were forced to teach subjects which would enable their students to pass the English Cambridge examination (Ferneyhough 1974:37).[3]

The English emphasis in the schools was more than a matter of necessity due to the examination structure. It also reflected the traditional importance attached to education as a means of upward mobility through the English colonial civil service. An English study of agriculture on Nevis from the 1970s thus found that the education system in general paid only "lip service to the role it could play in fostering an improved attitude toward agriculture" and saw its main role as that of preparing children for careers in white-collar jobs, a rather unrealistic goal for the vast majority of the children (Ferneyhough 1974:17, 34, 73; *Report for the Years 1959–62* 1966:4).[4]

The most impressive cultural development in the first decades after the second world war occurred in the dramatic increase in new churches. An unofficial count of the island's churches carried out in the early 1980s, with the help of a leader in the Caribbean Council of Churches on Nevis, included the Anglicans (with 5 churches on the island); the Methodists (7 churches); the Wesleyan Holiness Church, formerly called the Pilgrim Holiness Church (5 churches); the Seventh Day Adventists (4 churches); the Brethren (3 churches); the New Testament Church of God (1 church); the Church of God of Prophesy (1 church); the United Pentecostal Church (3 churches); the Apostolic Faith Mission Trinitarian (1 church); the Church of God (1 church); the Jehovah's Witnesses (1 congregation); and the Catholic Church (1 church). This enumeration of 33 congregations and 13 denominations, probably did not include all religious institutions on the island, and the number has undoubtedly continued to increase during the 1980s.[5]

Several of these new churches are offshoots from American fundamentalist churches. They maintain close ties with their parent church, which supplies religious literature and crusading Evangelists who tour the Caribbean. Due to their emphasis on the otherworldly life, and their affiliation with American institutions, these churches are little oriented toward the local community. Much of the literature distributed through the churches is written for American congregations and is oriented toward American mores and culture. These churches have thus tended to orient the islanders towards the Western world—and its "other world"—and away from the immediate economic and social concerns of the local community. The American orientation of many of the new fundamentalist churches has been further strengthened by the broadcasting of American religious programs through Caribbean based radio and TV stations, such as Radio Paradise on St. Kitts and the Trinity Broadcasting Network. The latter sends by satellite, and since the middle of the 1980s it has rebroadcast via a transmitter on Nevis. Apart from a brief weekly news program, which sums up the main events in the community, this television station broadcasts only American religious programs and wishes, according to its manager, to be only "in the community, not part of it".

This focus away from the local society may have been one of the strengths of these churches. They have constituted a haven of hope on an island otherwise dominated by a general situation of decline. Furthermore, many of these churches, like their predecessors during the early part of the century, have provided respectable institutional frameworks within which local people have been able to assert themselves, even in positions of leadership as fully ordained preachers. Access to leadership roles in these churches is facilitated by the fact that many of them regard salvation and spiritual fervor, rather than the acquisition of degrees, as the most important qualifications for the assumption of religious leadership. Some Nevisians, who never had an opportunity to complete a formal education through the school system, have thus found that these churches offer the possibility of holding positions of respect, which would otherwise be unobtainable. Furthermore, as was the case with the Wesleyan Holiness Church, many of these churches allow the incorporation of Afro-Caribbean performative styles in the service, and this gives them an added attraction.

At the same time as these otherworldly churches have become increasingly popular, the older established churches have sought to become more oriented toward the local Afro-Caribbean community. Today they are not directed from European headquarters, but organized in West Indian circuits, and most of the ministers are West Indians, rather than Englishmen. Many of the West Indian clergymen have apparently, however, found it difficult to assert a position of authority in the old established churches, where leadership was traditionally associated with White Englishmen. One way in which West Indian ministers have attempted to obtain respect from their parishioners is by furthering their education, a time tested method for gaining upward mobility within colonial society. While this emphasis has produced a number of notable intellectuals, some Nevisians were of the opinion that it has not necessarily produced better preachers, or persons with a better understanding of the local parishes and their needs.

The established churches have also sought to become involved in the local communities through the Caribbean Council of Churches, a West Indian ecumenical body which promotes, and partially funds, socioeconomic projects which seek to further community development on particular islands. Even though all churches were invited to join the Christian Council on Nevis, only the Anglican, Methodist and Catholic Churches had become members by the early 1980s. Despite all good intentions on the part of the church organizations, such membership has not necessarily led to increased engagement in community affairs on the part of the local congregations. One Nevisian, who was active in the Council, expressed disappointment at the lack of involvement in the work by leading members of the churches, particularly the clergymen, who, he found, were more interested in academic matters than the daily lives of the people. This possible lack of interest in the local community on the part of the ministers may, however, also be due to the tradition of moving ministers to new pastoral assignments after a few years in one location—a tradition which can be traced back to colonial times when the local churches were governed from Europe, and which does not encourage engagement in local affairs.

THE ESTABLISHMENT OF A TRANSNATIONAL COMMUNITY

The new cultural institutions which have appeared on Nevis, despite giving a more visible role to the local population, nevertheless have not transcended the well-rooted tradition of seeking respectability through the adoption of foreign cultural forms. The external focus in Nevisian culture, on the contrary, has been strengthened by the fundamental, outward oriented, economic and demographic developments which have taken place. Beginning with the 1950s, the island experienced a virtual "exodus", as thousands of Nevisians sought to improve their life through emigration to Western countries with developed industrial economies. Though the magnitude of emigration had increased, along with the distances involved, emigration was nevertheless part of a long tradition which had emerged shortly after Emancipation. By the middle of the twentieth century, emigration had taken Nevisians to such varying destinations of economic opportunity as the sugar plantations in Trinidad and Demerara, and later in the Dominican Republic and Cuba; the gold mines in Venezuela; the construction of the canal in Panama; the dock yards in Bermuda; the domestic and industrial sectors on the North American East Coast, and the oil refineries on Aruba and Curaçao (Richardson 1983).

Migration accelerated dramatically, however, beginning with the 1950s. Out of a total population of approximately 55,000,[6] close to 15,000 emigrated from St. Kitts, Nevis and Anguilla during the decade from 1955 to 1965 to work in public services and the industries in Great Britain (Richardson 1983:156); and by 1976 at least 15,000 had left for the American Virgin Islands (*Annual Report* 1968–76) to work in tourism. A considerable number, furthermore, had gone to the British Virgin Islands as well as the Dutch island of St. Martin, where similar tourist related work has been available. While much of the early emigration had been of a temporary nature, tied as it was to passing economic possibilities in, for example, canal work or oil refineries, the more recent emigration to England and the nearby West Indian islands has been of a hitherto unprecedented scale and involved the more or less permanent settlement of the émigré Nevisians abroad. The main movements of the emigrants, in fact, have involved re-emigration to Canada and to USA from England and the American Virgin Islands.

This massive outmigration has taken a heavy toll on the local society. When Richard Frucht carried out his community study on Nevis during the 1960s, he found that more than half of the households that he studied had lost members to emigration, and almost 45% consisted of grandparents and grandchildren with over 70% of household heads above 50 years of age. This age structure was also reflected in a survey of agriculture, conducted in 1968, which showed that the average age of farmers was 54 years. Farming was an occupation for older people, who no longer regarded themselves as part of the labor market, but devoted their efforts to the reproductive sphere of the household. Those who attempted to organize cooperative ventures to improve the agricultural economy, such as a cotton growers' cooperative, or credit unions, faced severe difficulties, as leading members kept leaving the island. Due to this heavy outmigration, many of the social events and cultural traditions, which had been of importance to the rural communities, such as Christmas celebrations and the tea parties, also began to die out (Frucht 1972:279–81; Ferneyhough 1974:33; Abrahams 1983:10–18).

During the 1970s, the two islands of St. Kitts and Nevis had the "dubious distinction" of surpassing "every Commonwealth Caribbean country in the rate of net emigration as a percent of the natural rate of growth of its people" (Mills 1985:1). Nevis accounted for most of this emigration, in that St. Kitts actually had a 4% increase in population during the period from 1970–80, while a 16.5% decline in population had occurred on Nevis during the same period (*Project Report to the Government of St. Kitts-Nevis* 1982:51). The effects of this depopulation were clear when a group of agricultural development specialists attempted to do a survey of the island's agriculture in order to assess its developmental potential. They found it extremely difficult to locate the 100-plus farmers whose names they had been given by the government because "some were deceased, others had left the island, while no trace could be found of some persons". Of the farmers they did find, almost two thirds were above 56 years, and close to a fifth above 70 years (CARDI 1982:1, 3, 4).

The Nevisian population of 9,428 in 1980 (*Population Census of the Commonwealth Caribbean* 1980–81:19) was the lowest since the early history of the island, and this population was likely to decline even further, if the islanders had anything to say about it. This was reflected in a study of 157 Nevisian schoolchildren that I carried out in 1981,[7] which showed that less than a third of the children expressed a desire to remain on the island. The children's considerations concerning emigration did not revolve around whether or not it was a good idea to emigrate, but rather whether or not they would be able to secure a visa to emigrate to an attractive location (Olwig 1987b:159).

Even though emigration has led to a further weakening of the local society, it is incorrect to speak of a breakdown of the Nevisian community as such. Rather this community has been redirected to include and center on Nevisians living and working abroad. The economic base of this community is therefore now found to a large extent in the migration destinations, rather than in the local society of St. Kitts and Nevis. According to one account "outside remittances account for more disposable income on the two islands than any other source, including the St. Kitts sugar industry" (Richardson 1983:48). It has been estimated that in St. Kitts-Nevis "each household with migrants abroad received (in 1984) about US $1,435 in cash (with a standard error of $440), about $568 in foodstuffs, about $337 in clothing, and about $185 in other household goods". In comparison the estimated gross national product per capita for 1982 was $950 (Mills 1985:39–40).

This influx of material goods and money from migrants has made an expectably significant impact on the material standard of living on Nevis. While most islanders, a couple of decades ago, lived in two-room wooden houses with no modern amenities, today, many of the old houses have been expanded and renovated so that they are now equipped with running water, electricity, telephones, and indoor kitchen and bathroom facilities. These households display such modern consumer goods as gas or electric stoves, electric blenders and mixers, color televisions, cassette recorders and stereo sets, while the members of such households eat imported frozen or canned foodstuffs and wear a variety of clothing that is factory made in Western countries. Most of these material goods have either been purchased with money sent by émigré relatives or given directly by migrants to their Nevisian family.

The several thousand migrants from Nevis who work in the American and European controlled tourist industry in the nearby Virgin Islands and Dutch West Indian islands are able to ship many goods directly to their families on Nevis by local boats which specialize in this sort of cargo. In a study of migration from Nevis the Nevisian geographer, Carolyn Liburd, has documented the increase in this transportation on the part of local cargo boats from 61 calls on Nevis in 1969 to 163 calls in 1979. A closer examination of the contents of one boat revealed such basic household necessities as beds, tables, chairs, plastic buckets, mops, brooms, and foodstuffs, as well as luxury items such as antennas, cake mixes and liquor (Liburd 1984:57, 59–60). Many of the goods are also brought to the island by migrants who return for brief visits to see their families and friends. It is a mark of the migrants' success abroad that they are able to display great generosity towards family and friends through liberal donations of material goods and money. A certain amount of prestige also accrues to the households which are relatively well-off and able to display an impressive array of consumer goods from Western countries

Émigré relatives are of fundamental social and economic importance to those who remain behind on Nevis, even if they live thousands of miles away in Europe or North America and rarely visit the island themselves. This was quite apparent in my study of Nevisian schoolchildren (Olwig 1987b). Not only did close to a third of the children have at least one parent abroad, but 96% of the children were able to enumerate a great number of more distant relatives who lived off Nevis. They were able to specify their location, even though, in some cases, the relatives were scattered across several different countries and continents. Thus one boy listed among the absent relatives his mother in St. Martin, his father in Trinidad, an aunt in Puerto Rico, an aunt in Dominica and an uncle in England, while a girl noted such relatives as her mother in the United States, her father in St. Kitts, two aunts in England and a grandmother in Puerto Rico. One student enumerated no less than 22 specific relatives living in such disparate locations as St. Thomas, Tortola, St. Croix, St. Kitts, St. Martin, Florida, New York, Texas and England.

These absent relatives provided not only much of the material basis of life for the households in which the children lived, but they also often acknowledged their ties to the children by sending them individual gifts. Close to 90% of the children had received presents from abroad in the form of for example money, clothes or books. These émigré relatives were so important to the children that they were regarded as members of the children's households, even though they were far away. In fact, it seems that the children did not operate with a concept of the household as a residential unit, but rather saw it as that group of people who contributed to the daily support of the home in which they lived. For this reason many of the children experienced difficulty delimiting exactly who lived in their household, and several children included relatives in their household, who, it later turned out, were not physically present.

The orientation toward Western societies and their material culture, which has been generated by migration, has in some ways merged with the old tradition of granting prestige and high social status to the English culture of the colonial masters. Thus, an imported factory made dress, sewn out of inexpensive material, is preferred to a dress which is sewn locally, even if it is made out of superior materials. This is because a homemade garment signifies poverty and low social status, while one imported from a Western country is associated with wealth and upper-class culture. A Nevisian woman who had sewn an embroidered blouse in a sewing project, received many compliments for this blouse, because it looked as if it had been purchased in the United States. Similarly, imported foodstuffs are preferred to local ones. A survey of the eating habits of members of three youth clubs showed that imported foods such as frozen chicken, cheese and macaroni dishes and white potatoes were among the most popular, while local chicken as well as breadfruit and cassava, both plentiful and inexpensive sources of starch produced on the island, were rarely, if ever, eaten by most youngsters. When asked in a later discussion of the survey why they did not eat these foods, the youngsters replied that they considered them to be "slave food" (Olwig and Olwig 1984).

The old tradition of associating Afro-Caribbean culture with a degraded slave life of low social status, while regarding European and North American culture as synonymous with privileged upper-class life of high status, has been further strengthened by the many television programs from the United States which can be seen on the local government station as well as on television stations transmitting from neighboring islands. Several series depict a life of material wealth which is entirely foreign to Nevisians. These series, particularly the soap operas, are quite popular, and Nevisians can discuss the details in such a personal and engaged way, that one can easily be misled to believe that they are talking about close personal friends.[8] It seems that for many Nevisians, series like *Another Life* on the intricacies of life among a group of well-situated North Americans are not fiction, but a realistic portrayal of another life in the United States. In this respect, conceptions held by many Nevisians concerning the material and social conditions under which the general population lives in the United States are hardly realistic.

Misconceptions about North American and British life are reinforced by the tourists who visit Nevis. The type of tourism which has been developed on the island, through the construction of smaller, exclusive hotels on the old plantations, has tended to cater to upper middle-class North Americans and Europeans. All tourists, furthermore, are relatively much better off than most Nevisians, and this impression is strengthened by the fact that tourists, generally speaking, affect a lifestyle of leisure and luxury, which they cannot afford in their daily life at home. Tourist behavior thereby contributes to generating the impression among Nevisians that most people in Western countries live in conditions of great wealth. The behavior of the emigrant Nevisians, who return for vacations on their home island, does little, of course to contradict this view because they try to make the best impression possible by flaunting material goods and money which they have accumulated abroad.

If many individual Nevisian families had succeeded in improving their own material condition of life by the early 1980s, little of this wealth benefitted the island society as such. Not only did the island lose its traditional agricultural economy, but no major new industrial development occurred. This is related to the fact that the island's infrastructure was poorly developed. The many families who invested in the installation of showers and flush toilets in their homes often found that there was no "government water" in the pipes and therefore had to use buckets of rain water collected in their own cisterns. Similarly much of their fancy electric equipment was inoperable due to shortages of electricity which led the government to close down the electric system in various parts of the island at regular intervals.

When during the early 1980s the Institute of Social and Economic Studies at the University of the West Indies, Barbados, published a general survey of conditions in the associate state of St. Kitts and Nevis (as well as three other island states) they concluded that the: "greatest single problem facing the state of St. Kitts-Nevis is the run-down, underdeveloped condition of the economy of Nevis" (*Project Report to the Government of St. Kitts-Nevis* 1982:153). It was at this very time when the local social and economic basis of Nevis society seemed to have disintegrated entirely that serious negotiations were initiated to make the British associated state of St. Kitts-Nevis an independent nation.

DEVELOPMENT OF AN INDEPENDENT NATION

The movement towards independence began in 1967, when the associated state of St. Kitts-Nevis was established, granting internal self-rule. During the 1970s, the British government sought to complete negotiations for the granting of total political independence within the British Commonwealth to St. Kitts-Nevis. As long as the Labor Party maintained political control on St. Kitts, Nevisians refused to participate in any sort of independence talks and threatened to secede. When the Labor Party lost several seats to the conservative People's Action Movement on St. Kitts in 1980, this party formed a coalition government with the Nevisian Reformation Party and the way was paved for independence. In September 1983 St. Kitts-Nevis was declared an independent nation.

Though this new nation had little economic or social basis for any sort of independence, a local bureaucracy was created to undertake the rather mammoth task of building up a new country out of the shambles left after more than a century of economic decline on the islands. They were aided in this by the willingness of foreign aid agencies to help fund improvements in the infrastructure as well as projects seeking to develop the local economy. With political independence new possibilities also emerged for attracting so-called offshore institutions, which operate on the island with a pro forma base provided by special legislation. During the first year of independence a number of development projects were initiated, and close to 20 people were stationed on Nevis to help develop the island. Most of them were Americans recruited through the Peace Corps or British working through Voluntary Service Overseas, and they were primarily engaged in agriculture, fishing, mechanics, handicrafts, health, and education. The island, furthermore, was receiving a steady stream of development specialists who were paving the way for the initiation of new projects, or evaluating those already started.[9]

Most of those who plan these projects have seen underdevelopment on Nevis as being largely an economic problem, which should be solved by the improvement of the infrastructure and the marketing of local products. Developing the Nevisian economy therefore primarily meant recognizing the economic potential of small farming, including animal husbandry, fishing and industries using local products such as coconuts. On Nevis, where the Afro-Caribbean way of life has been associated with low status, and where any sort of social mobility has been associated with a Euro-Caribbean outer appearance, it has been rather difficult, however, to market the attraction of projects which promote an economy tied to life in the rural villages (Olwig 1985c).

The promise of economic rewards clearly is not a sufficiently motivating force for people who live in a society where high social status has been measured not by the economic means of people, but by the obtainment of white-collar jobs, primarily in civil service, and the lifestyle associated with these positions. An irrigation project involving 10 acres of land at the old estate of New River, which was funded by British Development Division at the cost of about US $10,000 per acre, and which employed two agricultural officers on a full-time basis, thus attracted few young people who wished to undertake farming as a career, despite the high unemployment in the area. The few who finally acquired plots treated the project as a welcome opportunity to expand the backyard gardening, which provided a traditional supplement to wage employment. This was entirely against the intentions of the project: to provide the equivalent of a government salary, provided it was pursued as a full-time occupation according to the cultivation guidelines suggested by the project directors. This, however, would have necessitated intensive year-round irrigation farming, which involved strenuous field labor in the hot sun, standing in the mud watering and caring for the crops, a type of work which offered no social prestige, despite the promise of good economic remuneration (Olwig 1985c:39–44).

At the same time as several well-funded projects which sought to work with the local economy had to struggle to keep going, Nevisians flocked to those opportunities which offered the semblance of socially respectable work, even though they, generally speaking, offered rather low wages. This has been particularly apparent in the introduction of various factory enterprises on the island. During the 1980s, several outfits have appeared which use the island's relatively well educated, but inexpensive, work force to perform work or produce items for Western countries. These firms, which have been attracted to Nevis by tax incentives and other special legislation catering to offshore enterprises, have primarily produced clothing and electronic equipment, or they have offered such services as typing or the packaging of Nevis postage stamps, which are produced and sold by an English firm. Many of these operations have had a fairly short life span on Nevis since they service ephemeral Western financial interests or markets. This was the fate, for example, of an electronics plant which produced parts which apparently became obsolete shortly after its establishment on Nevis, and of a medical school geared to students from the United States, which never really seemed to have gotten off the ground due to mounting "onshore" criticism of "offshore" medical schools in the Caribbean (Olwig 1985c:50–54).

Women, in particular, have sought work in the new firms, because they offer employment that is not physically demanding and which is located indoors, usually in fairly modern buildings. Although the wages have usually been minimal, the glamor of wearing nice, clean clothes and doing either office work or light factory-type work seems to override the poor remuneration. Even though the best paid employees at these firms did not receive wages which were as high as the income that could have been derived from a serious agricultural enterprise at the irrigation project, Nevisians clearly were not tempted to exchange office work for farming (Olwig 1985c:44–47).

By the 1980s farming, and local economic activities in general, seemed to have such a low social status that many Nevisians preferred doing absolutely nothing to cultivating a plot of land. This was apparent when the Department of Community Affairs attempted to initiate a project for women in the St. James parish in 1984. The intention was to improve and further develop already existing local economic activities through the involvement of young women. The area chosen was one of the poorest on the island with few possibilities for local employment or education. Transportation to wage labor employment was limited and expensive, and the area had experienced severe depopulation during the 1970s due to emigration.

The 40 or so local women, who were interviewed about their interest in participating in a local development project, were in general completely disillusioned with regard to the possibility of achieving any sort of local economic improvement. Having failed to obtain the English exams necessary to get a white-collar job, they saw few career possibilities for themselves on the island. They expressed an interest in wage labor, but were not desirous of learning or upgrading skills that would help them become self-employed. They did virtually no farming and only little work in terms of handicrafts or sewing. Most of the young women helped around the house, but otherwise they did nothing but visit friends and "relax". For economic support they relied on relatives, many of them living abroad. The few women who had passed secondary school exams were waiting for a government job, and the fact that the participants in the project came from a government office was seen by some of them primarily as an opportunity to express their desire to get such a job.

When the possibility of initiating a community project was discussed with the women a few weeks after the survey they were sorely disappointed when the leader of the project encouraged them to engage in a "help for self-help" project in which they were expected to initiate locally generated economic activity with the help of her department, as well as the agricultural extension service. She suggested that they started producing something using local materials, such as preserves or handicrafts, and offered to help find a place in the area that might be used for the purpose. She also offered to find a skilled person to help train them and said that she would receive organizational assistance from Women And Development, a Caribbean organization which attempts to strengthen the role of women. As soon as agriculture was mentioned, the women complained that this was nothing but "fork and hoe" on Nevis, and in general they displayed little interest in engaging in any entrepreneurial activities on their own and instead requested that she try to have a hotel or factory constructed in the area, which could provide them with proper employment. If that could not be done, they wanted the government to put up a new building, where they could do some kind of work. For the women the suggestion that they stay in their home community and make a career out of domestic industry was not to be taken seriously.

"CLAY AIN'T DIRT"

One of the few projects which has achieved some success demonstrates the necessity of removing the local economy from its marginal position in the lower segments of society, if it is to be accepted by the Nevisians. The project is the Newcastle Pottery, which was constructed during the early 1980s with American and Canadian funds, and which sought to develop the old Afro-Caribbean tradition of pottery making on Nevis.[10]

When Gordon Merrill conducted his historical geographic study of St. Kitts and Nevis in the mid-1950s, he found in most homes locally produced pottery in the form of coal pots, cooking vessels, dishes and water jugs. This pottery was made by women from the Newcastle area who dug the clay locally, shaped it into the desired forms by hand using the coil method and fired it over open flames of burning coconut shells (1958:128). The trade, which had been passed on from mother to daughter for many generations, was relatively lucrative, in that pottery had a ready market on the island, but as was the case with other aspects of the Afro-Caribbean local economy, it had low social status, because it involved dirty and hard physical work. In pottery making this meant digging the clay, forming the pots and firing them by the strong heat in the open. Women therefore only worked as potters when they had no other means of support. When Platzer studied Nevisian potters in the mid-1970s, aluminium cooking ware and imported plastic and metal kitchen utensils had replaced the local pottery in most households, and less than a dozen potters were still plying their trade (1979:34).

In 1981, a training center for young potters was opened in a new building in Newcastle. It included the teaching of wheel-thrown pottery making, glazing and the techniques of kiln firing. Several young women were recruited for a six-month paid training period and a young, well-educated Nevisian, who had learned the trade from her aunt, was hired to train the women. A year later 5 full-time potters were working at the project, and 3 years later, in 1984, the number had expanded to 12. A Peace Corps volunteer who was trained as a potter was secured to teach glazing and kiln firing and to help run the business. Due to a shortage of electricity which prevented usage of the oven, the potters continued to produce unglazed pottery by the old methods, but they also added figurines, ashtrays and candleholders to the traditional repertoire. The simple Nevisian pottery turned out to be a success with hotels and tourists, who were interested in local crafts, and the potters were able to earn good incomes from the sales.

When interviewed about their pottery profession the women did express pride about the fact that their wages were equivalent to, or higher than those earned by women holding high status office jobs. They also emphasized the importance of the change which had occurred in the popular image of their trade. It was no longer regarded as "dirty", but respectable, even artistic. The simple fact that the work had been moved from the private potters' backyard to a building constructed with foreign aid gave the trade the aura of the highly desired "factory work". The new souvenir items were seen by some to be "artful", and the presence of the ware at exclusive hotels had not gone unnoticed by the Nevis public. Furthermore, the tourists' interest in the potters' work evidenced by their visits to the pottery made a great impression. As one of the potters stated, "People come here from the States and say that they also work with pottery and that makes me feel like I do worthwhile work".

The economic success of the pottery was undoubtedly an important factor in its popularity among Nevisians. Even more important, however, was the fact that the project managed to remove the social stigma attached to pottery making by turning it into a modern occupation, dissociated from the local community and its backyard economy, and recognized and respected by Western society. The project was successful because it developed an aspect of the Afro-Caribbean local economy by displaying and promoting it within a Western framework, for example a "factory", hotels and Western tourism. The new physical and social framework for this traditional occupation somehow cleansed it of its former associations—a sign on the wall reads, "Clay ain't dirt". In this respect, the Nevisian population continues the pattern of expressing locally generated cultural forms within a foreign medium, which they have established throughout their several centuries of suppression.

COMING TO TERMS WITH AFRO-CARIBBEAN CULTURE

The great difficulty which the Nevisians have experienced in coming to terms with their Afro-Caribbean cultural background is apparent in the cultural politics of the new country of St. Kitts-Nevis. This has, to a great extent, been inspired by the larger islands of Jamaica, Trinidad and Barbados where independence was declared during the 1960s. In these nation-states there has long been an increasing awareness of the importance of establishing a national identity which is separate from that of the old colonial mother country. An important aspect of this assertion of a non-English identity has been the development of a Caribbean curriculum which emphasizes knowledge of West Indian history, geography and literature and subjects relevant to West Indies existence. West Indian cookery and tropical agriculture are also part of the curriculum, both from a theoretical and practical point of view, and the subject of English includes West Indian literature and dialects. This curriculum is organized on a regional West Indian basis and prepares students for the Caribbean Examination System (CXC) which functions as an entrance examination for the

University of the West Indies. During the early 1980s, when independence was being negotiated for St. Kitts-Nevis, the state began to convert to the Caribbean curriculum as it adopted a new policy of placing greater emphasis on the Afro-Caribbean heritage of the nation.

Even though Afro-Caribbean culture has become incorporated into the school curriculum, many of the Afro-Caribbean cultural practices that go with it are still not highly regarded. While the schools on Nevis are expected to teach practical as well as theoretical agriculture, those preparing for the CXC do it primarily with an eye to continue their interest in agriculture through further studies at a university rather than through the application of their knowledge in practical work. The performance of the physically demanding work necessary to make agriculture a career continues to be neither attractive nor socially acceptable. Similarly, the addition of West Indian literature and poetry written in dialect and portraying Caribbean life, appears to be primarily an expression of academic deference to the local culture. The official language in the schools and the public administration on Nevis, as on the other former British West Indian Islands, remains standard English, or proper English as it is called locally, even though very few Nevisians completely master it.[11] There is, furthermore, the same manifest lack of sympathy for the mores of traditional Afro-Caribbean society depicted in this literature, and Nevisian schools still attempt to maintain the strict moral standards of respectability characterized by the former colonial era. Girls are thus still immediately expelled from school, never to be allowed to return, if they are found to be pregnant. The strictness of the code, oddly enough, reinforces traditional behavior patterns because the social stigma attached to their attending the free family planning clinic is so great that they prefer the risk of getting pregnant.[12]

The new-found interest in establishing a local West Indian culture is not, fundamentally, concerned with the recognition of the Afro-Caribbean culture imbedded in social relations and economic practices which have for so long been delegated to a socially marginal position. Interest rather focuses on the creation of a national culture which the local elite can call its own. The civil servants of today do not wish to distinguish themselves through their knowledge of British culture, as was the case formerly, when Shakespeare and piano concerts were cultivated by the local upper class. Today, knowledge of Caribbean history, geography and literature is important for the educated middle class, and it is no coincidence that the Caribbean curriculum has been introduced in the schools primarily at the upper, secondary level in connection with the preparation for the CXC examinations which are necessary to obtain a civil service job.[13]

The importance of developing a local Caribbean culture to replace the colonial English culture was recognized already during the 1950s, when two Nevisian schoolteachers started the Nevis Drama Group. They produced several plays locally and began participating in the Leeward Islands Drama Festival, where drama groups from St. Kitts, Nevis, Montserrat and Antigua met together on one of the islands and presented plays. These festivals had ceased by the 1970s, however, and the Nevis group became dormant, partly because several members of the group had emigrated from Nevis, partly because some drowned in the sinking in 1970 of the *Christena*, a ferry that sailed between St. Kitts and Nevis. In 1973, the group was reorganized in the form of NEDACS, Nevis Dramatics and Cultural Society, which also cultivated an interest in the folk culture of Nevis and organized performances of local folk songs, poems and various sketches on Nevis folk life. It also continued the drama tradition and produced plays written by Nevisian or other West Indian writers. Since 1974 this group has concentrated its efforts on the organization of a cultural festival, Culturama, during the week of August Monday, the holiday celebrating the Emancipation of the slaves (see Chapter Eight).

Though the educated middle class of civil servants has displayed an interest in developing a cultural heritage of Nevis, this heritage has not been made a part of the "established" image of Nevis promulgated by the nascent tourist industry and the government. This situation is clearly related to the structure of international power relations within which Nevisian society must operate, even within their own territory. As long as tourism and even the production of postage stamps are in the hands of non-natives, it is difficult to promote an island image which deviates from the colonial norm. Nevisians, therefore, still seek to promote their society through the vehicle of external cultural forms. Little emphasis has been placed on the Afro-Caribbean contribution to the island's culture and history in the presentation of the island to the outside world. The European background of the island still is perceived as the only historical and cultural attraction worthy of any note in Nevis. *The St. Kitts & Nevis Tourist Guide*, published in April 1984, recommends that the tourist to Nevis "take a taxi to Fort Charles, where Nelson kept a lookout for approaching ships. Then visit the Bath House and dip your feet in the warm, sulphurous, healing waters of the Bath Stream. Continue on to Fig Tree Church, where the original marriage certificate of the wedding of Lord Nelson to Fanny Nisbet can be seen. Visit the New River boiling house where you can get a detailed tour of the old steam process of making sugar." A similar approach to the main attractions of the island is taken in the *Walking and Riding Tour of Nevis*, published by the Nevis Historical and Conservation Society, which describes virtually only buildings connected with the White presence on the island, such as old merchant houses, plantation buildings, churches and forts. Little mention is made of the many rural villages which dot the island and which still include many fine examples of Afro-Caribbean architecture.[14]

The tendency to emphasize the White colonial history of Nevis also reflects the notion that this constitutes the only way of winning any recognition for Nevis on the part of the Western world. This is illustrated by the Island Assembly building. It is housed on the first floor of a building which has been erected on the supposed site of the birthplace of Alexander Hamilton, the architect of the American Constitution and one of the founding fathers of the United States of America (*Independence Magazine* 1983:64). Alexander Hamilton lived the first few years of his life on Nevis, but was taken as a small child by his mother to the Danish West Indian island of St. Croix, from where, as a young man, he moved to the United States. Whereas few Nevisians know who Alexander Hamilton was—understandably enough considering the fact that his role in Nevis history was virtually nil—every American schoolchild has heard his name. By naming the most central building in post-independence Nevisian history after an entirely minor figure in Nevis history, who happened to become a great American statesman, the Nevis local government has underlined the necessity of finding approval for Nevisian claims to a national culture through the vehicle of Western cultural recognition. Much as the adoption of the culture of respectability was rewarded economically by colonial society, this modern adaptation of local cultural interests to foreign forms also has its rewards. The local government received a grant from the American foreign aid agency, USAID, to reconstruct Alexander Hamilton House.

NON-RESPECTABILITY AND THE DOUBLE BIND OF A CULTURAL DILEMMA

The many problems which plague the local community on Nevis as it seeks to establish a viable nation-state with a cultural heritage of its own are, to a great extent, solved within the Nevisian transnational community. I shall argue, in the following chapters, that one of the primary reasons why migration is seen by Nevisians to lead to a better life is found in the way in which it resolves the irresolvable conflicts with which Nevisians are confronted in the local society. Furthermore, I shall suggest that even though migration has led to a collapse of the local rural communities and their associated cultural practices, Afro-Caribbean culture remains a vital basis of the transnational community which has developed upon its ruins. The mutual rights and obligations that tie Nevisians situated in distant locations together in global networks are thus informed by Afro-Caribbean culture, in particular its family system. The cultural identity which sustains the Nevisian global community draws, to a considerable extent, on the Afro-Caribbean rural life which has formed the context within which Afro-Caribbean culture has emerged.

NOTES

1 Two modern concrete hotels built by Nevisians are an exception to this pattern. These hotels are located at Pinney's Beach and cater to visiting government officials, returning Nevisians, who have no close family with which to stay, as well as ordinary tourists. Many Nevisians find it difficult to understand the attraction of hotels built out of old ruins. As one Nevisian stated, "To me the plantation buildings look old and dilapidated, but the tourists seem to think that they are antique!" One of the hotels which was most popular with Nevisians during my stay on the island in 1989 was a modern building which overlooked the airport.

2 Much of the dissatisfaction with St. Kitts was directed against Robert Bradshaw, the leader of the Labour Party and the local government.

3 The English orientation of the curriculum, naturally, has been reflected in the exam questions, a problem which has seriously handicapped West Indian students taking the exams. According to one schoolteacher, an exam question asking students to write about "moving house" had created a great deal of confusion, because the West Indian students interpreted it to refer to the moving of actual houses, a common West Indian practice, rather than the movement of household.

4 The study found a similar lack of commitment to the local community in the government radio station which had begun broadcasting in 1961.

5 Much of the material which forms the basis for this and the two following chapters is drawn from my field notes and is therefore not foot-noted.

6 The local population on the island has not declined as much as would be expected due to a very high birth rate. The estimated population of St. Kitts and Nevis of approximately 50,000 in 1950 had declined to less than 45,000 when a census was carried out in 1970 (Richardson 1983:146).

7 The study was based on a questionnaire survey of 5 schoolclasses, where I examined the attitude of the children toward their island community, the socioeconomic network in which they lived, and the impact of emigration on their lives. Finally, their career goals were ascertained. The sample included two sixth grades with students 11–12 years old, representing the senior group in Prospect School and Gingerland Primary School, two rural primary schools. There were also two fifth forms and one sixth form, which were the senior classes in Gingerland High School and Charlestown Secondary School, the two secondary schools on the island. The students in these grades were 16–19 years old. The three-page questionnaire contained a total of 25 questions.

8 When during my fieldwork on St. John I heard a Nevisian explain to a friend what had happened to a number of persons during the friend's absence from the island, I found myself busy taking mental notes on the unusual family patterns, until I realized that they were talking about a TV soap.

9 This study forms the basis of the following discussion of development on Nevis during the early 1980s. For a more detailed report of the study see Olwig 1985b.

10 I have analyzed the Afro-Caribbean pottery on Nevis in greater detail in Olwig 1990.

11 The problems caused by the failure to master standard English have been analyzed in a Ph.D. dissertation (Ralston 1979). It argues that the shame experienced by Nevisians when they find that they are unable to speak standard English leads many of them to stutter. The Afro-Caribbean celebration of verbal performance, analyzed in *The-Man-of-Words*

(Abrahams 1983) therefore has a reverse in the colonial denial of proper English verbal performance in a man "Without Words".

12 The girls are not readmitted because they are seen by teachers and parents alike as a serious threat to the discipline and morality in the classroom. A similar official condemnation of sexual relations out of wedlock was also followed until recently with regard to unmarried female civil servants who became pregnant. The policy of dismissing these women from their employment was first abandoned at the time of independence. This occurred, in my view, largely because of pressure for equal rights among men and women, rather than because of any acceptance of pregnancy out of wedlock. Apparently it was out of the question, or too complicated, to administer a policy which attempted to uphold the morality of male civil servants. Such considerations of sexual equality have not been taken into consideration as far as the schoolgirls are concerned, perhaps because many schoolgirls are impregnated by older boys who therefore do not attend school. If the conditions of unwed young girls are still difficult, the status of illegitimate children has improved with the status of children act passed at the independence which grants illegitimate children equal rights with legitimate children. This means that children born out of wedlock, for the first time, have a legal right to inherit from their fathers.

13 Even though some changes have been made in the primary schools, secondary school teachers often complain that primary schools to a great extent still function by the old English rote learning system and that their graduates are poorly trained for the secondary schools. Learning difficulties in the primary schools have been so severe that a study was commissioned to examine the problem in the mid-1980s. Among the problems found to be causing the poor performance of the students at school was absenteeism, the watching of television while (or instead of) doing homework, lack of interest in the local schools on the part of parents because they were unemployed or in the process of leaving the island (Edwards n.d.).

14 The only exception is a mention of the community of Newcastle which is described as having been at one time "a leading port of Nevis". Its buildings are seen to be "some of the most ornate in the state" reflecting the "degree of wealth that existed among its inhabitants". The pamphlet is published with the help of funding from the Organization of American States. This emphasis on grand buildings of the past is, of course, not unusual in tourist brochures.

CHAPTER SEVEN

The Global Community

In December 1980 I arrived for the first time on Nevis in order to do fieldwork on the effects of migration on the island society. The day after my arrival I went to Charlestown in order to change the American dollars that I had brought with me to the local Eastern Caribbean dollar. By using local currency I hoped that I would not be taken for one of the American tourists who visit the island at that time of the year. It turned out that I was in good company in the local bank. Judging by the long lines there, it seemed that half the islanders were busy changing money ranging from American and Canadian dollars to English pounds and Dutch guilders. I was, in fact, participating in one of the most important Christmas rituals on the island. Only, I had brought the money myself, while most Nevisians were changing the money that had been sent to them by relatives working abroad.

In the several years of research that have followed, it has become clear that the Christmas changing of foreign currency that I witnessed on Nevis was part of a large transnational network of exchanges of money and Western material goods involving Nevisian migrants and their families on Nevis. It further became apparent that the island society that I had come to study did not constitute an important entity in and of itself, but rather an important focal point in a global community of relations which extended between Nevisians throughout the world. The Nevisian community, therefore, was to be found between, not only within, the various localized settlements of Nevisians. This realization played havoc with my plans for traditional anthropological fieldwork in a local community.

The great importance of the global community to Nevisians is related to the role which remittances of money and material goods to family members on Nevis play as a means by which some of the most fundamental contradictions in the local society are resolved. These contradictions arise from the coexistence of the cultural frameworks of sociability, connected with communitywide relations of sharing and cooperation, and respectability, associated with self-sufficient nuclear families. These two frameworks make it difficult for Nevisians to maintain and further develop their way of life within an Afro-Caribbean cultural context, while gaining, at the same time, acceptance and respect for it in the local communities as well as the modern society of the nation-state. This is particularly apparent as far as family structure and social mobility are concerned. The global community therefore has come to override local Nevisian society, both in terms of its overwhelming

PLATE 9   *Mr. Lionel Thompson with granddaughter Tascha on Nevis. Photo, Karen Fog Olwig, 1982.*

significance as a socioeconomic field of life, and in terms of its capability of freeing Nevisians from the "double bind" in which they have been placed in island society as it has evolved under colonial rule.

THE AFRO-CARIBBEAN FAMILY

If the Nevisian community at first sight seemed amorphous and without clear boundaries, it soon became apparent that it was not lacking in organizational principles and structure, in that the Afro-Caribbean family network was at its very backbone. This network which had evolved and sustained the Nevisian population since the days of slavery, had led a shadow-like existence unrecognized by colonial society. It only became visible as a bearing element in Nevisian society with the development of the transnational community extending to migration destinations abroad. Emigration therefore can be seen as a means whereby Nevisians have been able to assert and further develop an aspect of Afro-Caribbean culture which hitherto has not found acceptance within the local, "respectable", Nevisian society.

The Afro-Caribbean notion of the family has been seen to be one of a network of ties between relatives and affines, who receive and offer one another recognition by sharing economic resources, just as they are a resource of help in economic activities and the raising of children.[1] The basic building block in the Afro-Caribbean family is the tie between parent and child. The parent-child relationship involves, on the one hand, the obligation to clothe, feed and care for the child and, on the other, the right to receive help and support from the child as soon as it is able to contribute in any way. On Nevis, as in the West Indies in general, the parent-child tie tends to be concentrated on the mother-child relationship because youths engage in sexual relationships, while they are still living in their respective natal homes, with the result that children often grow up in their grandmother's home. The relative unimportance of the father-child tie is reflected in a survey of Nevisian schoolchildren carried out in the mid-1980s, which showed that single mothers cared for the greatest proportion of children (38%), followed by grandparents (29%) and both parents (26%) (Edwards n.d.:44). The female bias in the parent-child relationship is strengthened by the fact that children are reared in the female sphere of the household and its yard, an enclosed area where many household activities take place.[2]

From an early age children provide an important source of labor power. They do much of the domestic work, and when they become old enough to obtain wage employment they are expected to contribute significant support as a measure of gratitude towards the person who has raised them. One woman explained:

> I have no bankbook, my children are my bankbook. I spend all I can on them, and they do all right. [...] It is my duty to raise them, and they will then raise

their children. They can never pay me back. But if they, out of the goodness of their hearts, want to help me, knowing that their mother worked hard for them and that they have money, this is fine.

The mother-child tie forms a basic model upon which economic and social relations of vital importance are generated. Thus children always have a strong obligation to help those who have reared them, whether grandmothers, aunts, or, in more cases, persons who are not related to them.[3] They will also have obligations towards those who have grown up with them, whether siblings, cousins or more distant relatives, because they have shared in the basic exchange of mutual help and support which takes place between the older and younger generation.

While the family receives concrete expression in the group of people who belong to a yard, the notion of the family is not based on a residential group of people, but on a network of relatives, who recognize their family ties by giving each other various goods as well as mutual assistance in the daily chores of life. According to this concept of the family, children are not regarded as dependents to be reared into self-sufficient adulthood, but are seen as links in a network of relations which must be nurtured before it can be relied upon. Likewise, sexual partners are not only regarded as conjugal spouses, but seen as important new links in the family networks, as well as the means through which children are born and the network expanded.

The tight network of interrelationships involving people of different generations who have rights to receive and obligations to help is, in many respects, what defines family as distinct from friends. Only those non-relatives, who have been involved in such exchange relations, may achieve a kin-like status. A woman who has reared a child from infancy becomes like a mother to the child and will therefore have more claims to help from that child than will the biological mother. Even a child who remains in the mother's home but spends much of the childhood in a neighbor's yard with the children there, perhaps because the child does not get along well with its own mother, can achieve status as a sort of cousin to these children. Persons who have not been involved in such networks of exchange during childhood, but are merely adult friends, will not be relatives and should not act as such. Thus one woman, who had no children of her own, was frowned upon by her relatives for sharing the generous economic support which she received from her sister in England with a neighbor, rather than with her family, who also lived nearby. As her niece explained:

It is wrong to give to strangers and not to family. If something happens to you, then the family will look after you. But strangers, they will not help the same way, they will just forget you.

Despite the important role of the family network in the Nevisian daily life, it has remained largely invisible in the island society. The Nevisian family is most prominently displayed in public through the institutions of marriage and the home, which are seen to offer an officially recognized framework for family life. Marriage is thus the only socially acceptable way in which a new home may be established, just as it is a precondition for marriage that a house has been secured by the man as a physical sign of the provision of a proper framework for family life.

The importance of the house as a center of family life, especially for women, can be seen to conform to the central role of the home in a respectable life style. Adult women are expected to be guardians of the home and its moral virtues, an important function of this being to hinder young female members of the household from becoming pregnant out of wedlock as this brings disgrace upon the family. Young women are expected to stay within the yard as much as possible, especially after dark, and are only encouraged to leave it in order to attend school and church or youth clubs organized by the churches or local leaders involved in community work, such as civil servants.

Respectability based on private life within the confines of the yard is, however, counteracted by the demands for public sociability amongst peers within the community. Today, the public sociability in the rural communities is most apparent in the importance of informal gatherings by men "liming" or hanging around at rum shops or the street corners drinking, playing, joking and engaging in loud discussions in the Nevisian dialect.[4] Through their participation in social life, male members of the household situate their family within the local community and show themselves thereby to be real men.

To a great extent the Afro-Caribbean family offers a middle ground between the extreme exclusivity of the private nuclear family, the ideal of the culture of respectability, and the extreme inclusiveness of the wide ties of community based friendship, emphasized by the tradition of sociability. The family networks demarcate a more limited field of rights and obligations than do the peer groups, where a great number of friends can lay claim to a person's resources. Furthermore, they recognize different kinds of interrelationships of rights and obligations with the mother-child tie usually being the most intensive, whereas the ties between distant relatives usually will be dormant. While kinsmen are important because they are persons on whom one can count when in need, claims to help from kinsmen may be refused if a kin tie has been neglected. A person who is generous towards a friend rather than close relatives who live nearby and are in need, has, in effect, denied the presence of this family and thus forfeited any claims of support later on, which would otherwise be expected from such relatives. The Afro-Caribbean family network therefore offers a framework which circumscribes a smaller circle of those who can really be counted on for help and who should be granted help. This form of family has not been seen as of any cultural value nor has it been granted any social recognition within the local society. The significance of the family network has become apparent, however, with emigration and the development of a global community, which is based upon, and highlights, the mutual ties of rights and obligations operating particularly between parents and children, but capable of being extended to a wider range of relatives.[5]

Parents are usually intimately involved in the entire migration process. They often decide who is going to emigrate and make the practical arrangements necessary for a son or daughter to leave the island and become established in a new destination. It is usually parents, who help with the necessary funds to purchase tickets and tide over the migrants during the first period in the migration destination, just as they often make the necessary arrangements to have relatives meet the new emigrants there. Many of the young people only have access to relatives abroad through their parents.

Young Nevisians are quite eager to emigrate largely because migration presents to them a means through which they will be able to fulfill their contradictory obligations. They will thereby be able to help their family, and, at the same time, establish a degree of independence as adults. By emigrating they can accomplish this without damaging the public image which they are expected to adhere to as young women and men within the traditions of respectability and sociability. Women of course are dependent upon men as procreators of their children, through whom they can build up their own family network. Men are also an important potential source of economic support which can make possible the establishment of a home, where the youngsters will not be under the close surveillance of older relatives. Women may, however, be reluctant to become publicly involved with men, unless they are willing to commit themselves to marriage and family life, since this may mean a loss of respectability. Men, on the other hand, are under pressure to spend much of their income (and time) on liming with male friends on the street corner and at the rum shops and may be unwilling to assume the responsibilities which are associated with marriage. At the same time, however, they may desire sexual contact, and domestic life, with women.

The importance of migration as a means of dealing with the conflicts which confront one another within the context of the family is reflected in the fact that many of the actual migratory moves occur in connection with some conflict between the older and younger generation. Conflicts over young people's sexual life may, for example, lead to emigration. Young women who have illegitimate children are often sent away, partly to avoid their burdening the household economy with still more illegitimate children, partly to enable them to help support their children, who often, at least initially, stay behind in the grandparental home. Migration also offers a way of helping young women who have given birth to illegitimate children because they will have difficulty pursuing attractive careers on Nevis. As one mother explained:

> A daughter of mine became pregnant while she was in school. I wrote an aunt in
> Michigan, asking whether my daughter could go there to learn something,

because I didn't intend to support my daughter and her baby. My aunt said to send her right away, and so she went, and after she had the baby, she went to Catholic High school and graduated from there.

Young men are more frequently sent away for other reasons, such as failure to hold proper employment and the habit of doing too much liming. One young man, who was living in his grandmother's house, was sent to a nearby island, not so much because he had produced two children out of wedlock, as because he did not have a job and thus was not able to offer any support for his own family or that of his children.

Since the bulk of the migrants are young people, who leave from their parental home, they are heavily indebted to the parents, not just for their having reared them, but also for their having arranged for them to emigrate. As one migrant in England explained:

> I came to England, because my parents suggested it. I had no work, and my parents didn't want their children to work as hard in the blazing sun as they had done. They wanted better for their children. They told us that we should broaden our outlook on life and make ourselves better.
>
> I was the first one to leave, and my family got the £65.00 together for my passage: sold some sheep, borrowed from an uncle, and friends and family gave a little. My auntie in America sent me clothes. I didn't have a clue what to expect in England. I hoped to get work to help my parents. All I could think about was to help my parents who worked so hard in the blazing sun.

While all migrants are expected to send remittances to their families on Nevis, and will be frowned upon if they fail to do this, men and women regard their obligations toward their home somewhat differently in accordance with the different way that they are integrated into the family.

In a study of emigration from Grenada, Tobias suggests that "manliness and liming are central to Grenadian migration" and that "freedom implies the ability to leave Grenada with the least fuss, leaving the fewest obligations behind" (1975:135, 214). For the men, who may not be tied to one particular domestic unit, with its social and economic obligations, but who are allowed or even expected to spend much of their time outside the home, migration can be regarded as a natural extension of their wide array of extra-domestic activities, and it may offer them a certain amount of personal freedom and mobility. This was emphasized by a migrant in the Virgin Islands who said:

> I have no commitments, I want to be totally free. No ifs and buts. If the grass is greener elsewhere, I want to go there. I am not tied to any place in particular, and I want to be wherever I feel like.

The situation for the women is rather different. Due to their close association with the domestic sphere, most women migrate as vital members of a household, usually their mother's, and feel a strong obligation to support it. This is accentuated by the fact that many of the women, when they emigrate, leave one or more children behind in the care of their mother. This had been true for more than a third of the Nevisian women that I interviewed on St. John, although virtually all of them had succeeded in sending for the children within a few years. The women, furthermore, felt strongly indebted to the mothers for enabling them to emigrate. While some of the men, who were subject to fewer domestic demands than the women, had been able to save some of the money needed to emigrate, women often were entirely dependent upon their parents for the fare. Emigration, somewhat paradoxically, tended to strengthen the importance of women to the household, and it did not, as often was the case for men, lead to a lessening of their commitments to it. They did, however, find some freedom from their parents' immediate control by leaving the household.

Though men and women often use migration as a way of living up to their respective gender roles,[6] it rarely provides a means for men to attain the sort of ideal "no strings attached" reputation described above. No male migrant, who still has close family on Nevis, is, in fact, free from any commitment. Most of them do send regular remittances to this family on their own accord, and if they do not, they are usually easily pressured to give money. It is, for example, common that a sister, living in the same migration destination as her brothers, asks them to give her money to send home, when she is writing letters to their family on Nevis. The men accept the responsibility to provide for relatives on Nevis, not only because they, too, feel an obligation towards their family, but also because they will lose status both on Nevis and in the emigrant destination, if they do not help maintain their family in a decent manner.

The extension through migration of the family network from the local society to a transnational community has brought to light some of the most significant social and economic ties and cultural values associated with Afro-Caribbean family relations. They include fundamental intergenerational ties of rights and obligations between close relatives, in particular parents and children, and complementary gender roles which situate men primarily in the wider community context, women in the closer knit domestic unit. These family relations can be seen to be celebrated through the consumption of Western material culture which flows to Nevis through the global family network.

DISPLAYING THE AFRO-CARIBBEAN FAMILY THROUGH MATERIAL CULTURE

During the 1950s and 1960s England and the American Virgin Islands constituted the two major migration destinations for Nevisians. During the 1970s and 1980s, when visa restrictions were instituted there, the British Virgin Islands and the Dutch island of St. Martin became important destinations. The American Virgin Islands still remain an important point of entrance, however, because of regulations which favor immigration on the part of relatives of resident aliens.

The Nevisians who emigrated to England, generally speaking, had great expectations due to England's historical background as the imperial mother country, and its close association with the culture of the Nevisian upper class. One Nevisian, for example, remembered how the English Anglican minister had depicted England in such glowing terms that she daydreamed about travelling to this place full of green parks and streets "paved with gold'. For Nevisians, leaving for England meant going to the center of the powerful old empire with its high culture and great wealth. Instead they found a racist society with serious economic problems, which, much to their surprise had a White working class which made a living by doing hard physical labor. The migrants therefore had to be satisfied with the worst of these laboring jobs, even though they would hardly have considered taking them on their home island. One man who started his career in England, shovelling hot ashes from a pit, remembered thinking to himself, as he donned wellies and gloves to begin a day of shovelling, "If my mother saw this, she would die!"[7]

The rapid expansion of the tourist economy during the 1950s and 1960s, led the American Virgin Islands to admit foreign laborers under a special labor certification program. This program allowed the hiring of aliens on a temporary basis, provided they were guaranteed 40 hours of work and the American minimum wage. Most of the immigrants entered the American territory on tourist visas and hoped that it would be possible for them to find work which would qualify them to become certified laborers before their tourist visas expired, usually after three months. The labor certification program began to be phased out in 1972, but until the late 1970s, when all certified laborers obtained status as permanent immigrants, most Nevisians lived and worked under the tenuous conditions of the certification program as "bonded laborers", as they were called in the Virgin Islands. For many years, the Nevisians, along with immigrants from other West Indian islands, therefore remained in a position of limbo, not knowing whether their visas would be terminated if they should lose their jobs and force them to return to Nevis. This was a fate that befell quite a few. In order to keep their visas many therefore agreed to illegal working conditions, typically involving the acceptance of wages which were lower than those stipulated by the law. One woman, who had emigrated to St. Thomas, thus managed to obtain tourist visas during a period of one and a half years, before she finally succeeded in acquiring a job that allowed her to receive labor certification. During this time she had to leave the American Virgin Islands every time her tourist visa expired, and incur the expense of travel to the British Virgin Islands. She survived by taking intermittent work under the minimum wage. Others simply overstayed on their tourist visas and became illegal aliens. Since the Virgin Islands had a highly inflated tourist economy, the standard of living which could be maintained on such reduced wages was meager to say the least. While the migrants' willingness to work under substandard conditions in the tourist industry made them popular with the Americans who controlled tourism on the islands, they became quite unpopular among the native Virgin Islanders who had to compete with them on the labor market.[8]

Most of the Nevisians, whom I interviewed in the American Virgin Islands and in England, were initially disappointed by the economic and social situation with which they were faced, and many wished to return to Nevis. The financial and social obligations that the migrants had incurred toward their family back home, however, prevented them from doing so. Furthermore, returning empty-handed to Nevis after only a brief, unsuccessful stay abroad, was a disgrace that few wished to experience. The migrants therefore endured conditions that made Nevis look like paradise on earth.

While the immigrants in England had a secure legal status, they experienced social discrimination and extremely poor living conditions. It was common for several people to live crammed up in small rooms, or "bed-sits", and to have to share kitchen and bathroom facilities with all the other roomers in the house. The houses were located in the most run-down urban districts, the only areas where rooms were rented out to "coloured people". Many of the Nevisians who had believed that the Anglican and Methodist Churches would provide an important religious and social center of life in England, as they had done on Nevis, found that they received a very cool welcome by the English congregations. I was told that it was common for White English congregation members to transfer to churches in White areas in order to avoid worshipping with West Indians. Due to this hostile atmosphere which particularly characterized the early period of immigration, many West Indians stopped attending church, or they founded their own churches. These were usually affiliated with fundamentalist denominations such as the Pentecostal or Baptist Churches. A similar pattern of joining fundamentalist churches also developed in the Virgin Islands, where the established churches of the local community also were seen to extend a less than warm welcome to the many immigrants.[9]

Migrants by and large accepted their lot in the migration destination, the primary purpose of their emigrating not being that of improving on their own individual situation, but rather that of helping their family on Nevis. Another factor which helped the immigrants to endure the social denigration was a greater orientation toward the social situation on their home island, than to that of the host country. The money and material goods which the migrants sent to their families on Nevis would provide the family with the material means to adopt a middle-class life style and a status of respectability within local society while at the same time remaining part of the rural folk community. The goal, however, was not just to help the family at home, but to pave the way for the migrant's own return home, through investment in traditional status items on the island: livestock, land and modern cinder-block houses.

The maintenance of proper relations within the global family network has become an important mark of prestige on Nevis and it grants a new sort of recognition, and visibility, to the family network within local society. It is important that families on Nevis receive sufficient economic support not just to maintain themselves, but also to surround themselves with Western material goods, which can announce the fact that the family is being well cared for by relatives abroad. The actual practical value of these goods may be rather limited. One family, for example, received a large gas stove from a daughter on St. Martin, which cost them several hundred EC dollars[10] in import duty. The stove had four pilot lights, which blew out, if the shutters in the kitchen were kept open, leaving a discomforting smell of leaking gas, or increased the temperature of the kitchen to unbearable degrees, if the shutters were closed. The oven needed both gas and electricity to function and thus was inoperable, when there was no electricity, which was a frequent occurrence. Within a few weeks, the family had decided to turn off the gas, whenever they were not cooking, in order to solve the problem of the pilot lights. The stove was used as little as possible and a coal pot, which was made out of the metal of an automobile wheel and which could be used in the yard, again constituted the main means of cooking. Though the stove proved to be so impracticable that it was left largely unused, it remained an important monument to the strength of the family network.

The role of the material goods as symbols of a well-functioning global family network was particularly important with regard to the household's standing within the community. An elderly lady thus had lived happily without a refrigerator for years, until she developed diabetes and was forced to keep her medicines in a neighbor's refrigerator. While this presented few practical problems, it was a source of embarrassment for her that the local community would then discover that she had no refrigerator, despite the many children she had abroad. She therefore asked the children to send money for a refrigerator, which they did, even though this presented a large, unexpected drain on their own economic resources. As one of her children in England noted:

> I feel that we must support our parents. If we didn't send money, we would

have a bad name in the village, and I am happy that the villagers see that my parents have a five bedroom house with TV, telephone and a fridge.

The migrants themselves also achieve personal recognition and prestige in their local community on Nevis if they are seen to provide well for their family on Nevis. They display this personal achievement by indulging in a grandiose and lavish lifestyle during their visits to their family on Nevis. Some Nevisians undergo a virtual transformation, when they arrive on their home island. I remember, for example, having trouble recognizing a woman, whom I knew well on St. John, when I encountered her on Nevis, because she was wearing elaborate costume jewelry and a garish outfit, in strong contrast to the way she presented herself on St. John.

The family is only obligated to share the remittances which it receives from abroad with close relatives; the migrants themselves, however, will be expected to share their reputed wealth generously, when they return for visits. Nevisians therefore try to travel with enough money and presents to shower family and friends with gifts. While women usually limit presents to family and godchildren, men will often be asked for presents by friends. In fact, visiting Nevisians may find that it is difficult to deal with the many requests that they are presented with, and one man, who apparently found it impossible to refuse anyone, gave away all his possessions, including his jacket, and his mother told me that she had to provide him with money so that he could leave the island again.

The problems of maintaining the appearance of success and affluence, even though the realities of life abroad often were quite different, were described vividly by one woman in the Virgin Islands:

> I would like to go back to Nevis, I was there five years ago, but I just got enough together for the fare, and this is not enough. I am a big woman now, since I have been outside Nevis, and I must behave accordingly, when I come home.
>
> When you go home on vacation it is almost necessary to carry a big bag of money and six suitcases of clothes. They all come and ask you right to your face to give them something. I bring something for my relatives. [...] I also have godchildren on Nevis, and I don't bring anything for them, but I may give them two dollars. They are fresh though, and they only want the American money. They all come to see you, when they hear that you are on a visit, and it is quite a rat race to go home. But when you go, you also get things from them. They give you fruit and provisions, which I then take back with me.

Remittances which are sent by individual migrants to their family for its benefit will be used to acquire material goods which are associated with a middle-class life style. They are, in other words, used to generate higher social status for the family on Nevis and thus greater respectability for the family network which sustains it. Those who do not belong to the family therefore have no right to these resources. Migrants who visit Nevis find themselves in a different situation. The eccentric self-indulgence which they project among friends on Nevis is directed toward their own aggrandizement and achievement among peers in the local community. They will therefore be challenged by this community to share their reputed wealth, and thus prove their claims to success.[11]

The important role of Western material goods in the local communities on Nevis suggests that Nevisians through Western material goods have found a means to aspire to upward social mobility and yet validate the "non-respectable" Afro-Caribbean family network. Nevisians are today exposed to Western material goods through several different sources, such as foreign investors, tourists, various foreign aid agencies, America-based fundamentalist churches and television programs. While foreign aid agencies have attempted to convince Nevisians that material welfare is a result of local development, foreign entrepreneurs leave the impression that development is identical with the presence of Western goods on Nevis. Foreign television programs and tourists have given Nevisians the idea that life in Western countries is equivalent to having an abundance of material goods to which everybody has free access, while the fundamentalist religious television programs give the message that the material wealth which is displayed on the TV screen is a gift from God, who has favored them because of their form of Christianity. None of these perceptions relate the presence of material goods to the workings of a Western capitalist system which, in nature, is contrary to the Afro-Caribbean context of life on Nevis.

Nevisians in general have little knowledge of the notions of capitalism and private enterprise and work discipline which are fundamental to material welfare in Western society. The productive implications and the economic significance of material goods in Western countries, where most of them are produced, are rather unimportant on Nevis, however, because these goods attain a "life of their own" here.[12] Nevisians, through their long tradition of migration, have brought most of the Western goods to Nevis themselves and, in the process, created their own interpretation of the cultural (and socioeconomic) significance of these goods. Nevisians therefore provide a good example of the way in which global flows receive new function and meaning as they are recontextualized in local communities throughout the world (Hannerz 1992). The Nevis case, furthermore, points to the fact that global flows do not just derive from expanding metropoles associated with the West, but are actively sought and incorporated within local systems as a means of addressing inherent contradictions.

The importance of migration as an avenue for asserting the importance of the family network, as well as the achievements of its individual members, is apparent in funerals held on Nevis, particularly for older people. As soon as a Nevisian dies, relatives abroad are notified, and the body is placed at great expense[13] in cold storage in a funeral home, so that there will be time for the migrants to return to Nevis in order to attend the funeral. The death is announced over the local radio station, which recounts the names and locations of the relatives, as well as the time and place of the funeral. The closest relatives, such as children and their eventual spouses, are always mentioned and identified by occupation if they have distinguished themselves in any way. The announcements are more select with regard to the rest of the family, especially if it is large. They will usually mention relatives abroad and those who have the most prestigious jobs on the island, but not necessarily others. In one case, the funeral announcement of an old man thus did not mention the grandson, who had looked after him during his last stage of life, probably because he was an "outside" or illegitimate child, but it mentioned a granddaughter, who was a nurse at the hospital even though she had not cared for him.

At a "good" funeral the body will be buried in a "proper" casket, decorated with flower arrangements made of plastic, so that they will last for a long time and provide decoration for the grave. On the day of the burial, the body is viewed at the funeral home, after having been prepared for viewing. The dead are usually made up and dressed in their best clothing. One Nevisian woman, who had lived in the United States for a number of years, was, for example, clothed in a fancy white and purple gown. The body may also be embalmed. It is brought to the church in a hearse followed by a long train of cars, carrying the mourning family and friends and the funeral train is accompanied by a loudspeaker broadcasting taped mourning music, which will be heard as the train passes through the island. At the funeral service in the church there are specially prepared printed programs with a picture and a brief obituary of the deceased. After the burial a tombstone is usually erected by the family on the grave. It is made out of concrete or stone, either plain or decorated with tiles or figures.

A burial provides an occasion where relatives who normally are scattered in distant migration destinations and therefore rarely see one another have a chance to meet and renew former ties. The days after the funeral are often characterized by a great deal of sociability on the part of family and friends, who have gathered in honor of the dead. One woman who had lost her husband a few weeks before I talked with her, thus recounted with great joy and pride that her husband's funeral had been attended by a great number of relatives who had come from England, Canada, The United States as well as several West Indian islands. They spent several weeks on the island afterwards and had a good time eating, drinking and playing dominos.

It is thought to be shameful if a person dies without anybody to provide at least a decent, if modest burial. In that case the dead must be buried by the government, which will not notify anybody of the funeral, but merely provides a simple interment at the public cemetery, involving only a minister and the necessary grave diggers. Such a funeral was the fate of an old notorious alcoholic, who died in the hospital after having caused his family (brothers and sisters and their children) considerable distress. He had lived by himself in a house, which was said to resemble a pig sty, and he was often to be found on the road, stupefied by liquor. All efforts to help him live a better life had been in vain, and he had failed to show up many times, when he was supposed to help fork the land for relatives, thus forcing them to hire strangers. When he died the hospital officials attempted to find relatives who would claim the body and provide it with a proper funeral, but the entire family refused to "response" for him and bear the heavy expenses of a funeral. After a few days, the government therefore buried the man without notifying the relatives. This was regarded by the villagers as a disgrace, because it signified the failure of the man to maintain good relations with his family, or to lead a decent enough life that a simple funeral arrangement could be made from his own means.

UPWARD MOBILITY

The social prestige accrued from remitting money and material goods from migration destinations to relatives on Nevis indicates that emigration also provides an important avenue of upward mobility in the island society which has been difficult because of local social contradictions. From the perspective of the tradition of respectability, social mobility is regarded as a consequence of individual hard work and industry, combined with a modest and virtuous lifestyle. The tradition of communal interdependence and sociability, on the other hand, has seen social mobility as a collective process, which must involve the entire community, since it is interwoven in a complex web of interdependent relationships. In Nevisian society this seems to have led to a conviction that social improvement is only possible through the institutions of respectability, which reward individuals, who complete their education successfully, with a higher position in the colonial hierarchy. Those who live and work in the local rural community, on the other hand, are prevented from achieving upward mobility because material wealth derived from success in the local economy of small farming is seen to have occurred at the expense of the rest of the community.[14] Social and economic improvement at an individual level therefore is difficult to achieve, without experiencing social sanctions, within this community.

The difficulty of advancing on the basis of local rural resources is reflected in the fear of "neighbors' grudge" held by many farmers. Several of the Nevisian government's agricultural officers, who were employed to promote new crops and farm techniques among farmers, found it difficult to get any information on how much the farmers produced. One of the Nevisian officials monitoring the agricultural development project at New River complained that the farmers were "not willing to release figures of return" from their fields in the project, while another found that Nevisians wanted to maintain the image that they were merely doing back yard farming, adding "Nevisians are jealous, don't like to see one having more or doing better". One elderly Nevisian woman who had a fine flower garden by her house had planted several "grudge bushes" by the fence which were supposed to turn away the damage which jealous people could do with their eyes, when looking at the garden.

This fear of neighbors' grudge is clearly tied in with beliefs in *obeah*, which have stayed with Nevisians through the centuries. These beliefs mostly concern the fear that envious people will "set *obeah*" against those, who are believed to prosper too much, and misfortune in the form of, for example, illness, death or bad luck in love may be attributed to *obeah*, and seen to be caused by persons who are envious of others who do too well. This again reflects the problem of accepting individual progress and affluence within the local farm economy. This is exemplified by an elderly woman who regularly asks her priest to pray for her, before she sells her produce in the town, not to get her produce sold, but in order that something may happen to those who grudge her because she has produce to sell.

Obeah is believed to work through manipulation of objects owned by the person targeted for *obeah*. Thus a hoe may be "worked on" to ruin the crops of the owner's field, just as a piece of clothing may be used to make the owner of the clothes sick. Money, the means of individual economic advancement, is dangerous if not given out of a good heart, in that it can do harm if it is "dressed". One elderly Nevisian man explained:

> The person, who you would take to be your best friend, would come down and give you a piece of money, and it would be dressed so that the person goes backward. It is always money that is dressed and given, nothing else.

He himself had received compensation for damages done by a neighbor's goats, after having gone to court. He felt, however, that the money was given begrudgingly, and therefore was too dangerous to use for his own purposes such as to purchase food. He therefore gave the money to others and since the money was not "set for them" nothing would happen to them. In other words, material goods and money, sources of wealth and prestige in the local community, which may be subject to *obeah*, can be neutralized by being given away and not used for personal advancement.

Many Nevisians had tried to come to terms with *obeah* by being "saved" and "washed in the blood of the Lamb", believed to offer protection against the Satanic powers of *obeah*. As one woman explained:

> On my husband's death certificate it said cancer, but that was not the real cause of his death. When he was getting really sick, he said to me, "Somebody throw it on us, but you being a Christian didn't get it, I did." But we all prayed for him through his illness, and I believe that he is now with the Lord.

> When he died, a man stayed with me during the night, and in the morning,
> before he went to go home, he went to a cousin, who used to fish with my
> husband, and told him that my husband died. The cousin said, "Yes, I know."
> How did he know? I believe it is because he burned the candle on him, and
> when the candle went out, he knew that my husband had died. He did this
> because he and my husband had their disagreements, when they fished
> together. The cousin didn't like that my husband was the boss on the boat,
> because he owned it.

The act of being saved might just imply receiving a sort of protective coating against all evil. The fact that those who were saved tended to be primarily preoccupied with their own religious well-being rather than with their social and material conditions also meant that they had, in essence, reconciled themselves to their earthly lot and were not concerned about social and economic mobility.[15]

Another solution to the problems presented by *obeah* can be found in migration. Material welfare which derives from external sources, i.e. from migrants who have sent it from abroad, is also freed from the feelings of grudge and the accusations of *obeah*. As one Nevisian stated:

> There is a lot of envy in this world, people are afraid in this country, so they
> leave. When they are outside, people here on Nevis don't know what they
> have, if they knew they would envy them.

The money that is sent back to Nevis usually passes through relatives, who either spend it on the family, or make investments on behalf of the migrant in Nevis:

> Those who are abroad usually send the money that they save there home for
> the family, because it is safer with the family. When it is the family that spends
> the money, those who grudge cannot know whose money it is, and then they
> cannot hurt the person who owns it. Eventually they may know, if the person
> returns to Nevis, but that will be much later. Plenty of people do it this way.

By leaving the island, Nevisians thus are able to escape local grudge and accumulate wealth. It is possible for the migrants and their families to secure a standard of living based on the consumption of Western material goods which will grant them all the external signs of social and economic mobility in Nevisian society. This is achieved without, on the one hand, posing a threat to the common resources of the local community with its many demands for redistribution and sharing, and without, on the other hand, having to fulfill educational requirements or conform to demands for respectability necessary for advancement within island society. Having derived from abroad, this wealth is not perceived to constitute a threat to the limited local resources, but can be displayed freely within the local community.

Most younger Nevisians today claim to know nothing at all about *obeah* and regard it as foolishness which only the old people worry about. This decline in belief in *obeah* has been attributed by islanders to such factors as better education on the island, the installation of electric lights which make people less fearful of jumbies, and the introduction of television which means that old time stories about jumbies and *obeah* are no longer being told at night. It may also, more fundamentally, be related to the fact that Nevisians by extending their context of life to a global community involving the flow of people, money, goods and images have found a means of coming to terms with some of the most fundamental conflicts connected with the local frameworks of sociability and respectability.

THE MIGRATION TRADITION

During the last decades several works have analyzed the migration tradition, or migration culture, which has characterized Nevis, along with most of the West Indies, since the Emancipation (Frucht 1968, 1972; Richardson 1983; Liburd 1984; Mills 1985, 1987). These studies have focused on socioeconomic aspects of migration, such as the social, economic and ecological implications of migration; the nature of the remittances sent to Nevis and their impact on the local society; and the emergence of migration as a way of life.

While my analysis certainly acknowledges the social and economic significance of migration, it has also viewed systems of values and beliefs as important shaping forces in the development of the migration tradition. These systems have been seen to have been informed by two different, and to a certain extent mutually exclusive, parameters for the display and codification of Afro-Caribbean culture in the island society. The importance of migration, from this cultural point of view, is that, by operating outside the confines of the local society, it has provided the islanders with a medium through which they can assert aspects of Afro-Caribbean culture which have not been granted any recognition in the local society. The transnational flow of people, money and goods has become a means of vindicating one of the most socially denigrated aspects of Afro-Caribbean culture: the family based on intergenerational ties of rights and obligations. This is perhaps most clearly demonstrated in the importance attached to the funerals of elders in the family, which have been seen to have played a central role in Afro-Caribbean communities in the New World, including Nevis since the earliest days of slavery.

Migration also has been seen to provide a means whereby the islanders can escape from the stifling double bind of the traditions of respectability and sociability, which have prevented most forms of local social mobility in the colonial society. Furthermore, it has provided a means of circumventing the serious restrictions on upward mobility within the local Afro-Caribbean community posed by the belief in *obeah* which holds that socioeconomic improvement within the peasant community occurs at the expense of others and therefore is the work of the devil. Such beliefs are not uncommon among people who, like the Nevisians, have experienced a long period of exposure to an externally imposed economic system without knowing the basic principles behind it. In his study of plantation workers in South America Taussig has seen similar beliefs to be present among social groups who accept only "use-value practices" because their "understanding of capitalist reason and the praxis that it embodies leads them to conclude that that system is contrary to the laws of nature, evil, and ultimately destructive of the conditions of objective existence" (1980:135, 139). Such an understanding would appear to constitute a fundamental insight upon which Nevisian culture is predicated, in that it developed within a plantation system, characterized by a capitalist reason and praxis which was "ultimately destructive" of the Afro-Caribbean population's "conditions of objective existence". By displacing "exchange-value practices" which are alien and contrary to this culture to migration destinations outside the island society, Nevisians therefore have maintained the "use-value" orientation of their culture. This may help explain why Nevisians have not invested remittances in economic development on Nevis, but have used them almost entirely to increase consumption.

The strengthening of certain aspects of the Afro-Caribbean community which has occurred through migration does not mean that Afro-Caribbean culture is, finally, becoming a predominant force. Its economic foundation has been severely threatened by the loss of labor power suffered from the emigration of young people, just as many of the local cultural and social forms of expressions have disappeared as life in the local villages has been disrupted with the massive outmigration and as the island has become flooded with Western material culture. Vital aspects in Afro-Caribbean culture, therefore, are rapidly disappearing and receding into the history of island society. Ironically, the very aspects which are losing their daily immediacy in local life are now being turned into reified cultural traditions to become socially recognized frameworks within which Nevisians can display their cultural identity and feeling of belonging. This is of particular importance to those migrants who have become settled with their own families in distant areas and thus have become increasingly alienated from their home island and its culture.

NOTES

[1] The concept of the Afro-Caribbean (and Afro-American) family as a network of relatives has been discussed by, among others, Stack 1974; R.T. Smith 1978a, 1978b, 1988; Sutton and Makiesky-Barrow 1977; and Olwig 1985a. It has formed an important supplement to earlier research on the Afro-Caribbean family which tended to examine it from the point of view of household structure or mating relationships. See, for example, Henriques 1953; R.T. Smith 1956; M.G. Smith 1962, 1966; Gonzalez 1969.

² This female bias has led some to characterize the West Indian family as matrifocal (R.T. Smith 1973; Gonzalez 1970).

³ The role of child exchange in West Indian family structure is discussed by Sanford 1975, 1976; Goosen 1972; Olwig 1985a.

⁴ The importance of liming as a male pastime in the Caribbean has been analyzed by Wilson 1971; Tobias 1975; Lieber 1976; Brana-Shute 1976; Abrahams 1983, and Eriksen 1990.

⁵ This discussion is based primarily on fieldwork with Nevisians in St. John, US Virgin Islands, and in Leeds, England. Structured interviews on the migration experience were conducted with 47 Nevisians (20 men and 27 women) on St. John in 1979–80, and with 26 Nevisians (16 women and 10 men) in Leeds in 1987.

⁶ I have discussed the special situation of female migrants in England and the Virgin Islands in Olwig 1992.

⁷ Various aspects of the West Indian migration experience in England have been dealt with in such works as Philpott 1973; Lamur and Speckmann 1975; Watson 1977; Foner 1979; Brock 1986; Carter 1986; Gilroy 1987.

⁸ The West Indian migration to the American Virgin Islands has been discussed by Green 1972; Lewis 1972; Miller and Boyer 1982, and Olwig 1985a.

⁹ The failure of Nevisians to join the already existing churches in the American Virgin Islands is also due to the fact that the major denominations there are the Moravian and the Lutheran Churches which are unknown on Nevis. Some of the earliest immigrants to Nevis, however, joined the Moravian Church and have become active members of it. As more migrants arrived, an Anglican and a Methodist church were established on St. John. While a number of Nevisians are active in these churches, most have joined newer fundamentalist denominations. This, of course, finds a parallel in recent religious developments on Nevis.

¹⁰ The exchange rate of the Eastern Caribbean dollar is c. EC $2.60 dollars to US $1.00.

¹¹ In an insightful analysis of fashion on Trinidad, Miller has argued that the fashion directed toward the home is conformist and concerned with respectability, whereas fashion that is outward-directed is more individualistic and concerned with reputation (1990).

¹² The cultural significance of the consumption of material goods has recently become a subject of increasing interest on the part of anthropologists. See, for example, the collection of articles *The Social Life of Things* ed. Appadurai 1988[1986] and the special issue of *Culture and History* on "Consumption", vol. 7, 1990.

¹³ Richardson (1983:53) estimated that, during the early 1980s, a funeral involving relatives from the Virgin Islands cost c. EC $600, whereas one involving relatives in the UK might cost upwards of EC $2000. The great difference is due to the high cost of keeping the dead under refrigeration until relatives are able to return.

¹⁴ This is related to the image of limited good, which is found in many peasant societies (Foster 1965).

¹⁵ Most of the fundamentalist churches accepted *obeah* as the evil workings of the devil. One local minister thus expressed the opinion that it was possible to work with evil spirits, as this was stated in the Bible, and he thought, for example, that the sinking of the passenger boat *Christena* in August 1970 was caused by *obeah*, which had been intended only for the captain and the crew, but which, in fact, killed more than 200 Nevisians.

CHAPTER EIGHT

Global Culture, Island Identity

A central theme which has emerged in this historical anthropological analysis of the Afro-Caribbean community of Nevis has been the global nature of its culture. This was seen to involve the appropriation of external, or foreign, institutions or traditions as frameworks for the display of locally developed contexts of life. As the Afro-Caribbean community has become removed from localized, rural life on Nevis, many aspects of Nevisian village culture have receded into the past and become cultural forms which can be employed to display cultural identity focused on Nevis. During the last few decades Nevisians at home and abroad have celebrated "folk" or "ethnic" culture which formerly was an integral part of Afro-Caribbean life on the island. As examples of this institutionalization of culture this chapter discusses two annual cultural festivals in which Nevisians are active participants, the Leeds carnival in England and Culturama on Nevis, and the fairly recent cultural tradition of family reunions which began among second generation Nevisians in the United States. The reification of a culture of the past, which these cultural celebrations represent, is not a unique phenomenon. It can be seen to be part of a more general interest in cultural identity, ethnicity and roots which has emerged as people look for local identities in a world which is increasingly experienced as a global ecumene.

The celebration of Nevis culture, not surprisingly, first began among Nevisians abroad. Though most Nevisian migrants experience a lessening of social and economic ties to their home island, as they settle abroad and their parents on Nevis die, Nevis nevertheless has remained an important source of cultural identification for most of them. Indeed it seems that as the migrants lose their "natural" ties to Nevis, they try to strengthen the cultural ties. And as cultural belonging turns into cultural heritage and ethnicity, Nevisians have begun to display it. They have here joined forces with other émigré West Indians, and the West Indian carnival has become an institutional framework within which West Indian cultural identity has been asserted, and maintained, abroad. Since the 1960s, a number of West Indian carnivals have appeared in England, USA and Canada, where there are sizable West Indian communities. The largest and best known are the Brooklyn carnival, the London carnival and the Caribana, held in Toronto.

The Brooklyn carnival grew out of carnival festivities which began in Harlem during the 1920s. The early celebrations were mainly private dances, but in 1947

PLATE 10   *Caribbean Women's Dramatic Society perform "The Journey to England"*
written by Gertrude Paul, originally from St. Kitts. West Indian Centre,
Leeds. Photo, Karen Fog Olwig, 7 July, 1987.

Trinidadian immigrants organized a street carnival in Harlem on Labor Day, which also drew participants from other West Indian islands. This carnival was stopped by the city authorities after a disturbance in 1964, but in 1969 permission was granted to hold a carnival in Brooklyn, which by then had a large community of West Indians. It has been held in Brooklyn every Labor Day weekend since then and attracts as many as two million people. Even though this festival has remained basically peaceful, the street parade is heavily guarded by armed policemen (Hill and Abramson 1979; Kasinitz and Freidenberg-Herbstein 1987; Nunley 1988).

Caribana in Toronto started in 1968 and was an outgrowth of an ethnic parade organized in connection with the celebration of the Canadian Centennial in 1967. Local authorities have continued to support the carnival, which is held every year during the first weekend of August and draws about half a million people (Nunley 1988).

The London carnival also emerged from a multiethnic cultural festival, but this event was organized privately by a local community leader of mixed ethnic origin who saw in it "a revival of the Notting Hill Annual Fayre that had been traditionally held in the area until it was stopped at the turn of the present century" (Cohen 1982:25). At the first carnival, which was held in 1966, one West Indian steel band appeared in the procession. Within a few years West Indian participation grew, and during the 1970s the carnival became a West Indian festival and its association with old English traditions was dropped. Insofar, however, as West Indians have carried on medieval festival traditions within their own carnival tradition, it might be more correct to state that the Notting Hill Carnival also represents an unintended renewal of European tradition, rather than the substitution of a foreign tradition. This festival has been in conflict with the authorities since its inception. The mayor, thus, withdrew his promised support of the first carnival apparently because he feared that political agitators were involved. While that carnival was peaceful, several later carnivals have witnessed violent struggles between participants and police, as tensions between the Black community and the local authorities have increased. The carnival which is held during the last weekend in August, a British bank holiday, has remained a popular festival, however, and it attracts about half a million people (Cohen 1982; Nunley 1988).

Nevisians have participated in these festivals, either individually or through Nevisian organizations formed abroad. At the Caribana, for example, different troupes in the parade are organized by island groups, including one from St. Kitts-Nevis (Nunley 1988:176). This event is not only attended by West Indians in Canada, but West Indians, including Nevisians, travel individually and in chartered buses to Toronto in order to attend it. The one festival, which Nevisians have been the most active in organizing, and which is the most influenced by Nevisian culture, is the carnival celebrated since 1967 in Leeds, which holds one of the largest communities of people from Nevis and St. Kitts.

LEEDS CARNIVAL

During the 1950s and early 1960s, several hundred Nevisians moved to Leeds in Northern England. After the institution of the immigration act of 1962, further immigration to England virtually ceased, and when I did fieldwork in Chapeltown during the late 1980s, second and third generation West Indians outnumbered the original migrants. The West Indians had settled in Chapeltown, a formerly affluent area with many spacious houses that could be subdivided and rented as bed-sits to newcomers who had little choice about where to live. As a result of this overcrowding and exploitation, the houses deteriorated even to the point that many had to be abandoned. While Chapeltown still contains some boarded-up houses, many streets have now been subject to urban renewal and today contain modern flats and terraced houses that can be rented or purchased at reasonable rates.

Many Nevisians did not wait for urban renewal to get a home on their own, but purchased houses as early as possible, no matter how run-down they might be, and renovated the buildings themselves. This, to them, was the only way in which they would be able to lead the kind of life that they desired in a society, where they were unwanted in the public arenas of the pubs and streets, and where rented housing was of miserable quality. Many Nevisians therefore acquired houses, even though this meant great sacrifices with husbands working overtime and wives caring for children during the day and working the evening or night shift. But the reward was, for the men, getting a place, albeit within the home, where they could associate with other West Indians the way they wanted to, playing calypso, having domino games and drinking; and for the women, reconstructing a domestic space of their own.[1] This relocation of male activities to the home did not mean the final "domestication" of the West Indian man, however. As the Nevisians became more settled in Leeds they began to create more public spaces of social life.

They were aided in this by the presence of a strong and distinct West Indian community in Leeds, which, besides the large Nevisian component, also includes a great number of Kitticians as well as a fair number of Jamaicans and Barbadians.[2] On the basis of informal gatherings in private homes some of the West Indians formed social ties which crosscut island affiliation and organized the United Caribbean Association. During the late 1950s and 1960s, this organization held Saturday schools for West Indian born children of migrants, many of whom were brought to Britain a number of years after the arrival of their parents, in order to prepare them for the entrance examination which they had to take before being placed in the English schools. The Saturday school was later expanded and offered classes for adults who wished to improve their education. The United Caribbean Association also held dances on holidays such as Easter, Whitsun Tide, August bank holiday and they held a Christmas party, where they gave presents to the children. They had great success with their ladies' night, where the women were treated to dinner and given a present. Later the organization was active in the construction of the West Indian Centre, a social club for West Indians opened in 1982, which has become the center of West Indian life in Leeds.

During the first decade abroad most of the West Indian community seemed preoccupied with establishing an acceptable life within English society by adapting to English cultural norms, including speech patterns. During the late 1960s, however, a few West Indians became interested in organizing a carnival, which would not just be a social and cultural event for the West Indians, but also a public festival where they could display their own culture and share it with other people. The idea of holding a carnival was conceived by a Nevisian, Arthur France, who had been fascinated with the costumes, dances and music, which he had seen on Nevis during his childhood. He had not been able to join in the fun due to a strict religious upbringing within the culture of respectability, but saw in England an opportunity not just to participate in this revelry but to also introduce it to the English. He approached the United Caribbean Association in order to gain their support, but discovered that many members of the association were rather embarrassed by the idea of holding a carnival. While they had been eager to improve the situation of West Indians in British society through education and to hold such respectable functions as formal dances and ladies' nights, they were hesitant to organize an event where they would take to the streets in costumes, dancing, playing music and drinking. Arthur France, therefore, organized the first carnival in 1967 largely with the assistance of African and Trinidadian students at Leeds University. It was held during the last weekend of August, which is a bank holiday.

The main events at the carnival were a queen show, where women appeared in fancy and elaborate costumes; a calypso competition; a steel band competition; and a road parade of troupes who competed for the best costumes. The organizers were careful to make the carnival a respectable event, which would be acceptable to the West Indian community and make a favorable impression in British society. The parade, therefore, went from the heart of the West Indian community in Chapeltown to the town hall in the city center, where prizes were awarded and a ball held. Unlike the London carnival, the Leeds carnival was organized in collaboration with local authorities. The police, though present, maintained a low profile. Furthermore the Trinidadian High Commission showed a great deal of interest in the carnival and dignified it with the presence of a representative. Leeds carnival became a great success, and it has remained a joyful, essentially peaceful yearly festival since then. When the London carnival, which is held during the same weekend, began to be institutionalized as a West Indian festival, the Leeds carnival had to give up the calypso competition, since there were not enough bands to sustain two competitions at the same time. Other features have been added, however, such as a prince and princess competition, a junior version of the queen show. After a few years, the carnival ceased to take place in the center of Leeds, but stayed in the Chapeltown area, and after the erection of the West Indian Centre, the shows and balls have been held there. Leeds carnival, today, attracts as many as 40,000 people.[3]

To a certain extent the Leeds carnival most of all resembles a Trinidadian carnival. The fantastic and intricate costumes made out of shiny and spectacular materials are clearly inspired by those designed for the carnival on Trinidad, and Trinidadians have often been involved in the making of costumes for the Leeds carnival. The steel bands are likewise of Trinidadian origin. This is in keeping with the fact that Trinidad is the spiritual heart of modern West Indian Carnival, insofar as Trinidadian traditions and Trinidadian Calypsonians dominate the carnivals held in the Caribbean.

The Leeds carnival, however, also has close ties with the old Christmas sports which developed on Nevis and St. Kitts. The parade thus also includes groups of people (troupes) and individuals, who are dressed up in costumes and dance to music, very much within the tradition of the sports. This can be seen, for example, in the popularity of troupes which are dressed up as (American) Indians, a costume which was also popular in the islands. At the very first carnival a troupe called "Shionina Indians" organized by Arthur France won first prize, and at the carnival that I attended in 1988 the largest troupe, which had more than 100 participants and which won first prize for best costumes, was called "Fancy Indians". It was organized by two women from St. Kitts, who had used the Indian theme several times before and regarded their participation in the Leeds carnival as a "natural" continuation of what they had done on their home island.

Another type of costume, which has deep roots on Nevis and St. Kitts and which dates back to at least the nineteenth century, is that worn by the masqueraders. This troupe is organized by a Nevisian, who is nicknamed Captain in the West Indian community because the leader of a masquerade troupe is called a captain. As in Nevis and St. Kitts the masqueraders are dressed in long-sleeved shirts, trousers with short aprons, and capes, decorated with small mirrors, palettes, colorful ribbons and bells. On the head they wear peacock feathers, and they are equipped with tomahawks. The members of the troupe dance accompanied by a fife, kettle drum and big drum, partly in various patterns which they call the quadrille, partly in individual "wild" dancing where they throw the tomahawks in the air, chase each other and dance in a more forceful way. Though Captain interprets the masquerade as being of African origin, masquerading and some of the dance steps can also be traced to early British customs on the island, and the costume bears some resemblance to mummers' costumes used in Britain. This group has participated in the parade since the first carnival, and it has attracted many young people of Nevisian and Kittician heritage, who like the vigorous, frightening dancing to the fife and drum. The group is also popular with those who come to watch the parade, and it was awarded second prize at the carnival in 1988.

Another aspect of the parade which is known from Nevis and St. Kitts is "*neaga* business", individuals dressed up in costumes involving the reversal of gender and social roles. This role reversal was also apparent in the Christmas troupes described by Antonia Williams, where men were dressed in "European skirt and apron" (see Chapter Five). In 1988 one of the male paraders was dressed as a woman and was wearing high heeled shoes and nylon stockings, as well as a snugly fitting dress which revealed a rather shapely figure. He carried a handbag and flirted outrageously with any man he could lay his hands on. Another individual was a man dressed as a king in a long red velvet costume, equipped with a crown and scepter. He walked in a slow, dignified manner, and bestowed benign greetings on his people, the crowds of people who had gathered to watch the parade. These included, besides West Indians, many British people who had gone to Chapeltown to watch the parade, as well as a great number of Asian residents in Chapeltown, who watched the parade with an apparent mixture of amusement and bewilderment.[4]

The carnival is not just a repetition of traditions known from the West Indies. As was the case on Nevis, it is characteristic of the sports, and the carnival, that new cultural elements are incorporated into the festivities both as new frameworks of cultural expression, and as new forms of commentary on contemporary issues. This is the case in Leeds, in particular as the younger generations born in England have become involved in carnival.[5] The Leeds carnival of 1988 thus featured an African troupe, organized by a youth club, which paid homage to Nelson and Winnie Mandela. This youth club is patronized by second and third generation West Indians, who generally speaking do not identify strongly with the West Indies, but rather regard themselves as Black British. This identity involves a strong political statement. Thus it refers to all non-White residents of Great Britain, including Asians and Africans, who are seen to share political and economic oppression in British society, as witnessed by their relatively poor education and high unemployment rates. This is quite apparent in Chapeltown, where unemployment in the late 1980s was as high as 40% for Afro-Caribbean men between 20–24 years of age (Lennard 1988:18). For these youngsters, carnival therefore was not just a time to cultivate cultural roots, but also a time to point to the need for a struggle to improve the situation of Black people, whether in England or South Africa.

The participants in the parade can be seen to work within the tradition of the sports and carnival, by combining old troupes and costumes with new themes. The parade itself has displayed a similar combination of old and new patterns. The fact that the parade has not been directed toward the West Indian community alone, but more generally towards the English society, of which the West Indians form a part, can be regarded as a continuation of old traditions. Just as the participants in the

Christmas festivities in the West Indies took their sports from the villages to the estate houses of the upper class, the first parades of the Leeds carnival began in the heart of the West Indian community in Chapeltown and went to the center of Leeds, ending at the Town Hall. In this way, the West Indians can be seen to have sought recognition of their community and culture within English society by taking their parade right to the center of the city. This involvement of British society in the carnival has continued even after it has ceased to take place in the town hall, in that special invitations for the main events such as the queen show are sent to such English dignitaries as the Lord Mayor and the head of police, as well as to the leaders of West Indian organizations in the local community. The carnival committee also seeks to involve local institutions in the West Indian community in the organization of troupes, such as community centers and churches, and in 1988, one of the Anglican Churches in the Chapeltown area sponsored a queen and troupe.[6]

During recent years the parade has reflected the West Indians' increasing concern with their native heritage and their rights as an ethnic minority. It now takes a circular route around the main section of Chapeltown, blocking traffic on some of Leeds' main traffic arteries in the process, thereby demarcating the West Indian community *vis-à-vis* the rest of the city. In this circumscription of their local community, West Indians may at the same time be following old traditions carried out within an English framework. Thus annual perambulations of parish boundaries in order to establish the social and economic rights of local populations are known from English rural society and was among the English traditions which were brought to the West Indies by the early English settlers. Nevisian holiday traditions, recorded by Abrahams in the 1960s often made a point of demarcating village boundaries, and Christmas sports involved the spatial circumscription of the island. The English authorities who allowed the parade and the English policemen who seemed to go out of their way to mingle with the crowd and to make the parade a success may be granting the West Indians a form of recognition which is the outcome of parallel British and Caribbean tradition.

Even though the Leeds carnival can be seen to have European roots, as far as some of its formal aspects are concerned, this is, generally speaking, not acknowledged by its participants. As one Nevisian explained:

> The English brought just working positions to the West Indies, no culture. They showed us how to work, what they could do. But we had to make the culture for ourselves.

The carnival and the sports, quite naturally, are associated with the culture and heritage of the West Indian community and seen as an expression of "Westindianness", which dates back to slavery and Africa. For the older generation of Nevisians, this culture has provided a sense of continuity despite the uprooting from their home island that they have experienced. One first generation Nevisian who is active in the carnival stated:

> The masquerade was not in this country, but was brought here by people from the West Indies, just as it was brought to the West Indies from Africa by old time people. They took it there as a culture, and the young ones picked it up, and they continued it, as they grew up and passed it on to the younger ones. In this way the masquerade goes by generation all the time.

To the younger, second generation, the sense of continuity inherent in the sports of the carnival is more directed towards the contemporary situation of Black people and the feeling of togetherness they should share. One young woman whose parents came from Nevis and St. Kitts explained:

> Masquerade is a cultural dance, it runs in the Caribbean, and Black people do it. It is part of where our parents came from. They did things together, and it is like Blacks are one big family when we do it, and this is the way it should be all the time.

In this association of carnival with Black togetherness, the woman, in fact, pointed to one of the most important results of the Leeds carnival. Every year thousands of West Indians, not just from Leeds but also from West Indian communities in other cities, meet in Chapeltown to celebrate carnival together. Some of them come in troupes or in music groups which participate in the parade, others just come to see friends and enjoy the West Indian music, dance and food. The fact that a number of carnivals have been organized in other major West Indian communities in England since the Leeds carnival began in 1967 has led to the creation of a carnival "circuit" which can sustain intercommunity efforts.

If the large-scale emigration which brought Nevisians and other West Indians to England and North America could be regarded as an escape from the social and economic marginality which was associated with village life, this very marginality has given rise to a form of cultural creativity which, today, makes this culture an important source of identity. Furthermore, while the Afro-Caribbean culture of the past tended to be displayed within institutions or traditions associated with the dominant English colonial power, today, the totality of cultural expression is regarded as Afro-Caribbean, if not African, as the West Indies seek to establish their own cultural heritage within Western societies.

CULTURAMA

The emergence of cultural festivals as acceptable institutional frameworks within which to display cultural identity and roots has not gone unnoticed on Nevis, and in 1974 Nevis developed its own festival in the form of Culturama. Culturama was started through the efforts of a group of young Nevisians, most of whom had been abroad in connection with further education and training. One of them, Calvin (Cabo) Howell, returned to Nevis in 1970 from St. Thomas and Canada and helped reorganize the then dormant Nevisian drama group as the Nevis Dramatic and Cultural Society. The group of people who worked with Calvin Howell found that many of the traditional customs, such as the Christmas sports, had all but died out and felt a need for a cultural revival on the island. The government on St. Kitts in 1971 had instituted a national carnival at Christmas, but Nevisians boycotted it for political reasons. Nevis lacked a formal framework of its own within which cultural activities of the past could be resuscitated and preserved. As the presidential message in the *Culturama Magazine* of 1977 noted:

> In many Caribbean Islands, much of the culture is no longer enjoyed by the locals. Instead, it is geared towards entertaining the many tourists on our shores. Hence, the youths do not have a chance to look into the past and see what their great-grand parents used to enjoy, what was "their own". There is now a total lack of cultural awareness in our midst; we have no values, nothing to call "our own" any more.
>
> It was because of this "lack of cultural awareness" that the idea of Culturama was born. [...] Sure, we do want all to enjoy Culturama, but at the same time, we would still like to see people become aware of this culture and develop a sense of responsibility in reviving a dying interest in our traditional folk art, and customs (Richards 1977:4).

The first Culturama was held in 1974 during the weekend of August Monday, the holiday celebrating Emancipation of the slaves. It was such a success that it became an annual festival. The main features of Culturama are the calypso show; the queen talent show where Miss Culturama is crowned among young women who display their talent in, for example, singing, recitation or dancing, while wearing an appropriate costume, and model a gown; food sales, troupes and bands (including the old Christmas sports); an arts and crafts display; a local recipe competition; a drama, and school song competition. The guiding principle behind these activities is that they must portray "traditional" Nevisian culture. At the food sale, the canned juices and sodas, that many Nevisians ordinarily relish, must give way to drinks made out of local juices and roots; music is supposed to be dominated by string bands and calypsos, rather than brass bands and electronic disco rhythms; and the competitors for the queen title must wear costumes made out of natural materials such as cotton, coconut fibers or shells, not synthetic fabrics or shiny materials. At the Culturama that I attended in 1984, a contestant for the queen title, appearing as a potter from Newcastle dressed in old-fashioned peasant clothing and entering the stage through a little thatched hut, was better received than one portraying a fisherman's daughter in a colorful carnival-like costume filled with glitter and tinsel.

In accordance with the global, inclusive character of Afro-Caribbean culture most of the elements which make up the cultural traditions, celebrated at Culturama as authentic Nevis culture, can be seen to have come to the island from the outside. Certain aspects of Nevisian culture such as the big drum or the masquerade dancers date several centuries back to the early days of slavery. Others, however, have appeared in fairly recent times, and were just barely part of the life of the great-grandparents of the present generation of youngsters. As the Nevisian Joyah Sutton has noted in her BA Thesis on Culturama, string band music, which today accompanies most of the troupes and sports, derives from Latin America and probably came to Nevis via returnee migrants who had worked in Panama and Cuba during the early part of this century. The calypso, in its present form, is Trinidadian and probably also came via returning migrants during this century. The troupes which perform at carnival include fairly recent themes, such as the "The Red Cross", where the participants are dressed as soldiers, doctors and nurses and enact war scenes using texts and songs from English school books brought to the island during the 1930s (Sutton 1986:19, 28, 31–32).

That which makes culture traditional and authentic is not so much its long history on the island or its lack of any external cultural influence. Rather culture seems to become Nevisian, when Nevisians have appropriated it and made it "their own" by imbuing it with their "own values". While I would argue that much of the more recent material and popular culture brought to Nevis from the outside is in the process of being made Nevisian, this is not apparent to present-day Nevisians, and therefore the more recent cultural expressions are not yet acceptable at Culturama. This rejection is not just a reaction against the fact that they still have only been partially incorporated into Nevisian culture. It also reflects a creation through Culturama of Nevis culture which is seen as distinctly different from Western culture as well as the culture that is found on other West Indian islands, such as Trinidad where the popular carnival received its modern form.

Despite the fact that Culturama seeks to define a particularly Nevisian cultural space, the people behind Culturama are not hostile to cultural performances from other West Indian islands. Culturama usually features guest appearances on the part of calypsonians from other islands such as The Mighty Sparrow from Trinidad as well as special shows such as the winners of the Best Village Competition on Trinidad who performed at Culturama in 1984. Nevertheless, the organizers of Culturama clearly see its primary purpose to be that of promoting culture unique to Nevis. In this way Culturama may become an important institution through which a national Nevisian culture can be established, which the present-day residents in the island society can call their own. Furthermore, Culturama is regarded as an important means by which the Nevisians abroad can keep in touch with their home island and maintain a cultural identity of their own.

This dual purpose merges today for many educated middle-class Nevisians, for whom emigration and/or return migration always seems a possibility. Most of them have been off the island in connection with their further education and may return only temporarily to Nevis in order to fulfill the work requirements attached to the government stipends which have funded their education. Those who work abroad usually keep close ties with the island society in order to leave open the possibility of returning to positions in civil service or business later on. For the educated, the possibility of leaving Nevis or returning to the island therefore is always present. Culturama has, to a great extent, been the creation of this transient group of people and several in the original group behind Culturama have emigrated from the island. To a certain extent, Culturama celebrates the Nevis which may be associated with the childhood of this group of people, before the undoing of village life and the drastic influx of Western material goods and tourism. This is reflected in essays in the *Culturama Magazine* such as "Nevis is", which clearly expresses the nostalgic theme in the Culturama celebrations. It begins:

> The writings of visitors to Nevis usually claim that the island is quiet, quaint and friendly. Those descriptions of the island may be true, but Nevis is much more, especially to Nevisians at home or abroad. To all of us there is a special something about Nevis—call it sentiment, love, feeling, or maybe it is just that our navel strings are there.
>
> Nevis is the games we played in the villages as young boys and girls—worksmart, green bush, hoop, etc. But Nevis is much more. Nevis is the stories about jumbiees, jack-o-lanterns, obeah, and of course Gingerland and Eden Brown. But Nevis is much more. Nevis is those scare o-yea! o-yea that made the children scrunch-up, as the death of a villager was announced during the wee hours of the night. But Nevis is much more. It is the mule cart, and the first car. It is also the Lady who when she saw the first plane ran and shouted that God had sent a big bird to eat the people up. But Nevis is much more. Nevis is those village weddings when almost everyone carried real or imitation pampee to throw at the crowds; and when almost everyone had a long toast for the newlyweds. But Nevis is much more (Browne 1981:14).

Culturama cannot, however, be reduced to nostalgia for the past. Calypso singers, in particular, have acted as critics of cultural conditions on the island, as evidenced by The Mighty Chevy, whose calypso "Let Them Know" appealed for more cultural education of the young generation and criticized the islanders' failure to recognize their African heritage (The Mighty Chevy 1981:18–19).[7] When in 1982 the obligation to sing about only cultural matters was removed, the calypsonians also began to deal with more political and economic matters. Most noteworthy is the calypsonian Dis and Dat, whose song "Freedom" was written in response to a government statement to the effect that St. Kitts-Nevis is the freest nation in the world. This song was censored by the government and therefore not played on the public radio station, when it covered the calypso competition.[8] A similar fate has befallen several other songs that he has written (Sutton 1986:22–23, 46). Nevertheless, by inviting such calypsonians to present their songs on stage, the organizers have attempted to incorporate social criticism into the festival.

The desire to make Culturama a platform for contemporary issues can also be seen in several articles in *Culturama Magazine*. One article "The Value of Vegetables in the Diet" thus contains a rather lengthy discussion of the nutritional value of local vegetables and suggests various new ways in which to use them (Amory-Manners 1984:n.p.). In a similar vein, the article "The Dilemma of Culturama" by one of the key organizers of the festival for several years, sees the main aim of Culturama to be that of making people "appreciate the things which are indigenous to us" such as local foods and music, and regards the festival as a failure as long as a dance with a brass band will be "jam packed", while one with a string band will be poorly attended (Richards 1984). Another article discusses the cultural aspect of development, criticizing politicans in "developing countries" for accepting uncritically a Western development strategy without examining its cultural implications (Howell 1982).

An important aim of Culturama may be the creation of greater cultural awareness and recognition of local resources and their development potential. For most Nevisians, who live in a transnational community which is closely integrated into the modern Western world, accepting the Afro-Caribbean village culture as a source of cultural identity is a far cry from adopting this village culture as a means of livelihood and social identity. The fact that one of the most famous talent shows was based on a portrayal of illegal rum making in the bush thus has not made it more legal to produce rum. The acceptance of rum distilling as a cultural activity to display on the stage rather reflects the fact that it is less common today and therefore receding into the past—ready to be included in the island's cultural heritage.

The significance of Culturama as a means of establishing a national cultural identity is apparent in the emphasis that the organizers have attached to the procurement of a building complex, where the main activities of Culturama can be held. An important dimension of this goal was realized when the open air stage within a fenced-in area was completed by the time Culturama celebrated its tenth anniversary in 1984. By creating a new setting for Nevis culture, Culturama has played a major role both in the recognition and redefinition of Nevisian culture as folk art, which can be presented on the stage. At the Culturama in 1984, the old sports were mainly performed on the stage for an audience, rather than on the road, where they traditionally took place.

This transformation of the old village culture to folk art and a medium for cultural identity, which has occurred under the auspices of Culturama, may be one reason why the festival is so popular among Nevisian migrants. Émigré Nevisians, especially in the Virgin Islands and North America, have constituted some of the main supporters of Culturama from its very inception. Hundreds of Nevisians travel to Culturama every year, and they have sponsored several of the events either through individual contributions or through organizations that Nevisians have formed abroad to promote Nevisian interests, such as "Nevisians in America", "Nevisian Benevolent Society" on St. Thomas, or "Nevisian Cultural Association" on St. Croix. Culturama has become an important means by which migrants can maintain their West Indian heritage, even though they have lost touch with the Afro-Caribbean culture associated with village life in Nevis.

In the Virgin Islands, Nevisian migrants have also actively promoted Culturama in order to attract more visitors to the festival, not just fellow Nevisians, but also other West Indians, particularly Virgin Islanders, who are beginning to show a greater interest in their Afro-Caribbean roots. Since the Virgin Islands have been heavily Americanized after 75 years of American rule and several decades of American mass tourism, many of the native Virgin Islanders have become interested in the West Indian culture of those islands which have been less exposed to influence from the United States. Some of them have therefore visited Culturama, and similar cultural festivals on the former British islands, often accompanied by Nevisian friends who are going home. In this way Culturama has become a sort of cultural preserve for other islanders as well.

Even though the émigré Nevisians return home to celebrate traditional Afro-Caribbean culture, the clothing which they wear and the amount of money which they spend at the festival does not exactly remind one of village life on Nevis. Many visiting Nevisians wear outlandish outfits and walk around with cameras, in a sense behaving like tourists who have arrived in a foreign place. This heightens the feeling that what is being celebrated is a culture which belongs to a distant past and which is merely being put on display for people to watch, not to share. This may, indeed, increasingly be the situation for some visitors, and Culturama has been patronized by a number of second and third generation Nevisians, who have no close family on Nevis. For them Nevis is mainly the island in the Caribbean where they can find their cultural roots outside the country in which they have lived their entire lives.

FAMILY REUNIONS

While most Nevisians in the Virgin Islands and England still have close ties to their home island through family and friends there, this is no longer true for some of the Nevisians, or descendants of Nevisians, in the United States. One of the old, established Nevisian communities, where personal contact with the island of Nevis has been lost, as far as the majority of the population is concerned, is that in New Haven, Connecticut.[9] Most of the Nevisians arrived in New Haven during the first decades of this century, before 1924 when the United States instituted an act which severely limited further immigration to the United States (Richardson 1983:134–35). In 1930, the community of West Indian immigrants constituted c. 400, most of whom were Nevisian (Warner 1969[1940]:124). Many found work at Yale University, which had a tradition of "Negro service" (Warner 1969[1940]:246; Lanker 1989:65) and settled in the inner city close to the university. They attended St. Luke's Episcopal Church nearby, which quickly became dominated by the West Indian immigrants. The Nevisians formed an exclusively Nevisian club (Warner 1969[1940]: 194), but the Antillean Friendly Association, which was also started by a Nevisian and which was open for all West Indians, became the primary West Indian organization in the city. It purchased a building, where meetings and various social events could be held.[10]

In general the Nevisian immigrants and their descendants in New Haven have been highly successful socially and economically and today can be described as solid middle-class Americans. According to a recent study of the Nevisian community in New Haven, more than half have received higher education, and most have white-collar jobs working in the teaching profession, health sector, public administration or business (Rogers 1987:52–53). Most Nevisians have acquired their own house, initially in the inner city area around Yale, later moving to the suburbs. Despite "Americanization", however, Nevisian emigrants have remained in touch with the Nevisian community through the Antillean Friendly Society as well as St. Luke's Episcopal Church. In 1987, when I visited the Nevisian community in New Haven, the Antillean Friendly Society was busy preparing the annual Christmas party for children, and St. Luke's Episcopal Church, which remained strongly "West Indian" and had a Barbadian rector, was celebrating the dedication of a new pipe organ.[11]

While St. Luke's Episcopal Church and the Antillean Friendly Society have been important focal points in the Nevisian community of New Haven, making the American born of the younger generations aware of their West Indian background, most of them had no direct contact with Nevis. As the older generation of original immigrants had died, those who knew the island and the family there had disappeared. The second generation, who had grown up in the United States and inter-married with Black Americans, was only distantly related to remaining relatives on Nevis and not able to maintain the ties to Nevis on a personal basis. This did not mean that they were not interested in their Nevisian heritage, and when I was introduced at St. Luke's Church as an anthropologist who was interested in Nevis and the culture of the Nevisian community in New Haven, I was met with enthusiastic applause.

During the early 1970s, as the second generation Nevisians were beginning to realize that they had lost their family relationship to Nevis, they began to create what they termed "clans", family institutions which consisted of all the descendants of a known, named ancestor on Nevis. These clans held family reunions and helped maintain the Nevisian heritage of the members. A number of clans, which hold annual or biannual reunions, have now been organized around major Nevis families. The Huggins family, for example, decided to organize a family reunion, when relatives scattered in different areas of the United States congregated in New Haven at the funeral of an elderly aunt, and in August 1974, 184 Huggins relatives met at the Holiday Inn in New Haven for a three day weekend together.[12] One of the clan members had researched the family history by consulting church records on Nevis, and this was presented at the clan dinner where members appeared in long evening dresses and suits (The Huggins Cousins 1974:18). According to this history, the Huggins clan can trace its family tree to a freed slave, who was baptized at St. John's Anglican Church on Nevis in 1836, and who in 1974 was survived by 33 great-grandchildren, 86 great-great-grandchildren, 93 great-great-great-grandchildren and 10 great-great-great-great-grandchildren (Motley n.d.).[13] This clan was also, although half in jest, equipped with a coat of arms, when one of the organizers of the reunion found a Huggins coat of arms in a book at the New Haven library.

The family reunions, held mostly in various parts of the United States, have in and of themselves been a great success. As one second generation Nevisian explained:

> Family reunions are important in order that later generations like my son's will get a better understanding of who they are—their West Indian heritage, from where they came, and who their relatives are.

The two reunions, which have taken place on Nevis in 1976 and 1984, both at the time of Culturama, have been particularly important for the Huggins clan. At the very first New Haven reunion, it was decided that the clan should embark on a "pilgrimage home" in order to find "its roots", and in 1976, more than 100 pilgrims, members of the Huggins clan and some Nevisian friends, travelled to Nevis. Besides the Culturama activities, which would offer a taste of the local culture, the program also included Sunday service at St. John's Parish Church, where members of the clan presented a commemorative plaque with individual family name plates to the Church.

The overwhelming feeling of being in the native land of their parents or grandparents and of experiencing a rather different sort of "Westindianness" than expected was recalled at the 1979 reunion of the Huggins Clan. Among the noteworthy memories were the fabulous banquet, where the native cuisine consisted of "chicken necks and peas and carrots"; the dance after dinner accompanied to steel band music where some clan members did "a version of the Quadrille dance"; the ordering of a "screwdriver" at a bar, which led the bartender to produce a "carpenter's screwdriver"; the queen show, where "they asked" two clan members to "help judge de queen" and where the pilgrims "learned to use inverted chairs as umbrellas"; and the searching for roots, which began after the service at St. John's Parish Church, where the Huggins clan "walked through the ancient grave yard, spoke with passersby and engaged drivers to help track down family leads. Huggins covered the entire island in search of roots" (*Clan Huggins Reunion, 5 Years Later* 1979). The world of the sophisticated urban second and third generation Nevisian Americans was clearly quite different from that of the Nevisians in Nevis, where they had come to look for their roots.

Most of the American born Nevisians realize that they are basically Black Americans and that they would never find life on Nevis attractive. One second generation Nevisian thus found that it was great to visit Nevis with the clan, but boring to go there alone:

> It was very touching, after hearing about Nevis for so many years, to be there. It was sentimental to be in the place where my father and mother were born. I liked the quietness, I liked seeing where my family was born, just being there was special—where the family roots are from. I later visited Nevis over a long weekend on the way back from Barbados. I then thought that Nevis was extremely quiet. I stayed at the hotel all by myself, and I got scared, thinking that if something happened, nobody would hear me. But I also realized that Nevis was so quiet, nothing would happen, and that this was an American fear. [...] I didn't like being there on my own so much—it is too quiet. It is better with the clan.

Some of them also realize that their cultivation of Nevis roots is very much part of their being Americans, who feel the need to find their roots outside of the United States. American society in the 1970s was characterized by an interest in ethnic heritage and roots (Lowenthal 1985). Among the Afro-American segment of the population some went to Africa, as reflected in Alexander Haley's bestseller *Roots* (1977), which formed the basis for an enormously popular television program.[14] This did not mean, however, that Black Americans found it easy to identify with Africa, and for some the West Indies provided a viable alternative. One third generation Nevisian explained the importance of the Nevisian heritage in this light:

> Many Americans don't have their own identity associated with a culture. Black Americans don't necessarily consider their African background as their heritage, most of those I know don't, and then they have nothing to identify with. I, on the other hand, have a West Indian background. Certain traditional dances that we were taught at our first family reunion in New Haven are part of it, some of the old time music, like the string band. [...] Nevis is like a second home, it is a connection to another place.

Family reunions and "clans", first organized as part of the rooting and search for a cultural identity of second generation middle-class Nevisians in the United States, are no longer just an American phenomenon. Family reunions have also become popular among Nevisians elsewhere, and reflect the increasing affluence of many of the Nevisian migrants and the ease of transnational transportation today. They are often held at Culturama time, when Nevisians from the entire world gather to celebrate their culture and roots. Through the organization of clans and the holding of reunions, the migrant communities, which formerly became absorbed by the host society and thus lost contact with Nevis, now are presented with an opportunity to maintain their ties to Nevis through several generations. From the Nevis point of view, the clans are also important, because they create a more permanent tie to some of the most influential Nevisians abroad. The family clans therefore constitute an important consolidation and further development of the Nevisian global community.

THE CELEBRATION OF NEVISIAN CULTURE

The celebration of Nevisian culture that has taken place during the last few decades can be seen to have finally granted to Afro-Caribbean culture a form of recognition and respect that it was denied for several centuries. Music and dance, long condemned as licentious and riotous, is now seen to be an integral part of the islanders' Afro-Caribbean heritage and presented as folk art. Local economic activities, such as peasant farming, pottery and illegal rum making, which have been regarded as lowly and degraded work, are now portrayed on stage as manifestations of Nevisian history and culture. The family network, which has been characterized as immoral and loose by colonial officials, ministers, not to speak of social scientists, has been codified as clans with family trees and coats of arms.

To a certain extent, this celebration signals the decline of the importance of Afro-Caribbean village culture in the rural communities in the daily lives of the Nevisians. As long as the sports were a vibrant festival in the villages, there was no need to put them on the stage or to organize formal parades where they could be displayed. Those Nevisians who make a living cultivating the land, producing pots, or distilling illegal rum would not dream of presenting these means of making a livelihood on the stage as culture. And no Nevisian who has just emigrated in order to help the family back home has time for, or any interest in, reunions with unknown family members. The celebration of Nevis culture therefore reflects the reification of this culture, which has occurred as Nevisians have removed themselves from, and externalized, their culture and institutionalized it as traditional folk art or cultural heritage.

The celebration of Nevis as cultural identity may, indeed, reflect the demise of many aspects of the village culture, which was dominant in the rural communities until the middle of this century. This does not mean, however, that the islanders have become Western in outlook, or that Nevis today is merely an outpost in the Western world. Nevis culture remains distinctly non-Western in its global character. The large-scale emigration and heavy influx of Western material culture should not be seen as a sign of Nevisians having, finally, succumbed to Western culture after several centuries of exposure to it. Like the traditions of sociability associated with early colonial history, and the institutions of respectability introduced during the late slave period, migration and Western material culture represent important frameworks, associated with the conditions of life in the present-day world, within which Nevisians can position themselves and display Afro-Caribbean culture. These frameworks are therefore a sign of the islanders actively confronting, within their own cultural context, the inherent conflicts and contradictions generated by the various global flows which have met on their island. The emergence of a transnational community of Nevisians straddling migration destinations in several different nation-states, exploiting a variety of economic niches, yet remaining fiercely loyal to the family back home on Nevis and to everything it stands for, represents a departure from mainstream Western cultural norms. The members of this community are aware of this and have sought to express their special cultural identity through such "cultural inventions" as festivals and family clans. The fact that Nevisian village based culture has changed through this impressive display of globalism, does not make it any less Afro-Caribbean. That Nevisians, through this experience, have learned to see their own heritage as an appropriate means of asserting their cultural identity, certainly does not make the present-day culture any less authentic. It is rather indicative of the new-found recognition of their own cultural background that the Nevisians are achieving.

As the celebration of an island identity rooted in locally developed ways of life becomes an increasingly important focal point in the global community Nevis may turn into a sort of cultural reservation for Nevisians living and working in various migration destinations abroad. The creation of Culturama, spearheaded by educated Nevisians several of whom had been abroad, may be seen in this light. Furthermore, many Nevisians are becoming aware of the cultural importance of the childhood home on Nevis to the migrants. They realize that there is an inherent conflict between their great consumption of Western material goods, which gives life on the island a Western appearance, and the Nevis which returning migrants wish to experience when they return. They therefore actively engage in a sort of cultural management for the benefit of migrant relatives. Much of the farming on Nevis today probably should be seen as a cultural, not an economic venture, the primary purpose being to maintain a home on Nevis for the global family network. As one elderly

Nevisian explained, he did not keep goats and sheep for his own dietary needs—they were met almost entirely by canned vegetables and imported frozen chicken—but so that he could give his children and grandchildren a "taste of home" during their brief stays on Nevis. The island identity which is celebrated by Nevisians therefore is predicated on a sense of home which must be cultivated globally from a distance, whether a geographical distance in the case of the migrants, or a cultural distance in the case of those who live on Nevis. Home is where you leave it.

NOTES

[1] Today a rather large proportion is living in the council housing which has been constructed in Chapeltown under urban renewal. According to the 1981 population census, 52% of the households with a head of West Indian origin lived in council housing, 39% in owner-occupied houses, 9% in other types of housing. The relatively high dependence on council housing was seen as being caused by the West Indians having "a low marriage rate, an above average divorce rate and high proportions of lone parent households and unmarried couple families" (Leeds City Council 1985/86:2, 4).

[2] In 1981, 8,193 people were reported to live in households with a head of West Indian origin. Though the West Indian population is small in number, it is concentrated in a small area of the city. Close to three quarters of the first generation West Indian immigrants lived within 4 wards of the city, the majority living in Chapel Allerton (Leeds City Council 1985/86:10).

[3] The first Leeds carnival is described in *Leeds Westindian Carnival* 1987 and *Leeds Other Paper* 26th August 1988.

[4] The colorful and shiny synthetic fabrics and materials, which are sold in Indian shops in Chapeltown, have also been used to make costumes for the parade.

[5] In 1981 55% of the population of West Indian origin in Leeds was born in the United Kingdom (Leeds City Council 1985/86:4). This figure must have increased a great deal, as the original West Indian immigrants die and a growing number of second and third generation West Indian children are born.

[6] So far, the two Anglican churches in the Chapeltown area have been the most responsive towards carnival. The West Indian churches, generally speaking, are fundamentalist and therefore strongly against carnival, which they regard as licence to immoral behavior.

[7] This calypso began:

> If you really want to have a real Cultural Festival
> Here is a suggestion to improve our celebrations
> A say we need more education in de Culture ad Arts form
> Especially the youths of tomorrow
> Teach them the things that they should know
> Let them know our Roots are back in Africa
> Let them know we were brought as slaves over here
> An the struggle that we met to get our freedom today
> So we could have Culturama in our own splendid way.

[8] This calypso included these lines:

> Freedom to Nevisians is a lie
> Freedom is still in the Nevisian's cry.

9 Structured interviews were carried out with 17 persons of Nevisian descent in New Haven in 1987: 5 men and 12 women. Of these persons, 5 were first generation, 10 were second generation, and 3 were third generation Nevisians.

10 The Antillean Friendly Society was formed in 1934. According to one Nevisian, this was occasioned by the death of a fellow West Indian from Montserrat, who died without any family to bury him. In order to avoid burials by the government, which are frowned upon, a friendly society was formed, which could help in such situations.

11 The Barbadian rector, Victor Rogers, had just completed a PhD Dissertation on the Nevisian community which made up a large part of his congregation. For this study he was able to locate 191 persons of Nevisian descent in the New Haven area. He was a great help to me during my research in New Haven.

12 The first Nevisian family reunion in New Haven probably was held by the Esdaile clan in 1973.

13 The historian of the Huggins clan, Constance Baker Motley, is one of the most outstanding examples of the success which many of the New Haven based Nevisian families have had in the United States. The 9th of 11 children born to Nevisian immigrants, she attended Columbia Law School and joined in the civil rights struggle in the South. In 1964 she was elected to the New York Senate as the first Black woman, and later became the first female Borough President of Manhattan and the first Black female Federal Judge (*The Voice of Nevis* 1978:13; see also Lanker 1989).

14 One of the main actors in this series, Cecily Tyson, is of Nevisian heritage and is one of the Nevisian Americans who has paid a visit to their ancestral island.

PLATE 11   *Leeds West Indian Carnival filmed by ZIZ, the government television station on St. Kitts, for broadcast on St. Kitts and Nevis. Photo, Kenneth Olwig, 1988.*

Toward an Anthropology of Cultural Complexity

During my first period of West Indian fieldwork, on St. John in the Virgin Islands, I became friends with a woman from the island who had been educated at an American college where she had taken a few courses in anthropology. She was very interested in my research but asked me whether I had been disappointed when I learned that the islanders were not more primitive? At the time I found her question amusing. Anthropological fieldwork was rather well-established in the Caribbean at this time—the mid-1970s—and it was even becoming increasingly common in the heart of the industrial West. Anthropology clearly was not just the study of primitive cultures as she had been led to believe in the college courses that she had taken during the early 1960s. The perception of anthropology which my friend expressed seemed to me, then, to be curiously old-fashioned and naive. Nevertheless, it has had a profound influence on the field, molding the development of theory and method. This is not unproblematic when studying an area which has been characterized as one of "the most Westernized of the modern world" (Mintz 1971[1966]:37).

Contemporary culture and society in the Caribbean emerged out of a colonial encounter which involved the decimation of the aboriginal population and the introduction of new populations from Africa, Europe and Asia. As a result, the area today displays no heirs of former tribal natives, as does most of the Third World, but is populated by descendants of those who were brought there to labor in plantation systems based on slavery and other systems of forced labor. In the Caribbean, rural communities therefore have a long history of modernization and integration into the Western world system and are not the repositories of cultural tradition and continuity which my friend saw as the prime object of anthropological studies.

Even though most anthropologists have agreed that slavery constituted an important institutional framework for the early development of Afro-Caribbean culture and society, up to the 1970s few did actual research on slavery. In a review essay of slavery in general Kopytoff (1982) finds that anthropologists almost entirely ignored slavery until the 1970s. He suggests that this is caused by the concern of anthropologists, during the formative period of the field from 1920 to 1960, with the explication of the culture on the basis of field data. This heavy emphasis on fieldwork provided little information on institutions such as slavery which are primarily of a historical nature, and led anthropologists to situate their analyses in a changeless ethnographic present. Furthermore, due to their eagerness to present an internal, sympathetic view of the culture under study, there was little incentive to focus on such unsympathetic institutions as slavery, even where it still could be found. In the Caribbean this has meant that the close historic link between slavery and the processes of modernization and Westernization, and the implications of this for cultural development, have not been central themes of study.

The failure to focus on modernization and Westernization can also be seen to be related to the difficulty of applying to the Caribbean the anthropological concept of culture which has been developed in the study of primitive societies. A basic problem revolves around the notion of culture as constituting distinct wholes which provide the framework for the thinking and action of particular groups of peoples. As argued in recent critical discussions of the concept of culture within anthropology, the idea of clearly defined and bounded cultural entities is an anthropological construct which is extrinsic to the people studied (Barth 1989; Kahn 1989). While it may have been an useful analytical concept in the study of small-scale, highly integrated societies, it is an entirely unsatisfactory point of departure in the study of societies which have emerged out of the very meeting of many different cultural flows such as occurred in the Caribbean. By taking a point of departure in cultural interaction and reflexivity rather than in cultural essence and uniqueness the anthropologist does not have to bemoan the impossibility of ever uncovering the "true" nature of primitive cultures existing prior to colonial times, which will always be beyond our reach and grasp. Far from being a problematic location to do fieldwork, the Caribbean therefore ought to epitomize the sort of cultural characteristics which promote anthropological understanding.

The island societies, with their industrial plantations organized around the production of export crops, appeared as rational, well-integrated entities predicated upon a European colonial order. This colonial order, however, belonged only to a small plantocracy, who regarded the bulk of the population, the Black slaves, as non-persons outside the social ranks of society (Kopytoff 1982; Patterson 1982). Due to this marginalization of the Black population, Afro-Caribbean culture has not revolved around the establishment of an autonomous, organic, distinct sociocultural system, but has emerged out of the constitution of an Afro-Caribbean context of life within an oppressive colonial system. Furthermore, the display of Afro-Caribbean culture in the wider colonial society has become an important means of negating the social marginalization imposed by this colonial order. Afro-Caribbean cultural contexts of life can be seen to have developed primarily in the crevices left for the Black population within the plantation society. The conditions for cultural development and display depended, naturally, on the socioeconomic conditions of the colonial society. In the course of the long colonial history of the Caribbean this society underwent a fundamental change from the inclusive hierarchical, patriarchal order of the early colonial period to the exclusive, egalitarian order associated with the late colonial period. The study of Afro-Caribbean cultural continuity and change therefore must be guided by a notion of cultural complexity involving the continuous constituting, developing and assertion of culture within multiple frameworks rather than a concept of self-contained, cultural wholes.

CULTURAL COMPLEXITY IN THE CARIBBEAN

In this book I have focused on the cultural processes which have taken place as the Afro-Caribbean people of the island of Nevis have struggled to establish their cultural presence within the varying socioeconomic frameworks of life available. Originally imported from Africa to work as slaves on the European owned plantations they arrived as individuals who had been torn away from their natal sociocultural milieu. Afro-Caribbean culture thus can be seen to have developed out of the common ground which the African slaves were able to establish with one another in the situation of oppression which they experienced. This common cultural ground was in many respects radically different and separated from the Euro-Caribbean culture of the colonizers. Yet, because they were denied the possibility of expressing their cultural identity through institutions of their own, they employed colonial institutions to which they gained access as frameworks within which they could formalize and make visible a culture which they saw as their own. The Afro-Caribbean slaves therefore sought to establish their cultural presence through institutional frameworks which belonged to a foreign culture. In the process they created a global culture, characterized by the ability to cultivate and promote a system of values and practices of their own by appropriated colonial cultural forms.

The historical records, written by representatives of the colonial power, can be seen to bear witness to this "cultural struggle" between colonizers and colonized. Most of the records—ranging from eighteenth century memoirs describing the slaves' Sunday market, to nineteenth century missionary letters reporting on tea meetings, to twentieth century travel accounts depicting Christmas sports—share a more or less uneasy recognition of the Englishness of these institutions or traditions. At the same time the European observers also recognized that these cultural forms were no longer English but had undergone a transformation as they had become appropriated by the Afro-Caribbean people. The partial understanding and un-comfortable feeling which historical accounts reveal thus represent an important means for the uncovering of the cultural development which was reflected in this asymmetrical colonial dialogue.

The colonial frameworks employed by the Afro-Caribbeans can be seen to have developed, themselves, in connection with the cultural reflexivity and codification which took place in Europe and North America as modern Western society emerged out of locally based rural communities. The social and cultural context within which the Western institutions emerged in Western society therefore had a bearing on the sort of codification which could be sought through these institutions in the colonies. The tradition of holiday sports had emerged in the hierarchical English society. Through seasonal rituals involving the rich as well as the poor they gave expression to the dependence on the natural and social resources of the local community which these two groups shared. Even though African performative traditions in some ways dominated the way in which the sports came to be presented in Nevis, many elements of the English rural tradition were maintained and incorporated into the rituals enacted by the Afro-Caribbean population. The sports disappeared in many parts of England during the eighteenth and nineteenth centuries as the country witnessed the decline of the English rural society with which they were associated. They survived, however, well into the twentieth century in the West Indies as a tradition which had been employed by the Afro-Caribbean people to assert a sociocultural presence in the colonial society and served as reminders of a system of social and economic relations less repressive than that of plantation slavery.

In England the community based mutual rights and obligations associated with "traditional" English rural society can be seen to have given way to the institutions of respectability introduced from the late eighteenth century. They were closely related to the rise of the middle classes who sought to establish traditions of their own which might reflect, and validate, their superior social status *vis-à-vis* the lower classes. In this way they can be regarded as a form of high culture in relation to the popular culture cultivated by the lower segments of the population in rural society such as the Christmas sports. In the West Indies the culture of respectability came to serve the purpose of establishing the privileged position of the small middle class within the colonial society which appeared at the time of Emancipation. The institutions and traditions associated with this culture were appropriated by the lower classes as frameworks within which to gain social recognition.

During this century these colonial frameworks have been superceded by extensive and massive cultural flows of goods, people and images deriving from Western metropoles as part of the expansion of the global ecumene. Much of this flow has occurred in connection with the system of migration which has de-territorialized the Nevisian community and turned it into a transnational network of relations. In particular material goods have come to play an important role as Western cultural forms through which Nevisians can seek social recognition for Afro-Caribbean culture in the local society. Thus possession of a wealth of Western material goods has come to signify the strength of the Afro-Caribbean network of family relations which has enabled the acquisition of these items. At the same time, the goods in and of themselves are associated with high socio-economic status in the local society influenced by the increasing importance of material goods in modern Western society. Material goods acquired through migration therefore have become a means of aspiring to upward social mobility outside the traditional avenue of respectability and without offending the rights and obligations inherent in the local system of sociability.

It has been possible to delineate a long Nevisian tradition of displaying cultural identity through Euro-Caribbean cultural forms, whether those associated with traditions of sociability deriving from the seventeenth century; institutions of respectability associated with the eighteenth and nineteenth centuries, or patterns of mass consumption developed during this century. The codification of Afro-Caribbean culture therefore has not seen the institutionalization of lived culture into reified culture, but a continuous cultural interplay, or struggle, between locally developed Afro-Caribbean cultural contexts of life and externally imposed Western frameworks of cultural display.

GLOBAL AND LOCAL STRATEGIES

While the result has been that Afro-Caribbean culture has remained alive and vibrant, this has been at a rather high personal and social cost. By employing institutions which were not just at variance with local contexts of life but also pitted against one another, the Afro-Caribbean people have been placed in a situation in which they have been faced with conflicts which cannot be resolved easily within Caribbean society. Nevis is not alone in the West Indies in having witnessed this cultural struggle in connection with the asserting of Afro-Caribbean culture within conflicting frameworks appropriated from colonial society. Throughout the West Indies local populations have been incorporated into European colonial structures as inexpensive labor power denied a social or cultural identity within the colonial order. During slavery only the runaway slaves who managed to escape to isolated areas where they could develop independent societies managed to institutionalize an endogenous framework of life (Price 1973). After Emancipation the freed on certain islands were able to develop their own villages or communities, where they could achieve a certain autonomy of their own and thus establish their own social institutions and tradition (Carnegie 1987).

These locally based institutions tended not to be recognized by the official colonial society, and the interplay between informal local cultural systems and external institutionalized frameworks can be seen to be a general theme in Caribbean societies. This is reflected in Wilson's influential discussion of the cultural values of reputation and respectability, and in the prolonged debate concerning whether Caribbean societies are structurally integrated or culturally plural (see for example R.T. Smith 1967; M.G. Smith 1965). The inherent contradictions in Afro-Caribbean cultural development constitute an important reason, I would argue, for the strength of the absentee tradition throughout the Caribbean. This tradition has involved the emigration of thousands of Caribbeans from their natal societies and resulted in the virtual deterritorialization of Afro-Caribbean communities. This migration should not be seen primarily as an escape from impossible local conflicts posed by the irreconcilability of co-existing traditions of respectability and sociability or as an inevitable result of the continued social marginalization of Afro-Caribbean culture within the local societies. It should rather be seen as a further extension of the tradition of globality whereby cultural constituating is, fundamentally, based upon incorporation and reinterpretation of reified, foreign forms of culture within continually negotiated cultural contexts of life. The massive exodus of Caribbean peoples from their natal societies therefore has not signified the abandonment of these societies. On the contrary, migrants by and large have remained in close contact with them through the families they have left behind, and they still regard them as their home. Nevertheless, the absentee orientation of most Caribbean people has led to the development of transnational socioeconomic fields which today constitute the primary contexts of life. This absentee orientation of Afro-Caribbean communities has become further strengthened by the increased dependence of the local Caribbean communities on Western material goods acquired primarily through remittances from migrants.

At the same time as the Nevisian context of life has become globalized through the deterritorialization of Afro-Caribbean communities, the island societies have gone through a process of decolonization which has led to the establishment of independent nation-states in the area. Having become independent the local intelligentsia now see the need to establish national Caribbean cultures. In this endeavor they have become increasingly interested in Afro-Caribbean village culture. As Afro-Caribbean people have seen their daily context of life expanded from the local rural communities to global fields of socioeconomic relations, the village culture has been perceived as receding into the past. It can now be cultivated as reified cultural form which can be used as a framework within which to assert and display Afro-Caribbean cultural identity, and already certain aspects of Afro-Caribbean culture have been turned into folk art which can be put on stage and celebrated as local tradition.

By adopting their own "past" culture as a framework within which to continue their struggle for cultural recognition a new form of reflexivity has emerged, where cultural recognition no longer needs to take place within institutional frameworks associated with foreign culture. The middle class formerly cultivated European culture through Shakespeare performances, piano concerts, cricket and netball. Today some of the middle-class civil servants in the new nation-state display their identity by helping to organize Culturama festivals or by being active in development projects based on traditional Afro-Caribbean economic activities. In this attempt to establish a unique Nevisian culture, the population seems to be adopting, as folk model, the Western, anthropological notion of culture as a clearly demarcated integrated whole underlined by shared values (cf. Kahn 1989).

Cultural reflexivity and assertment through external frameworks, associated with geographical or historical distance, represent a structuring principle in Afro-Caribbean culture. It is notably global, as demonstrated in the ability and willingness of Afro-Caribbean people to continuously adopt and employ such external frameworks. It is also fiercely local, as evidenced by the continuous appropriating of external forms to locally developed ways. The dual nature of Afro-Caribbean culture may be interpreted as a result of the particular history of the Caribbean as a modern society where cultural development has occurred within a situation of insti-tutionalized marginality. It may also, however, be seen to be a particularly clear example of the cultural interaction and exchange which is a natural consequence of the fact that people do not live in isolated cultural wholes but rather between various forms of external cultural influences which are dealt with in various ways. Where in modern Western society, for example, such influence has led to the closing off of national cultures, in the Caribbean it has led to a pattern of cultural incorporation and appropriation.

The interplay between global and local strategies is an important issue in the study of cultural development today, whether or not it pertains to the Caribbean. The importance which cultural display has been seen to attain in such contexts suggests, furthermore, that a more generalized study of cultural display within our globalized culture might be worthwhile. This might also help explain the peculiar attraction which Afro-Caribbean and Afro-American culture exerts globally today.

THE DISPLAY OF LOCAL CULTURE IN GLOBAL CONTEXT

The importance of cultural display for peoples who have experienced a process of socioeconomic marginalization by the Western world adds another dimension to the discussion of global culture. As noted in the introduction the widespread interest in cultural forms associated with the West on the part of people in the Third and Fourth World has been interpreted as a means whereby they "resist and play-back systemicity and order" associated with the dominant West (cf.

Featherstone 1990:2). The Nevis case study suggests that such local discourses on the West are not only concerned with challenging and breaking down of the constitutent elements of the dominant West. They are just as much concerned with presenting and representing local identities which are perceived to be fundamentally different from the identity, or lack thereof, accorded to Third World people within the global order of the West. Since the Third World is dominated by the West it is necessary to display this presence within a Western framework. Local discourses within a global framework therefore may well constitute attempts at displaying and thereby establishing, radically different local cultural identities in a world where Western concepts of equality leave little room for the recognition of other ways of thinking and acting.

References

PRINTED SOURCES

Abbott, George C.
1964   The Collapse of the Sea Island Cotton Industry in the West
        Indies. *Social and Economic Studies* 13(1):157–87.

Abrahams, Roger D.
1983   *The Man-of-Words in the West Indies.* Baltimore: The Johns Hopkins University
        Press.

Abrahams, Roger D. and John F. Szwed
1983   Introduction. In *After Africa*, edited by Roger D. Abrahams and John F. Szwed,
        1–48. New Haven: Yale University Press.

Acts of Assembly
1740   Passed in the Island of Nevis, from 1664 to 1739, inclusive. London: John Baskett.

An Agricultural Development Plan for Nevis
1957   Report of a Team of Experts Following its Visit in September, 1955. Development
        and Welfare in the West Indies. Bulletin, No. 33.

Amory-Manners, Annette
1984   The Value of Vegetables in the Diet. *Culturama Magazine*, n.p.

Anderson, Benedict
1983   *Imagined Communities.* London: Verso.

Annual Digest of Statistics for 1981
1982   The Statistical Office Planning Unit. Basseterre, St. Kitts: Prime Minister's
        Ministry.

Annual Report
1968–76 Immigration and Naturalization Service. Report of the Commissioner of
        Immigration and Naturalization. Washington, DC: US Government Printing
        Office.

Appadurai, Arjun
1990   Disjuncture and Difference in the Global Cultural Economy. *Theory, Culture &
        Society* 7(2/3):295–310.

1991   Global Ethnoscapes: Notes and Queries for a Transnational Anthropology. In
        Recapturing Anthropology, edited by Richard G. Fox, 191–210. Santa Fe: School of
        American Research Press.

Appadurai, Arjun, ed.
1988–   *The Social Life of Things. Commodities in Cultural Perspective*. Cambridge:
[1986] Cambridge University Press.

Ardener, Shirley G.
1973   Sexual Insult and Female Militancy. *Man* 8(3):422–40.

Austin, Diane J.
1983   Culture and Ideology in the English-Speaking Caribbean: A View from Jamaica.
        American Ethnologist 19(2):223–40.

Barker, G.H., comp.
1981   *St. Kitts-Nevis. An Agricultural Profile*. Caribbean Agricultural Research and
        Development Institute. Agricultural Profile Series. Small Farm Multiple Cropping
        Systems Research Project.

Barth, Fredrik
1989   The Analysis of Culture in Complex Societies. *Ethnos* 54(3–4):120–42.

Batie, Robert C.
1976   Why Sugar? Economic Cycles and the Changing of Staples on the English and French
        Antilles, 1624–54. *Journal of Caribbean History* 8:1–41.

The Beacon
1958   Students Magazine. Spring Gardens Teachers' Training College, Antigua.

Beckles, Hilary
1982   English Parliamentary Debate on "White Slavery" in Barbados, 1659. *The Journal of
        the Barbados Museum and Historical Society* 36(4):344–52.
1989   *White Servitude and Black Slavery in Barbados, 1627–1715*. Knoxville: The
        University of Tennessee Press.

Berleant-Schiller, Riva
1989   Free Labor and the Economy in Seventeenth-Century Montserrat. *The William and
        Mary Quarterly* 3rd Series, 46:539–64.

Besson, Jean
1987   A Paradox in Caribbean Attitudes to Land. In *Land and Development in the
        Caribbean*, edited by Jean Besson and Janet Momsen, 13–45. London: Macmillan.

Bettelheim, Judith
1988   Jonkonnu and Other Christmas Masquerades. In *Caribbean Festival Arts*, edited by
        John W. Nunley and Judith Bettelheim, 39–83. Seattle: The Saint Louis Art
        Museum in association with University of Washington Press.

Bettelheim, Judith, John Nunley and Barbara Bridges
 1988   Caribbean Festival Arts: An Introduction. In *Caribbean Festival Arts*, edited by
         John W. Nunley and Judith Bettelheim, 31–37. Seattle: The Saint Louis Art
         Museum in association with University of Washington Press.

Blackman, Francis (Woodie)
 1988   *Methodism 200 Years in Barbados*. Bridgetown, Barbados: No publisher.

Brana-Shute, Gary
 1976   Drinking Shops and Social Structure. Some Ideas on Lower-Class West Indian Male
         Behavior. *Urban Anthropology* 5(1):53–68.

Brathwaite, Edward
 1978   *The Development of Creole Society in Jamaica 1770–1820*. Oxford: Clarendon
[1971]   Press.

Bridenbaugh, Carl and Roberta Bridenbaugh
 1972   *No Peace beyond the Line. The English in the Caribbean, 1624–1690*. New York:
         Oxford University Press.

Brock, Colin, ed.
 1986   *The Caribbean in Europe. Aspects of the West Indian Experience in Britain, France
         and The Netherlands*. London: Frank Cass.

Browne, Whitman
 1981   Nevis is. *Culturama Magazine*, 14–17.

Burdon, Katharine Janet
 1920   *A Handbook of St. Kitts-Nevis*. London: The West India Committee.

Burke, Peter
 1978   *Popular Culture in Early Modern Europe*. New York: Harper & Row.

Bush, Barbara
 1981   White "Ladies", Coloured "Favourites" and Black "Wenches": Some
         Considerations on Sex, Race and Class Factors in Social Relations in White Creole
         Society in the British Caribbean. *Slavery and Abolition* 2(3):245–62.

Bushaway, Bob
 1982   *By Rite. Custom, Ceremony and Community in England 1700–1880*. London:
         Junction Books.

Bushman, Richard L.
 1984   American High-Style and Vernacular Cultures. In *Colonial British America*, edited
         by Jack P. Greene and J.R. Pole, 345–83. Baltimore: The Johns Hopkins University
         Press.

Byron, E.

1981   *More Families of Nevis.* Basseterre, St. Kitts: No publisher.

1987   Helen Bridgewater. A Nevisian Who Put Country Above Self. *Nevis Historical and Conservation Society Newsletter* 11:4–8.

n.d.a   *Some Nevis Families.* Basseterre, St. Kitts: No publisher.

n.d.b   *Millicent Theodora Byron.* St. Kitts-Nevis: No publisher.

CARDI—Caribbean Agricultural Research and Development Institute

1982   *Final Report, January 1980–November 1982: Small Farms Multiple Cropping Research Project 538 0015.* J.E. Lowery Country Team Leader. Nevis: Charlestown.

Carnegie, Charles V., ed.

1987   *Afro-Caribbean Villages in Historical Perspective.* Afro-Caribbean Institute of Jamaica Research Review, No. 2.

Carter, Trevor

1986   *Shattering Illusions. West Indians in British Politics.* London: Lawrence and Wishart.

Case in Nevis

1818   Charing Cross: Whitmore & Fenn.

Castle, Terry

1986   *Masquerade and Civilization. The Carnivalesque in Eighteenth-Century English Culture and Fiction.* London: Methuen.

Clan Huggins Reunion, 5 Years Later

1979   June 1979–June 1979. MS.

Clark, Peter

1978   The Alehouse and the Alternative Society. In *Puritans and Revolutionaries, Essays in Seventeenth-Century History Presented to Christopher Hill,* edited by Donald Pennington and Keith Thomas, 47–72. Oxford: Clarendon Press.

Cohen, Abner

1982   A Polyethnic London Carnival as a Contested Cultural Performance. *Ethnic and Racial Studies* 5(1):23–41.

Coke, Thomas

1811   *A History of the West Indies.* London: Printed for the Author.

Coleridge, Henry Nelson

1832   *Six Months in the West Indies in 1825.* London: John Murray.

Colonial Annual Report

1948   Leeward Islands. London: His Majesty's Stationery Office.

Cominos, Peter T.

1963   Late-Victorian Sexual Respectability and the Social System. *International Review of Social History* 8:18–48, 216–25.

Cox, Edward L.
1984   *Free Coloreds in the Slave Societies of St. Kitts and Grenada, 1763-1833.* Knoxville: The University of Tennessee Press.

Craton, Michael
1978   *Searching for the Invisible Man. Slaves and Plantation Life in Jamaica.* Cambridge, Mass.: Harvard University Press.
1979   Changing Patterns of Slave Family in the British West Indies. *Journal of Interdisciplinary History* 10:1-35.

Crosse, Maude
1962-   Education for Leisure in the Primary Schools with Special Reference to the
63   Charlestown's Girls' School. BA Thesis, University of Durham.

Culture and History
1990   Vol. 7: Consumption, guest editor Orvar Löfgren.

Davy, John
1971   *The West Indies Before and Since Slave Emancipation.* London: Frank Cass.
[1854]

Dirks, Robert
1987   *The Black Saturnalia. Conflict and its Ritual Expression on British West Indian Slave Plantations.* Gainesville: University of Florida Press.

Drummond, Lee
1980   The Cultural Continuum: A Theory of Intersystems. *Man* 15:352-74.
1981   Ethnicity, "Ethnicity" and Culture Theory. *Man* 16:693-96.

Dunn, Richard
1972   *Sugar and Slaves. The Rise of the Planter Class in the English West Indies, 1624-1713. Children in Nevis.* [No publisher].

Edwards, Elkanah D.
n.d.   *Socio-Economic Factors Contributing to Learning Difficulties among Primary School Children in Nevis.*

Eriksen, Thomas Hylland
1990   Liming in Trinidad: The Art of Doing Nothing. *Folk* 32:23-43.

The Excelsior School Quarterly Magazine
c.1928 Charlestown, Nevis.
1929   Charlestown, Nevis.

Featherstone, Michael
1990   Global Culture: An Introduction. *Theory, Culture & Society* 7(2/3):1-14.

Ferneyhough, Don
1974 The Agro-Socio-Economic Factors Influencing the Planning of Change in Agriculture in St. Kitts-Nevis—the Effects of History and Prospects for the Future. M.Sc. Dissertation, University of Reading: Agricultural Extension and Rural Development Centre.

Foner, Nancy
1979 *Jamaica Farewell: Jamaican Migrants in London.* London: Routledge and Kegan Paul.

Fortune, Stephen Alexander
1984 *Merchants and Jews. The Struggle for British West Indian Commerce, 1650–1750.* Latin American Monographs—Second Series, Center for Latin American Studies Book, Gainesville: University of Florida Press.

Foster, George
1965 Peasant Society and the Image of Limited Good. *American Anthropologist* 67: 293–315.

Friedman, Jonathan
1990 Being in the World: Globalization and Localization. *Theory, Culture & Society* 7(2/3):311–28.

Frucht, Richard
1966 Community and Context in a Colonial Society: Social and Economic Change in Nevis, British West Indies. PhD Dissertation, Brandeis University.
1968 Emancipation, Remittances, and Social Change: Aspects of the Social Field of Nevis, West Indies. *Anthropologica* 10:193–208.
1972 Migration and the Receipt of Remittances. In *Resource Development in the Caribbean*, 275–81. Montreal: Centre for Developing—Area Studies.
1977 From Slavery to Unfreedom in the Plantation Society of St. Kitts, W.I. In *Comparative Perspectives on Slavery in New World Plantation Societies*, edited by Vera Rubin and Arthur Tuden. Annals of the New York Academy of Sciences 292:379–88.

The Fulham Papers in the Lambeth Library
1965 American Colonial Section. Calendar and Indexes, compiled by William Wilson Manross. Oxford: Clarendon Press.

Galenson, David W.
1981 *White Servitude in Colonial America. An Economic Analysis.* Cambridge: Cambridge University Press.

Gaspar, David Barry
1985 *Bondmen & Rebels. A Study of Master-Slave Relations in Antigua.* Baltimore: The Johns Hopkins University Press.

Gay, Edwin F.

1964 Letters from a Sugar Plantation in Nevis, 1723–32. *Journal of Economic and Business*
[1928– *History* 1:149–73.
29]

Gellner, E.

1983 *Nations and Nationalism.* Oxford: Basil Blackwell.

Gilroy, Paul

1987 *"There ain't No Black in the Union Jack." The Cultural Politics of Race and Nation.*
London: Hutchinson.

Gonzalez, Nancie L.

1969 *Black Carib Household Organization.* Seattle: University of Washington Press.

1970 Towards a Definition of Matrifocality. In *Afro-American Anthropology: Problems in
Theory and Method*, edited by Norman Whitten and John Szwed, 231–43. New
York: Free Press.

1988 *Sojourners of the Caribbean.* Urbana: University of Illinois Press.

Goosen, Jean

1972 Child Sharing and Foster Parenthood in the French West Indies. Paper presented at
the American Anthropological Association, New York City.

Goveia, Elsa

1965 *Slave Society in the British Leeward Islands at the End of the Eighteenth Century.*
New Haven: Yale University Press.

Green, James W.

1972 Social Networks in St. Croix, United States Virgin Islands. PhD Dissertation,
University of Washington, Seattle.

Gullick, C.J.M.R.

1985 *Myths of a Minority. The Changing Traditions of the Vincentian Caribs.* Assen:
Van Gorcum.

Gumbs, Wycherly

1986 *Methodism: Its Roots and Fruit.* Nevis Circuit.

Haley, Alexander

1977 *Roots.* New York: Dell Publishing Co.

Hall, Douglas

1971 *Five of the Leewards 1834–1870.* Barbados: Caribbean Universities Press.

Handler, Jerome S.

1974 *The Unappropriated People: Freedmen in Slave Society of Barbados.* Baltimore:
The Johns Hopkins University Press.

Handler, Jerome S. and Charlotte J. Frisbie
1972 Aspects of Slave Life in Barbados: Music and its Cultural Context. *Caribbean Studies* 11(4):5–46.

Handler, Jerome S. and Frederick W. Lange
1978 *Plantation Slavery in Barbados. An Archaeological and Historical Investigation.* Cambridge: Harvard University Press.

Hannerz, Ulf
1990 Cosmopolitans and Locals in World Culture. *Theory, Culture and Society* 7(2/3): 237–51.
1992 *Cultural Complexity. Studies in the Social Organization of Meaning.* New York: Columbia University Press.

Henriques, Fernando
1953 *Family and Colour in Jamaica.* London: MacGibbon & Kee.

Heskith, Thomas
1702 *A Farewel-Sermon Preach'd in St. John's at Nevis in America, May the 25th, 1701.* London: Printed for Thomas Speed.

Heuman, Gad
1981 *Between Black and White: Race, Politics and the Free Coloreds in Jamaica, 1792–1865.* Westport: The Greenwood Press.
1985 Introduction to Out of the House of Bondage, special issue of *Slavery and Abolition* 6(3):1–8.

Higham, C.S.S.
1921 *The Development of the Leeward Islands under the Restauration, 1660–1688.* Cambridge: Cambridge University Press.

Higman, B.W.
1973 Household Structure and Fertility on Jamaican Slave Plantations: A Nineteenth-Century Example. *Population Studies* 27:527–50.
1975 The Slave Family and Household in the British West Indies, 1800–1834. *Journal of Interdisciplinary History* 6(2):261–87.
1977 Methodological Problems in the Study of the Slave Family. *Annals of the New York Academy of Sciences* 202:591–96.
1978 African and Creole Family Patterns in Trinidad. *Journal of Family History* 3:163–80.
1984 *Slave Populations of the British Caribbean 1807–1834.* Baltimore: The Johns Hopkins University Press.
1988 *Jamaica Surveyed. Plantation Maps and Plans of the Eighteenth and Nineteenth Centuries.* Kingston: Institute of Jamaica Publications.

Hill, Christopher
1984 *The World Turned Upside Down.* London: Penguin Books.
[1972]

Hill, Donald R. and Robert Abramson
1979   West Indian Carnival in Brooklyn. *Natural History* August/September, 73–85.

Hobsbawm, Eric and Terence Ranger, eds
1983   *The Invention of Tradition.* Cambridge: Cambridge University Press.

Horton, Robin
1971   Stateless Societies in the History of West Africa. In *History of West Africa*, Vol. 1, edited by A. Ajayi and M. Crowder, 72–113. London: Longmans.

Howell, Calvin Cabo
1982   Notes on Culture and its Relationship to Development. *Culturama Magazine*, n.p.

The Huggins Cousins
1974   *The Bulletin.* Southern New England Telephone, August, 17–19.

Iles, John Alexander Burke
1958   *An Account Descriptive of the Island of Nevis.* Norwich: Fletcher & Son.
[1871]

Independence Magazine
1983   St. Christopher and Nevis, 19th September.

Jayawardena, Chandra
1980   Culture and Ethnicity in Guyana and Fiji. *Man* 15:430–50.

Jeaffreson, John Cordy
1878   *A Young Squire of the Seventh Century.* London: Hurst and Blackett.
[1672–
82]

Johnston, J.R.V.
1965   The Stapleton Sugar Plantations in the Leeward Islands. *Bulletin of the John Rylands Library* 48(1):175–206.

Kahn, Joel
1989   Culture. Demise or Resurrection? *Critique of Anthropology* 9(2):5–25.

Kapferer, Bruce
1988   *Legends of People. Myths of State.* Washington: Smithsonian Institution Press.

Kasinitz, Philip and Judith Freidenberg-Herbstein
1987   The Puerto Rican Parade and West Indian Carnival: Public Celebrations in New York City. In *Caribbean Life in New York City: Sociocultural Dimensions*, edited by Constance R. Sutton and Elsa M. Chaney, 329–49. New York: Center for Migration Studies.

Keesing, Roger
1982   Kastom and Anticolonialism on Malaita: "Culture" as Political Symbol. *Mankind* 13(4):357–73.
1985   Kwaio Women Speak: The Micropolitics of Autobiography in a Solomon Island Society. *American Anthropologist* 87(1):27–39.

Kingsley, Charles
1871   *At Last: A Christmas in the West Indies.* London: Macmillan.

Kopytoff, Igor
1982   Slavery. *Annual Review in Anthropology* 11:207–30.

Kopytoff, Igor and Suzanne Miers
1977   African "Slavery" as an Institution of Marginality. In *Slavery in Africa. Historical and Anthropological Perspectives*, edited by Suzanne Miers and Igor Kopytoff, 1–81. Madison: The University of Wisconsin Press.

Kussmaul, Ann
1981   *Servants in Husbandry in Early Modern England.* Cambridge: Cambridge University Press.

Lamur, Humphrey E. and John D. Speckmann, eds.
1975   *Adaptation of Migrants from the Caribbean in the European and American Metropolis.* Co-publication of the Department of Anthropology and Non-Western Sociology of the University of Amsterdam and the Department of Caribbean Studies of the Royal Institute of Linguistics and Anthropology at Leiden, Netherlands.

Lanker, Krian
1989   *I Dream a World. Portraits of Black Women Who Changed America.* New York: Stewart, Tabori & Chang.

Laqueur, Thomas Walter
1976   *Religion and Respectability. Sunday Schools and Working Class Culture 1780–1850.* New Haven: Yale University Press.

Laslett, Peter
1988   *The World We Have Lost—Further Explored.* London: Routledge.

Lawaetz, Herman
1902   *Brødremenighedens Mission i Dansk-Vestindien 1769–1848.* Copenhagen: Oto B. Wroblewski.

Leeds City Council
1985/   *Urban Programme.* Seventh Annual Submission. Inner City Programme.
86

Leeds Other Paper
1988   Carnival 21 this week. 26th August.

Leeds Westindian Carnival
1987   Official Carnival Magazine. A Leeds Westindian Carnival Committee Publication.

Lemon, James T.
1984   Spatial Order: Households in Local Communities and Regions. In *Colonial British America*, edited by Jack P. Greene and J.R. Pole, 86–122. Baltimore: The Johns Hopkins University Press.

Lennard, Val
1988   *Project Fullemploy*. Leeds Feasibility Study Report for Chapeltown/Harehills Task Force.

Lewis, Gordon K.
1972   *The Virgin Islands. A Caribbean Lilliput*. Evanston: Northwestern University Press.

Liburd, Carolyn G.
1984   Migration from Nevis since 1950. BA Thesis, University of the West Indies, Mona, Jamaica.

Lieber, Michael
1976   "Liming" and Other Concerns. The Style of Street Embedments in Port-of-Spain, Trinidad. *Urban Anthropology* 5(4):319–34.

Ligon, Richard
1970   *A True & Exact History of the Island of Barbados*. London: Frank Cass. Cass Library
[1673]   of West Indian Studies, No. 11.

Lowenthal, David
1985   *The Past is a Foreign Country*. Cambridge: Cambridge University Press.

Lowery, J.E.
n.d.   Cotton Production—Nevis Statistics & Evaluation. Caribbean Agricultural Research & Development Institute, St. Kitts-Nevis. MS.

Lowes, Susan
1987   Time and Motion in the Formation of the Middle Class in Antigua, 1834-1940. Paper presented at the Annual Meeting of the American Anthropological Association, Chicago, November.

Malcolmson, Robert W.
1973   *Popular Recreations in English Society 1700-1850*. Cambridge: Cambridge University Press.

Marshall, Dawn
1983   Toward an Understanding of Caribbean Migration. In *US Immigration and Refugee Policy: Global and Domestic Issues*, edited by Mary M. Krintz, 113–31. Lexington, Mass.: Lexington Books.

Maurer, Bill
1991   Caribbean Dance: "Resistance," Colonial Discourse, and Subjugated Knowledges. *Nieuwe West-Indische Gids* 65(1/2):1–26.

Maynard, G. Oliver
1968   *A History of the Moravian Church, Eastern West Indies Province.* Trinidad. No publisher.

Maynard, Norman
1987   Nevis at the Turn of the Century. *Nevis Historical and Conservation Society Newsletter* 11:9.

Merrill, Gordon C.
1958   *The Historical Geography of St. Kitts and Nevis, The West Indies.* Mexico City: Instituto Panamericano de Geografia e Historia, No. 232.

The Mighty Chevy
1981   Let Them Know. *Culturama Magazine*, 18–19.

Miller, Daniel
1990   Fashion and Ontology in Trinidad. *Culture & History* 7:49–77.

Miller, Mark J. and William Boyer
1982   Foreign Workers in the USVI: History of Dilemma. *Caribbean Review* 11(1):48–51.

Mills, Frank
1985   *Determinants and Consequences of the Migration Culture of St. Kitts-Nevis.* Hemispheric Migration Project, Georgetown University & Intergovernmental Committee on Migration.
1987   Conditions in St. Kitts-Nevis that Promote Migration: A Predictive Model. Paper presented at the XII International Congress of The Caribbean Studies Association, May 27–29.

Mills, Frank and S.B. Jones-Hendrickson
n.d.   *Christmas Sports in St. Kitts-Nevis. Our Neglected Cultural Tradition.* No publisher.

Mintz, Sidney, W.
1971   The Caribbean as a Socio-cultural Area. In *Peoples and Cultures of the Caribbean*,
[1966] edited by Michael M. Horowitz, 17–46. Garden City, NY: The Natural History Press.
1974   *Caribbean Transformations.* Chicago: Aldine.
1985   From Plantations to Peasantries in the Caribbean. In *Caribbean Contours*, edited by Sidney W. Mintz and Sally Price, 127–53. Baltimore: The Johns Hopkins University Press.
1986   *Sweetness and Power.* New York: Viking Penguin.

Mintz, Sidney W. and Douglas Hall
1960   The Origins of the Jamaican Internal Marketing System. *Yale University Publications in Anthropology* 57:3–26.

Mintz, Sidney W. and Richard Price
1976   *An Anthropological Approach to the Afro-American Past: A Caribbean Perspective.* Philadelphia: ISHI.

Mosse, George L.
1985   *Nationalism and Sexuality. Respectability and Abnormal Sexuality in Modern Europe.* New York: Howard Fertig.

Motley, Constance Baker
n.d.   The Huggins Family Tree. MS.

Nicolas, Sir Nicholas Harris
1845   *The Dispatches and Letters of Vice Admiral Lord Viscount Nelson*, Vol. 1, 1777–1794. London: Henry Colburn.

Nisbet, Richard
1789   *The Capacity of Negroes for Religious and Moral Improvement.* London: James Phillips.

Nunley, John
1988   Festival Diffusion into the Metropole. In *Caribbean Festival Arts*, edited by John W. Nunley and Judith Bettelheim, 165–81. Seattle: The Saint Louis Art Museum in association with University of Washington Press.

Oldendorp, C.G.A.
1987   *A Caribbean Mission.* Ann Arbor: Karoma Publishers.
[1777]

Oliver, Vere Langford
1914   *Caribbeana*, Vol. 3. London: Mitchell Hughes and Clarke.

Olwig, Karen Fog
1981   Finding a Place for the Slave Family: Historical Anthropological Perspectives. *Folk* 23:345–58.
1985a   *Cultural Adaptation and Resistance on St. John. Three Centuries of Afro-Caribbean Life.* Gainesville: University of Florida Press.
1985b   Slaves and Masters on Eighteenth-Century St. John. *Ethnos* 50(3/4):214–30.
1985c   *The Culture of Development on the West Indian Island of Nevis.* Report to the Danish Council for Development Research, October 22, 1985.
1987a   Village, Culture and Identity on St John, V.I. In *Afro-Caribbean Villages in Historical Perspective*, edited by Charles V. Carnegie. African Caribbean Institute of Jamaica Research Review, No. 2:20–44.

1987b   Children's Attitudes to the Island Community—The Aftermath of Out-Migration on Nevis. In *Land and Development in the Caribbean*, edited by Jean Besson and Janet Momsen, 153–70. London: Macmillan.

1987c   Sport as Secular Ritual. The Case of Netball. *Folk* 29:75–90.

1990   Cultural Identity and Material Culture: Afro-Caribbean Pottery. *Folk* 32:5–22.

1992   The Migration Experience: Nevisian Women at Home and Abroad. In *Women and Change: A Pan-Caribbean Perspective*, edited by Janet Momsen. London: James Currey.

Olwig, Kenneth and Karen Fog Olwig

1984   "Off-shore" Dependence: Cultural and Developmental Consequences. Paper presented at the Institute of Latin American Studies, University of Florida, Gainesville.

Pares, Richard

1950   *A West-India Fortune*. London: Longmans.

Patterson, Orlando

1975   Context and Choice in Ethnic Allegiance. A Theoretical Framework and Caribbean Case Study. In *Ethnicity, Theory and Experience*, edited by Nathan Glazier and Daniel P. Moynihan, 305–49. Cambridge, Mass.: Harvard University Press.

1978   Migration in Caribbean Societies: Socioeconomic and Symbolic Resource. In *Human Migration. Patterns and Policies*, edited by W.H. McNeill and Ruth S. Adams, 106–45. Bloomington: Indiana University Press.

1982   *Slavery and Social Death*. Cambridge, Mass.: Harvard University Press.

Philpott, Stuart B.

1973   *West Indian Migration: The Montserrat Case*. London: Athlone Press.

Platzer, Eryl

1979   The Potters of Nevis. MA Dissertation, University of Denver.

Population Census of the Commonwealth Caribbean

1980–   St. Christopher/Nevis, Vol. 1.
81

Price, Richard

1973   Introduction. In *Maroon Societies*, edited by Richard Price, 1–30. Garden City, NY: Anchor Books.

1985   An Absence of Ruins? *Caribbean Review* 14(3):24–29, 45.

1990   *Alabi's World*. Baltimore: The Johns Hopkins University Press.

Project Report to the Government of St. Kitts-Nevis

1982   MAB Eastern Caribbean Project. Institute of Social and Economic Studies, University of the West Indies, Barbados.

Puckrein, Gary A.

1984   *Little England. Plantation Society and Anglo-Barbadian Politics, 1627–1700*. New York: New York Universities Press.

Ragatz, Lowell Joseph

1932   *A Guide for the Study of British Caribbean History, 1763–1834*. Washington, DC: US Government Printing Office.

Ralston, Lenore D.

1979   With and Without Words in Nevis: Aspects of an Ethnography of Speaking in a British West Indian Community. PhD Dissertation, Bryn Mawr College.

Ramsay, James

1784   *Essay on the Treatment and Conversion of the African Slaves in the Sugar Colonies*. London: James Phillips.

Ranger, Terence

1983   The Invention of Tradition in Colonial Africa. In *The Invention of Tradition*, edited by Eric Hobsbawm and Terence Ranger, 211–62.

Report for the Years 1955 and 1956

1958   St. Kitts-Nevis-Anguilla. London: Her Majesty's Stationery Office.

Report for the Years 1957 and 1958

1961   St. Kitts-Nevis-Anguilla. London: Her Majesty's Stationery Office.

Report for the Years 1959–1962

1966   St. Kitts-Nevis-Anguilla. London: Her Majesty's Stationery Office.

Report of the Wesleyan-Methodist Missionary Society

1821   London: Printed for the Society.

Richards, Lyra P.

1977   President's Message. *Culturama Magazine*, 4–5.

1984   The Dilemma of Culturama. *Culturama Magazine*, n.p.

Richardson, Bonham

1983   *Caribbean Migrants. Environment and Human Survival on St. Kitts and Nevis*. Knoxville: The University of Tennessee Press.

Robertson, Rev. (Robert)

1730   *A Letter to the Right Reverend of the Lord Bishop of London*. London: J. Wilford.

1732   *A Detection of the State and Situation of the Present Sugar Planters, of Barbadoes and the Leward Islands*. London: J. Wilford.

Rochefort, Charles

1666   *The History of the Caribby-Islands*. Trans. by John Davies. London: Thomas Dring
[1658] and John Starkey.

Rogers, Victor
1987   A Study of Assimilation of Nevisians/Nevisian Americans in New Haven, Connecticut. PhD Dissertation, Mississippi State University.

Rooke, Patricia T.
1979   "The World they Made"—The Politics of Missionary Education to British West Indian Slaves, 1800–1833. *Caribbean Studies* 18(3/4):47–67.

Rowlands, Michael
1985   Exclusionary Tactics in the Logic of Collective Dynamics. *Critique of Anthropology* 5(2):47–69.

Rymer, James
1775   *A Description of the Island of Nevis; with an Account of Its Principal Diseases.* London: T. Evans.

Safa, Helen I.
1987   Popular Culture, National Identity, and Race in the Caribbean. *Nieuwe West-Indische Gids* 61(3/4):115–26.

The St. Kitts & Nevis Tourist Guide
1984   April. St. John's Angitua: FT International on behalf of the St. Kitts & Nevis Tourist Board.

Sainton, Jean-Pierre
1982   The Historical Background: A Sketch. In *Kaz antiyé: jan moun ka rété (Caribbean Popular Dwelling)*, edited by Jack Berthelot and Martines Gaumé, 45–61. Paris: Éditions Caribéennes.

Sanford, Margaret
1975   To Be Treated as a Child of the Home: Black Carib Child Lending in a British West Indian Society. In *Sozialization and Communication in Primary Groups*, edited by T.R. Williams, 159–81. The Hague: Mouton Publishers.
1976   Child Lending in Belize. *Belizean Studies* 4(2):26–36.

Sargeant, Lincoln A.
1988   To Make Children Happy. *Nevis Historical and Conservation Society Newsletter* 12:10–24.

Seaga, Edward P.G.
1973   Parent-Teacher Relationships in a Jamaican Village. In *Consequences of Class and*
[1955] *Color*, edited by David Lowenthal and Lambros Comitas, 169–89. Garden City, NY: Anchor Books.

Sharpe, Barrie
1986   Ethnography and a Regional System. *Critique of Anthropology* 6(3):33–65.

Sloane, Hans
1707   *A Voyage to the Islands of Madera, Barbados, Nieves, S. Christophers and Jamaica.*
        London: BM for the Author.

Smith, Abbot Emerson
1947   *Colonists in Bondage. White Servitude and Convict Labor in America 1607–1776.*
        Chapel Hill: The University of North Carolina Press.

Smith, John
1910   *Travels and Works of Captain John Smith, President of Virginia, and Admiral of New*
[1629] *England 1580–1631.* Edited by Edward Arber. Edinburgh: John Grant.

Smith, M.G.
1962   *West Indian Family Structure.* Seattle: University of Washington Press.
1965   *The Plural Society in the British West Indies.* Berkeley: University of California Press.
1966   Introduction. In *My Mother Who Fathered Me*, by Edith Clarke, i–xliv. London:
        George Allen and Unwin.
1973   Education and Occupational Choice in Rural Jamaica. In *Consequences of Class and*
[1960] *Color*, edited by David Lowenthal and Lambros Comitas, 191–97. Garden City, NY:
        Anchor Books.

Smith, R.T.
1956   *The Negro Family in British Guiana.* London: Routledge and Kegan Paul.
1967   Social Stratification, Cultural Pluralism and Integration in West Indian Societies.
        In *Caribbean Integration: Papers on Social, Political and Economic Integration*, edited
        by S. Lewis and T. Mathews, 226–58. Proceedings of the Third Caribbean Scholars'
        Conference, 1966, Rio Piedras, Institute of Caribbean Studies.
1973   The Matrifocal Family. In *The Character of Kinship*, edited by Jack Goody, 121–44.
        Cambridge: Cambridge University Press.
1978a   The Family and the Modern World System. Some Observations from the Caribbean.
        Journal of Family History 3(4):337–60.
1978b   Class Differences in West Indian Kinship: A Genealogical Exploration. In *Family*
        and Kinship in Middle America and the Caribbean, edited by Arnaud F. Marks and
        René Römer, 335–85. Co-publication of the University of the Netherlands Antilles
        and the Department of Caribbean Studies of the Royal Institute of Linguistics and
        Anthropology, Leiden.
1987   Hierarchy and the Dual Marriage System in West Indian Society. In *Gender and*
        Kinship: Essays toward a Unified Analysis, edited by Jame Collier and Sylvia
        Yanagisako, 165–296. Stanford: Stanford University Press.
1988   *Kinship and Class in the West Indies. A Genealogical Study of Jamaica and Guyana.*
        Cambridge: Cambridge University Press.

Smith, William
1745   *A Natural History of Nevis.* Cambridge: J. Bentham.

Sobel, Mechal
1987   *The World They Made Together. Black and White Values in Eighteenth-Century Virginia*. Princeton: Princeton University Press.

Southall, A.W.
1970   The Illusion of Tribe. *Journal of Asian and African Studies* 5(1/2):2.

Stack, Carol B.
1974   *All Our Kin. Strategies for Survival in a Black Community*. New York: Harper and Row.

Starkey, Otis P.
1961   *Commercial Geography of St. Kitts-Nevis*. Bloomington, Indiana University: Office of Naval Research, Technical Report, No. 7.

Story, G.M.
1969   Mummers in Newfoundland History: A Survey of the Printed Record. In *Christmas Mumming in Newfoundland. Essays in Anthropology, Folklore, and History*, edited by Herbert Halbert and G.M. Story, 165–85. Canada: University of Toronto Press for Memorial University of Newfoundland.

Summary Report on the Census of Agriculture
1975   St. Kitts-Nevis-Anguilla.

Sutton, Constance R. and Elsa M. Chaney, eds.
1987   *Caribbean Life in New York City*. New York: Center for Migration Studies.

Sutton, Constance R. and Susan Makiesky-Barrow
1977   Social Inequality and Sexual Status in Barbados. In *Sexual Stratification. A Cross-Cultural View*, edited by Alice Schlegel, 292–325. New York: Columbia University Press.

Sutton, Joyah Junella
1986   Culturama: An Analysis of a Nevisian Festival. BA Thesis, University of the West Indies, Cave Hill, Barbados.

Taussig, Michael T.
1980   *The Devil and Commodity Fetishism in South America*. Chapel Hill: The University of North Carolina Press.

Thomas, Keith
1971   *Religion and the Decline of Magic. Studies in Popular Beliefs in Sixteenth and Seventeenth Century England*. London: Weidenfeld and Nicolson.

Thomas-Hope, Elizabeth
1978   The Establishment of a Migration Tradition: British West Indian Movements to the Hispanic Caribbean in the Century after Emancipation. In *Caribbean Social*

Relations, edited by Colin G. Clarke, 66–81. Liverpool: Centre for Latin American Studies.

1985   Characteristics and Implications of Caribbean Return Migration. *Population Mobility and Development Project Paper*, No. 3. Mona, Jamaica: Institute of Social and Economic Research.

Tobias, Peter M.

1975   How You Gonna Keep 'em Down in the Tropics Once They've Dreamed New York? Some Aspects of Grenadian Migration. PhD Dissertation, Rice University.

[Tobin, James]

1785   *Cursory Remarks upon the Reverend Mr. Ramsay's Essay on The Treatment and Conversion of African Slaves in the Sugar Colonies*. London: C. and T. Wilkie.

Tonkin, Elizabeth

1990   West African Ethnographic Traditions. In *Lozalizing Strategies. Regional Traditions of Ethnographic Writing*, edited by Richard Fardon, 137–51. Edinburgh: Scottish Academic Press.

Turner, Mary

1982   *Slaves and Missionaries: The Disintegration of Jamaican Slave Society 1787–1834*. Urbana: University of Illinois Press.

Turner, Victor

1982   *The Ritual Process. Structure and Anti-Structure*. Ithaca: Cornell University Press.
[1969]

Underdown, David

1985   *Revel, Riot, and Rebellion. Popular Politics and Culture in England. 1603–1660*. Oxford: Clarendon Press.

The Voice of Nevis

1978   Judge Constance Baker Motley: Ninth but First. August 3(1):13.

Walker, G.P.J.

n.d.   Cottle Church. An Incident in the Life of Pre-Emancipation Nevis. No publisher.

Walking and Riding Tour of Nevis

n.d.   Charlestown, Nevis: The Nevis Historical and Conservation Society, Alexander Hamilton House.

Warner, Robert Austin

1969   *New Haven Negroes. A Social History*. New York: Arno Press and the New York
[1940]   Times.

Watson, James L., ed.

1977   *Between Two Cultures. Migrants and Minorities in Britain*. Oxford: Basil Blackwell.

Watson, Richard
  1835   *A Defence of the Wesleyan-Methodist Mission in the West Indies.* In *Works*, Vol. 6.
  [1817]   London: John Mason.

Wells, Robert V.
  1975   *The Population of the British Colonies in America before 1776. A Survey of Census Data.* Princeton: Princeton University Press.

Williams, Alfred M.
  1896   A Miracle-Play in the West Indies. *Journal of American Folk-Lore* 9(33):117–20.

Williams, Eric
  1970   *From Columbus to Castro: The History of the Caribbean 1492–1969.* London: André Deutsch.
  1973   Education in the British West Indies. In *Consequences of Class and Color*, edited by
  [1951]   David Lowenthal and Lambros Comitas, 148–67. Garden City, NY: Anchor Books.

Wilson, Peter
  1969   Reputation and Respectability: A Suggestion for Caribbean Ethnology. *Man* 4(1): 70–84.
  1971   Caribbean Crews: Peer Groups and Male Society. *Caribbean Studies* 10:18–34.
  1973   *Crab Antics: The Social Anthropology of English-Speaking Negro Societies of the Caribbean.* New Haven: Yale University Press.

Yorke, Philip C.
  1931   *The Diary of John Baker.* London: Hutchinson & Co.
  [1751–57,
  1766–67]

Zelinsky, Wilbur
  1988   *Nation into State. The Shifting Symbolic Foundations of American Nationalism.* Chapel Hill: The University of North Carolina Press.

ARCHIVAL RECORDS

Great Britain
Public Record Office, Kew:
CO Colonial Papers
CO1 Colonial Papers, General Series
CO152 Leeward Islands, Correspondence, Original Board of Trade and Secretary of State, Nos. 37–39.
CO154 Leeward Islands, Acts
CO155 Leeward Islands, Sessional Papers
CO185 Nevis, Acts
CO186 Nevis, Sessional Papers

Public Record Office, Chancery Lane, London:
SP State Papers
SP16 vol. 151/20 State Papers Domestic Charles I. Letters and Papers 1–16 November, 1629
SP25 vol. 77 Council of State: Books and Accounts. Fair Order Book, 25 March 1656–16 September 1657

University of Bristol Library:
PP Pinney Papers
Miscellaneous, List of Deeds and Papers [. . .] Left under the Care of Joseph Gill, Esq., in the Island of Nevis, 14 June, 1783
Letter Books, No 3, John Frederick Pinney, 5 October, 1761–1 June 1775
Letter Books, No. 5, John Pinney, 9 September, 1778–30 April, 1784
Plantation Occurrences, John Frederick Pinney II's Plantation, Diary of Plantation Work, 11 January, 1798–25 July, 1801

Methodist Missionary Society Archives, Wesleyan Methodist Missionary Society (London)
Archive West Indies, School of Oriental and African Studies, London:
B Biographical, microfiches 27–109
C Correspondence, West Indies General, 1803–57, microfiches 1–727
CA Correspondence, Antigua, 1833–90, microfiches 989–1296
CR Correspondence, West Indies General, 1903–43, microfiches 728–883
CL Correspondence, Leeward Islands, 1907–46, microfiches 2710–2847

University of North Wales, Bangor:
BM Bodrhyddan Manuscripts, No. 3247
SC The Stapleton-Cotton Manuscripts:
Bundle 13, Russell's Rest, Plantation Accounts, 1745–52
Bundle 15, Nevis Plantation Accounts, 1770–74
Bundle 17, Nevis Affairs, Letters from Walter Nisbet, 1785–95(?)

National Library of Wales, Aberystwyth, Department of Manuscripts:
BC Bodrhyddan Collection, Bodrhyddan Correspondence, Vol. 1, Letters Relating to Sugar Plantations in the West Indies

The John Rylands Library, Manchester:
SM The Stapleton Manuscripts, Correspondence concerning West Indian Affairs, Sir William Stapleton, 4th Bart

Dorset Record Office, County Hall, Dorchester:
PM Pollard Manuscripts, Title Deeds, Plantations in Nevis, 1739–1863

National Library of Scotland:
HE The Papers of the Diplomatist, Hugh Elliot, Governor of Leeward Islands, 1810–13, MS 13058

West Indies
Nevis Archives at Alexander Hamilton Museum, Charlestown, Nevis:
Nevis Assembly Minutes, September 1823–April 1827
Nevis Blue Books, 1840–82
Leeward Islands Blue Books, 1891–1940
John Jones' Diaries, 1887, 1893–97

Court House, Charlestown, Nevis, Registrar's Office:
Probate Register B.2
Records of Nevis, Wills, Vol. 1–B, 1880–

Library, The University of the West Indies, Mona, Jamaica:
AW Antonia Williams, *A Tour through the West Indies, 1908–09*, MS

With the exception of the Colonial and State Papers (CO) and (SP), the abbreviations in the texts are my own.

Index

231